CITIZEN BOARDS AT WORK

New Challenges to Effective Action

Other books by HARLEIGH B. TRECKER

Group Process in Administration

Social Group Work: Principles and Practices

Supervision of Group Work and Recreation (*with Hedley S. Dimock*)

How to Work with Groups (*with Audrey R. Trecker*)

Social Agency Board Member Institutes: An Analysis
    of the Experience of Eighteen Cities

Education for Social Work Administration (*with Frank Z. Glick and John
    C. Kidneigh*)

Committee Common Sense (*with Audrey R. Trecker*)

Building the Board

Handbook of Community Service Projects (*with Audrey R. Trecker*)

Group Work: Foundations and Frontiers (*editor*)

Group Work in the Psychiatric Setting

New Understandings of Administration

Group Services in Public Welfare

CITIZEN BOARDS AT WORK

New Challenges to Effective Action

HARLEIGH B. TRECKER

University Professor of Social Work
School of Social Work
The University of Connecticut

ASSOCIATION PRESS

NEW YORK

CITIZEN BOARDS AT WORK
New Challenges to Effective Action

Copyright © 1970 by
National Board of Young Men's Christian Associations

Association Press, 291 Broadway, New York, N. Y. 10007

Standard Book Number: 8096–1757–9
Library of Congress Catalog Card Number: 73–93425

PRINTED IN THE UNITED STATES OF AMERICA

Contents

Policy Issues Boards Must Face
Board Responsibilities for the Period Ahead—
　　An Agenda for Action

Introduction

Boards of directors of the community service enterprise face unprecedented challenges today. In the fields of education, welfare, health, recreation, youth services, and others the problems of effective board functioning are grave. The "establishment" is under attack.

Hundreds of thousands of people contribute millions of hours to board service annually. Usually they work without salary and often at expense to themselves. They may receive little thanks or satisfaction from this giving of themselves. Their critics say they are the wrong people working on the wrong problems and with the wrong methods!

While that indictment may seem unjust, there is widespread agreement that community agency board members, officers, and staff who work with boards need to take a critical look at themselves and their ways of work today. Thoughtful evaluation and appraisal of board functioning is high on the priority lists of many community agencies as they seek to strengthen their services and strive creatively to do a better job of meeting community needs.

This book offers a realistic portrayal of the problems, challenges, and opportunities that lie ahead for these boards that sincerely wish to move ahead with greater efficiency and productivity. Hopefully, readers will find stimulation, motivation, and ideas to use in undertaking a thorough checkup of the "health" of the boards they serve on and work with.

11

For whom is this book intended? It should help men and women who are serving as board members or officers today or who will do so tomorrow. Perhaps they will see their jobs more clearly and may carry their responsibilities more effectively. Thus, *Citizen Boards at Work* is, as the title implies, a guidebook for citizen leaders. But it should also be of value to professional workers, administrators, executives, and staff members who work with boards and who need a fresh perspective on the vital roles they carry. In addition, teachers and students who are engaged in preparation for the staff role may find this a worthy and even basic text. Hopefully, the panorama portrayed herein may enable the general public to get a better grasp of the importance of boards in the vital decisions of community life.

I have been interested in and have been studying the board for over a quarter of a century. As a professional worker and educator I have tried to share with students the principles of effective board leadership and service. Perhaps more important are my many years of participation as a citizen member and officer of scores of national, state and local boards and commissions. It is hardly possible to count the hours that have been devoted to service of this kind. Perhaps by combining the theory of *how it ought to be* with the experience of *how it really is* I can make a genuine contribution. I hope that this is the case.

In spite of the fact that boards are historically well-established instruments and architects of community policy and program in this country and abroad, there is not an extensive body of literature about them. Research efforts have been relatively few and rigorous studies of their organization and functioning are likewise scarce. Consequently, board members are asking such questions as: Are we using our time on the most significant matters? Why have we failed to develop a broad base of board leadership? Why do we have frequent and recurring misunderstandings between board members and staff members? Why must we spend so much time on budget and finances and have so little time to think about our purposes and our programs? Why do many of our board members fail to get basic satisfaction from the work they are doing?

These questions and many others will be considered in the five sections and fourteen chapters of this volume. The first section is designed to give the reader a comprehensive picture of the importance of boards today and the vital functions they must perform. Next, we look at the crucial problem area of relationships between the board, the executive, and the staff. In the third section a careful look is taken at the board at work from the selection of members to the evaluation of effectiveness. The board in relation to the changing and challenging community is brought into focus in the fourth section. Finally, suggestions are offered for the strengthening of board service to meet the challenges of the unfolding future. The fourteen chapters are augmented by selected references for those persons who wish to do further study.

Many people have had a part in the development of material for this book. To acknowledge each one individually would be difficult if not impossible. Some would certainly be left out by accident. So, thanks are offered to major groups of people who have cooperated in this long task. They are my professional colleagues and my graduate students. The latter group gave great assistance in the numerous research projects I have undertaken. My fellow board and commissions members over the years have provided examples of dedicated service to the common good. The national, state, and local agencies and organizations that have invited me to serve as a consultant, researcher, institute or project leader have given me many opportunities to learn much. The board members who participated so willingly in our studies have given of their wisdom. I am also indebted to the good friends who replied to letters and supplied materials. Because so many have given so generously there is the ever-present hazard that I will not know for sure where ideas came from. I do not always know nor can I recall precisely the origin of a specific contribution. When one works on a subject for a long time and engages many people in it, the product is often a blend of knowledge and experience from many sources. Suffice it to say that many have helped but this final product can be attributed only to me, but only because so many have given so completely of their ideas.

Special thanks must be given to my wife, Audrey, and to my sons, Jerrold and James, and my daughters-in-law Janice and Barbara. They have done much to support me, sustain me, and encourage me to return to my writing. Without their love and devotion it would not have been possible for me to do this book.

—Harleigh B. Trecker

West Hartford, Connecticut
December, 1969

PART ONE

BOARDS—INSTRUMENTS AND

ARCHITECTS OF POLICY

1 *The Importance of Boards Today*

The citizen board [1] is one of society's most important instruments. It is used to determine social policy and is charged with the responsibility for providing all kinds of community services. Yet, the board and how it works is treated only sparsely in the literature. Also, it has been a considerable time since a comprehensive book about boards has been written. Perhaps this latter lag is fortunate because the world has changed so much in recent years that a fresh approach to the board and its responsibilities is needed. Boards and board methods of even a decade ago will not suffice in this era of rapidly mounting community needs.

The community service enterprise and the boards in charge of this enterprise face rapid and pervasive changes in the social order. Today the world is different, the community is different, the needs of people are different, and the volunteer and professional skills required to meet these needs are likewise different. As Harrison put it, "The universe is not orderly, it is dynamic. Everything about us is in ceaseless change. We think of the mountain of granite as an everlasting mass of inert material, but its atoms vibrate and some occasionally explode, and its days are numbered, though in the trillions. Man is being required to learn to cope with events that may happen a million times faster than the flash of a firefly or a million times more slowly than the recession of a glacier." [2] Frankel tells us: "It took man roughly 475,000 years to arrive at the agricultural revolution and another 25,000 years to come to the industrial revolution. We have arrived at the space age in a hundred and fifty years, and while we do not know where we will go from here, we can be sure

17

we will go there fast." This led to the sage observation by a character in an E. B. White story: "I predict a bright future for complexity. Have you ever considered how complicated things can get, what with one thing leading to another?" [3] Thus, it is certain that the rapidly accelerating pace of events and the explosive rate of change will bring complications compounded. Most of the human needs society endeavors to meet are incredibly complicated today. The rate of obsolescence with reference to knowledge is high; skills adequate for an earlier time no longer suffice. Boards are faced with the strong realization that procedures must be modernized, processes revised and speeded up, and new leadership found and trained.

In the face of this rapidly changing and complicated community situation there are some serious and unrelenting challenges. The critical and mounting shortage of professional personnel to man the human services is a problem of great concern to all boards. There are not enough professionally educated workers in any field to operate existing community agencies let alone to provide for services for a growing population. In addition, society has failed to finance the human services, either governmental or voluntary, to the extent of recognized current needs, to say nothing of projected needs. Consequently, there is a tremendous backlog of unmet human needs and a mounting toll of inevitable human breakdown and human wreckage all around us.

It would seem evident that society has failed to interpret the seriousness of these unmet needs to the decision-making bodies responsible for the quality of community life. It would appear that knowledge and skill already at hand have not been put to work with sufficient zeal to prevent many of the problems of human behavior which seem to be on the increase today. There is enough knowledge and enough resources to create healthy communities; what is lacking is the will to do so. Perhaps society will be called upon to devise a far different design for the operation and coordination of the community services of education, health, welfare, recreation, and the like.

If it can be assumed that it is the basic responsibility of boards to act as the sensitive conscience of the community, boards must now become the spokesmen for the community's goals and aspirations including the demands of articulate minorities. Furthermore, boards must take new leadership in guaranteeing that the best of knowledge and skill is brought to bear in the provision of human services.

An Inventory of Current Tasks

Across this country, boards are at work on vital tasks to meet the challenges of today and to plan skillfully to meet the even greater demands of tomorrow.

Boards are sharpening selection procedures and demanding the highest of qualifications for board membership.

Boards are broadening the base of representation and endeavoring to involve a much wider range of community interest and background in agency affairs.

Boards are striving to create an orderly flow of new leadership so that they will no longer be allowed to become ingrown or stagnant.

Boards are providing much better job orientation and training for their members and are making sure that every member is clear about the purpose of the agency and has conviction about the need it exists to meet.

Boards are working to clarify the roles and tasks of board members and professional workers. The primary energy of the board is being devoted to basic matters of agency and community policy and the provision of high-quality services.

Boards are working on broad community problems and striving to exercise influence upon the basic governmental processes where community decisions are made.

Boards Are Responsible for Both Private and Public Business

Here and abroad, citizen boards are responsible for both private and public business. Speaking from the standpoint of the business corporation, Koontz calls attention to the fact that "in the United States, over three-fourths of the state laws under which corporations are established require that the corporation be 'managed' by a board of directors, usually comprised of at least three members. . . . A board of directors charged with such responsibility is common not only in the United States. Boards, commissions, or committees in similar positions of responsibility exist in virtually every part of the world. It is an interesting commentary on human affairs that, except for relatively rare instances of monarchy or dictatorship, power over enterprises of all sorts has tended to rest in groups. Even in authoritarian societies, one finds groups holding considerable power over individual enterprises or segments of enterprises. This should not be surprising. It attests to the fact that people have historically distrusted placing too much power in the hand of an individual." [4]

In higher education, Martona observes that "the principle of placing primary responsibility for the direction of colleges and universities in the hands of boards of lay citizens has never been challenged. Instead, it has grown steadily in strength and public acceptance. This may be attributed perhaps not only to the advantages that have been observed to accrue to both the institutions and their constituencies through the principle of administration by lay boards, but also to the fact that the advantages of the same principle have been observed throughout the history of the nation in the government of public elementary and secondary schools." [5]

Sweden is but one of many countries that make use of boards. Rosenthal says, "A further demonstration of the Swedes' interest in their government is the widespread use of boards and committees in many fields of government activity at central, province, county and local government levels. Many people feel that they are part of the governmental process, and in fact they are, as they serve on local pension, welfare, child care, or other committees and boards. . . . The actual administration of central government activities is conducted by a number of central administrative boards known as Centrala Ambetsverk. The concept of administrative boards is very old in Swedish government and records have been found which indicate they existed as early as 1634. The Swedish tradition of independent administrative boards is a significant one in the administrative process. . . . The board consists of the director general as chairman and a number of senior officials, appointed by the minister of the department, who serve immediately under the chairman. In addition, laymen representing organizations or sections of the population having special interest in the board are included as members. For example, on the Social Insurance Board, workers and employers as well as owners of small enterprises and farms are included." [6]

Obviously, this form of citizen participation in both private and public business grows out of a philosophy of administration and in turn contributes to the evolving methodology of the democratic process. Since the people are ultimately in charge of and responsible for the services rendered, it follows that ways must be found to organize their efforts for maximum productivity.

Board Service Set in the Volunteer Tradition

In this country, from its very beginning, there has been a great tradition of citizen participation and volunteer service in community affairs. Among others, Cohen [7] calls "citizen participation the backbone of democracy." Service on boards is a part of this system of personal responsibility for meeting community needs. Seider sets it in a broad framework when she says, "Volunteers are a traditional and integral part of the American social welfare system . . . the specific duties assigned differ from agency to agency . . . these may be classified as: (1) identifiers of human conditions or problems requiring social welfare services; (2) initiators and makers of policy in agencies created to prevent, control, or treat these social conditions; (3) contributors of service based on knowledge, skill, and interest; (4) solicitors of public or voluntary support; (5) spokesmen and interpreters of agency program and problems to which they are directed; (6) reporters of community reaction, critical or positive, to the agency's program; and (7) collaborators in community planning activities for the purpose of modifying or designing services to meet changing social conditions." [8]

Increasingly, business is reaching out and offering its resources in the social realm.[9] Board service by corporation executives and officers is more and more the pattern as leaders call for "creative innovation" in community affairs.[10] Citizen groups, largely from the fields of business and industry, are providing a huge amount of service in the realms of research, study, and policy data input.[11] All of this is in keeping with the basic belief that every one has a never-ending obligation to contribute to the social good.

Millions Serve on Boards

It is not possible to discover precisely how many people serve on the boards of community agencies but it must run into the millions. In 1950 it was reported that there were 280,000 members of local boards of education.[12] In 1966 it was indicated that "every year 50,000 men and women take office as new school board members. Most of them serve only one or two terms." [13] In 1966 there was an estimate of 30,000 trustees of colleges and universities.[14] For 1967 it was reported that a total of 656,000 persons served on local and state boards of education and colleges.[15] When one thinks about the huge number of persons who serve on the thousands of library, hospital, and social service agency boards the total is staggering. Add to this the board personnel of religious, cultural, civic, service, and governmental agencies and the figure mounts steadily. Thus, it is readily apparent that the work of the community could not long continue without the millions of hours of board service and leadership provided by countless citizens. The importance of their contribution can scarcely be overestimated.

Another area where facts are lacking is the extent to which the same person serves on more than one board at the same time. Undoubtedly, this happens fairly frequently. Consider the newspaper announcement of the resignation of a Board of Education member who had served for eight years. In his letter of resignation he said, "It has reached a point where my plans for the coming year do not allow time to do justice to the board" and that he must either concentrate on the Board of Education and drop his other activities or resign. The story went on to report that the man was vice-president of the Rotary Club, director of the Family Service Society, treasurer of the Cancer Crusade and moderator and deacon of his church. He was doing all of these things in addition to his regular job of bank vice-president and secretary.[16] One does not know how many persons carry multiple community responsibilities but it must be many.

In discussing the reason why some persons refuse to serve on boards, an education reporter observed that "the real obstacle is the inordinate amount of time and physical presence at meetings which school board membership has often come to require. In cities such as New York the demands on the time of these unpaid people have become unmanageable. In times of crisis—and crisis has become almost the normal state of affairs—the duties of the board president require almost full-time effort, and most of the other members must be ready to sacrifice a substantial part of their daily lives to the job." [17]

Why Do People Serve on Boards?

Board service is clearly an important avenue of expression for many thousands of people. Why do they serve, or perhaps a better way of asking the question is, "Why do they *work* so hard?" because being on a board is hard work. The board is a task group, it has a job to do. It is not primarily a "need meeting" group insofar as the individual member is concerned although undoubtedly in some cases deep psychological needs are met.

The fact is that in this country and elsewhere hundreds of thousands of citizens voluntarily assume responsibility for furthering the quality of community life. In doing so they take on a role of trusteeship and have chosen to become creative partners dedicated to improving life. Towley, in discussing the matter of motivation, stresses the "warmly human motive behind board service, the wish to be needed, to count, to feel now and then not expendable; the human desire to be the determinant in a balanced or hung-fire situation to tip the scales; the wish to be a part of an identified, purposeful group activity, and one that both takes and gives; the wish to be creative, to build, and to see completion; the wish to be a controlled and disciplined influence toward the well being of numbers of people; the need of us all to affirm life and its meaning in the midst of much that is life-negating in our community life; the need to enlarge our own life to touch the lives of others and be touched by them." [18]

People who agree to serve on boards agree to behave responsibly. To behave responsibly means to become increasingly capable of responding to human needs in whatever form they present themselves. Board members, therefore, become the sensitive conscience of the community and the instruments and architects of public policy.

Board members agree to serve because they are willing to study community needs and problems and do the critical thinking required if sound solutions to these problems are to be found. As Simon points out, "Man is a problem-solving, skill-using, social animal. Once he has satisfied his hunger, two main kinds of experience are significant to him. One of his deepest needs is to apply his skills, whatever they be, to challenging tasks. . . . The other is to find meaningful and warm relations with a few other human beings—to love and be loved, to share experience, to respect and be respected, to work in common tasks." [19] Board members, therefore, are interested in seeing to it that the best of knowledge and skill are always brought to bear in solving the problems of the community.

People become board members because they believe deeply that community services should be provided to people as a matter of basic right. They feel that these services must be presented in ways that further the dignity and integrity of the individual. Like Faulkner, they are essentially motivated by faith and compassion; it was Faulkner who said, "I believe that man will not merely endure: he will prevail. He is immortal, not because he alone among creatures has an inexhaustible voice but because he has a soul, a spirit capable of compassion, sacrifice, and endurance." [20]

Board members, in addition, are interested in guaranteeing to the community that thoughtful plans will be made and that funds will be well spent so that needs will be met to the maximum extent possible.

In summary, board service is a matter of work and reward going hand in hand. The work is hard but the rewards are apparently sufficient to sustain the efforts of thousands of people year after year.

Power of Boards

One publication pointed out that university boards are "the unknown rulers . . . the men and women who are technically at the top of the nation's huge state-university system are the least known figures in academe's power structure. And the least rewarded. [They] read reams of reports, worry endlessly over their university's business, scurry to meetings and ceremonies. . . . As states expand their higher-education systems [their] role looms larger. . . . The selection methods do not guarantee that a regent will be particularly prepared for this job. . . . [They] vary on how deeply they delve into operational detail. Most try to confine themselves to setting broad policy and letting administrators carry it out. . . . [One board member] concedes that his service takes about thirty per cent of his time. . . ." [21]

In referring to the contribution made by boards, one university leader said, "Clearly, for all who will look at the evidence, any university can gain enormously from the judgment and guidance of a dedicated body of men who are not caught up in the day-to-day activities of the institution. Their value in the management and development of the University's financial resources is obvious. Beyond that, the advice and judgment of such a 'lay' body on almost the whole range of University problems can present a perspective unlikely to be found in any other quarter. But to perform that function they must have an informed sense of the problems and their contexts. What links, accordingly, should be developed and strengthened in order more effectively to supply that information to them? Without undermining the executive authority of the President, should not the Trustees and their committees be brought into closer and more continuous contact with representative groups of faculty and students, and advisory councils of alumni and interested friends? Trustees necessarily and properly can give only a portion of their time to University matters. Can ways be found, without unreasonably increasing demands upon them, to make their contacts with the University broader and more informative?" [22]

Boards—Trustees of Community Values

In addition to and probably more important than their managerial responsibilities, board members are the trustees of community values and the conscience of community life. Although they may represent private or voluntary agencies they have a public duty. As Tead said, "Trustees are, of course, in the last analysis, holding the operation of education in trust as a public service. Every college has now become in fact a public agency; and it is required to gain and hold public confidence. To do this means a two-way relationship and trust. The wider public has to realize that for it to perform its unique mission the college has to have its own special degree of freedom, of elbow room, of leisure time, and of absence of influence from outside pressures." [23] While this observation is made in terms of the field of higher education it has universal application to all of the human services. However, at the present time in the field of higher education and elsewhere the makeup of boards is changing partly because of pressure being applied by outside groups seeking a voice in the governance of the institutions. For example, students have been elected to college boards of trustees, clients have seats on welfare boards and advisory councils, youths are being added to trustee memberships and in many cases boards are striving to become more representative of the community.[24]

Major Criticisms of Boards

Like all human institutions, boards are subject to criticism sometimes justified and oftentimes not. Among the criticisms which arise from time to time are the following: boards are not broadly representative of the public. Their membership tends to be limited to older, upper-income, professional, employer, and managerial persons, and frequently a ruling clique of community leaders serve on many boards and have interlocking control of the community service enterprise. Boards are thus charged with being parochial and conservative in their point of view and express only narrow concerns for the agency they represent and fail to see the large picture. Boards are too far removed from the people their agencies are designed to serve and thus have no way of knowing "how it really is." Boards are merely rubber stamps and do only what the executive or professional worker tells them to do. Board members are essentially self-seeking and serve only because of the status such service brings to them. Boards meddle, impinge upon, and interfere with the administration of the agency rather than stick to their primary business of policy development. Boards are basically conservative in their outlook and lack the courage to innovate.

Despite these criticisms, and some of them may be justified, the board continues to occupy a place of major importance in the community welfare enterprise. Perhaps because of the barrage of criticism, but more likely because of the great changes occurring in society, there is a strong move afoot for boards to take a hard look at their ways of work.

In an Atmosphere of Change

Boards today carry on their continuous evaluation in an atmosphere of change. Today, the role of government looms larger than ever and the involvement of the several levels of government (federal, state, and local) in community affairs has changed the financial base of almost all agencies. With this change in the base of support has come the greater insertion of government in the policy-making realm and few agencies are completely independent to make their own policy decisions so long as they share in government funds. In addition, there has been a remarkable growth in the number of professional workers in all fields and this has tended to diminish if not eliminate the direct service role of the board member. He finds himself more and more working in partnership with a growing staff of paid workers to carry out the decisions of the board. Recent years have seen the growth of the community planning movement and the emergence of centralized program proposals for defined geographic areas. This calls for the board to redefine its role in relation to larger units of society. More agencies today are multiservice in that they offer a larger variety of services to a number of different clienteles. This, too, has made for modification in the board function.

Size and Complexity of Agency Operations

One of the greatest problems faced by boards today is the size and complexity of agency operations. With the urban population continuing to increase, many programs which were small a generation ago are now huge. They involve millions of dollars of capital and operating funds, thousands of staff workers, and hundreds of thousands of persons served. This problem is vividly underlined in this discussion of New York City and its educational responsibility: "The sheer size of the system and the administrative difficulties of managing it hamper its effectiveness . . . [the] system is a monstrous operation, employing more than 59,000 teachers and several thousand administrators and technicians, and serving close to 1,100,000 pupils spread out over the five boroughs of the city. New York is more like sixty cities than one, and the diversity of needs of its many subcommunities may be too great for a single centralized board to handle. The schools have been 'managed'—if one can call it that—by a nine-person lay board which is supposed to make policy, and the superintendent and his professional staff, who are supposed to carry it out. Actually, the professionals make policy and carry it out, and it is difficult to say just what the board does. It does not have the time, staff, energy, expertise, or political base to influence how the schools are run, and it is emasculated regularly by the professionals. Much of its time is taken up on administrative details . . . which cover everything from school maintenance and construction contracts to the purchasing of supplies. Whether planned that way or not, it is useful for the professionals that their board is bogged down in trivia. This keeps the board so busy that it doesn't have time to set policy, let alone find out what is going on." [25]

Administrative Philosophy and the Board

As Millett puts it, "Administration is not and cannot be a one-man show. No enterprise can be performed by one person, unless it is the most simple of endeavors. Administration usually involves the cooperative efforts of many persons. Indeed, administration is a system of people working together, it is a pattern of cooperative activity in which the specialized talents of various individuals are brought together to achieve a common purpose. By definition, I am disposed to say that administration is a team operation." [26]

In previous writings [27] the author has discussed and developed a philosophy of administration which is basic to the carrying forward of community services in the democratic framework where the board is an important, even essential element. The following concepts are offered as a review and summary of that philosophy:

1. *The Concept of the Work Group:* Community services are carried on by groups of people working together to solve problems, to make decisions, to establish legislation, to create policy, to determine needs, to develop programs and procedures. These *work groups* include the board, the staff, various committees, community groups and others. Some of these groups are established by the legal instruments of the agency, namely the articles of incorporation, the constitution, or the bylaws. Some of the groups are special ones set up to deal with special problems. Each group, whether it be regular or special, has authority, responsibility, and limits as granted by the legal articles or the appointing authority. While each group is similar to every other group, each group is also different. Some groups are made up of direct service participants and some are made up of representatives who are a number of steps removed from the services being rendered. Boards usually fall into this category, but increasingly, service participants and recipients of service are being included on boards.

2. *The Concept of Leadership:* The various work groups mentioned above require leadership if they are to accomplish their assigned tasks. None of these groups is leaderless. All of them require the efforts of people particularly prepared and particularly competent to enable them to understand their jobs and get them done. These leaders are both professional workers and volunteer workers. The methods they use should be essentially democratic.

3. *The Concept of the Leadership Team:* In most community agencies leadership is given to these work groups by teams of persons. The most usual team consists of the professional worker and the lay or volunteer worker. By this is meant the chairman of the board of education and the superintendent of schools; the chairman of the board and the social agency executive; the library board and the professional librarian. This team pattern proceeds across the agency structure with committee chairmen frequently teaming up with related staff workers and so on. Teamwork is the heart of democratic administrative leadership. In fact, the way the professional executive and the volunteer board president work together does much to set the tone for the entire organization.

4. *The Concept of Structure:* In every community agency there are many work groups going about their affairs simultaneously. Thus, it is necessary to arrange these groups into a form of organization or structure

which will show them as being interconnected and in communication with each other. Out of the continuous relatedness and communication of these work groups comes the totality of the agency or organization.

5. *The Concept of Time and Timing:* As the professional and volunteer team provide leadership for the work groups, the groups go through a cycle which can be plotted on a time continuum. Each session of the work group requires different leadership as the group becomes more able to fulfill its task role. Each session of the work group produces a product and subsequent sessions grow out of what has been accomplished before. The leadership needs of the work group change, making it necessary for the leadership team to redefine constantly the ways in which they will work. Leadership roles are dynamic and changing just as work groups are dynamic and changing.

6. *The Concept of Coordination:* Since the many work groups are engaged in a variety of tasks and are usually at different stages in their progress, they must coordinate their several separate efforts if maximum output is to occur. The task of providing the impetus for this coordination and the mechanisms for its occurrence is a primary one in the portfolio of the board president and the executive. Coordination skills are thus paramount in key leaders such as board presidents and agency executives.

7. *The Concept of Reporting, Decision Making and Implementation of Decisions:* As the many work groups carry forward their endeavors it is necessary to prepare reports for transmittal to the parent authority. Then decisions must be made and plans prepared for the implementation of the decisions. In all agencies, especially in large ones that have scores of work groups, the question of when to report, what to report, and to whom to assign follow-up is of great importance. Having done this, a new cycle of activity gets underway.

NOTES

1. Throughout this book the general term "board" will be used to refer to boards of directors, boards of trustees, boards of management, commissions, advisory committees and other groups responsible for the community service enterprise.
2. George R. Harrison, *What Man May Be* (New York: William Morrow, 1956), p. 9. © George Russell Harrison.
3. Quoted by Harlan Cleveland in pamphlet entitled, "The Social Fall-Out of Science." The Maxwell School, Syracuse University, 1958.
4. Harold Koontz, *The Board of Directors and Effective Management*

(New York: McGraw-Hill, 1967), p. 1. Used with permission of Mc-Graw-Hill Book Company.

5. S. V. Martona, *College Boards of Trustees* (New York: The Center for Applied Research in Education, Inc., 1965), pp. 5-6.

6. Albert H. Rosenthal, *The Social Programs of Sweden* (Minneapolis: The University of Minnesota Press, 1967), pp. 98-103.

7. Nathan Cohen, *The Citizen Volunteer* (New York: Harper, 1960), Chapter 3.

8. Violet M. Seider, "Volunteers," *Encyclopedia of Social Work* (New York: National Association of Social Workers, 1965), pp. 830-836. Reprinted with permission of the National Association of Social Workers.

9. "Beyond the Profits: Business Reaches for a Social Role," *New York Times,* July 3, 1966.

10. W. Homer Turner, *Stewardship Responsibility for Creative Innovation* (New York: United States Steel Foundation, 1968); Roger M. Blough, *The Public Life of Private Business* (Pittsburgh: United States Steel Corporation, 1968).

11. "Citizens Groups Help Statehouses," *Wall Street Journal,* July 1, 1966.

12. Charles E. Reeves, *School Boards—Their Status, Functions and Activities* (New York: Prentice-Hall, 1954), p. 3.

13. Gloria Dapper and Barbara Carter, *A Guide for School Board Members* (Chicago: Follett Publishing Company, 1966), p. vii.

14. Gerald P. Burns, *Trustees in Higher Education* (Independent College Funds of America, 1966), p. 75.

15. "The Magnitude of the American Educational Establishment (1966–1967)," *Saturday Review,* October 15, 1966, p. 75.

16. *Hartford Courant,* August 20, 1968.

17. Fred M. Hechinger, "Too Busy Bodies," *New York Times,* February 16, 1964.

18. Louis Towley, "The Dividends You Get From Board Membership," *Highlights,* June 1952; also in *Making Yours a Better Board* (New York: Family Service Association of America, 1954), p. 10.

19. Herbert A. Simon, *The New Science of Management Decision* (New York: Harper, 1960), p. 50.

20. "William Faulkner's Nobel Prize Speech," *Saturday Review,* July 28, 1962, p. 20.

21. "The Unknown Rulers," *Time,* May 12, 1967.

22. David B. Truman, "A Message to the Faculty and Teaching Staff of the University" (New York: Columbia University, June 4, 1968).

23. Ordway Tead, *Trustees, Teachers, and Students—Their Role in Higher Education* (Salt Lake City: University of Utah Press, 1951), p. 23.

24. M. A. Farber, "Negro Who Aided in Take-Over at Princeton Is Elected Trustee," *New York Times,* June 8, 1969, p. 1; Fred M. Hechinger, "Students to Gain a Voice in U.S. Education Policy," *New York Times,* June 1, 1969, p. 1; "A Declaration on Campus Unrest," American Council on Education, Washington, D. C., April 4-5, 1969; *A Proposal to Establish the Council of the Princeton University Community,* A Report

of the Special Committee on the Structure of the University, May 1969; Jay Brown, "Welfare Mothers Want Power in Vital Decisions," *Hartford Times,* February 27, 1969; C. Gerald Fraser, "Community Control Here Found Spreading to the Field of Health," *New York Times,* March 9, 1969; "Nine Young People Added to Trustee Membership, Five to Board of Directors, One to Executive Committee," *Memo to Members,* The National Assembly for Social Policy and Development, Inc., New York, N. Y., Number 7, May 15, 1969.

25. David Rogers, "New York City Schools: A Sick Bureaucracy," *Saturday Review,* July 20, 1968. Reprinted with permission of Random House from *One Ten Livingston Street* by David Rogers, 1968, pp. 47-48.

26. John D. Millett, "National Conference of Professors of Educational Administration," *The Community School and Its Administration,* Vol. IV, No. 1, September 1965, p. 2.

27. Harleigh B. Trecker, *New Understandings of Administration* (New York: Association Press, 1961).

2 Types of Boards and Their Functions

There are several different types of boards. Functions of these boards vary by the amount of authority and responsibility delegated to them. Unfortunately, the community is not always clear about what a board is supposed to do and sometimes board members themselves are not too clear. Staff members likewise may have misconceptions about the task of the board in relation to the task of the paid workers. A systematic review of the literature and an evaluation of current practice reveals wide differences in boards by both type and task.

Policy-making Boards

One of the major kinds of boards is the policy-making administrative board. As Fairlie remarked, "In the administration of public affairs extensive use has been made of boards. . . . Since the end of the Middle Ages boards have been used to some extent by most European governments. . . . In the American colonies in the 18th century there were councils to the governor but little other use of boards and committees. During the revolution the Continental Congress and the state assemblies set up committees and boards to administer the navy, the army, the treasury and foreign affairs, but in 1781 the Congress established a system of single headed departments. Although this system has in general prevailed in the national government, administrative boards have been established for various purposes, especially since 1913. . . . In colonial local government there were school committees and in some colonies boards of county commissioners or supervisors. Local boards of health were established in several states before 1800 and other boards for special purposes were set up occasionally after that time. . . . State boards came into use early in the 19th century for public works, for the equalization of tax assessments and for the management of penal, and later of charitable and educational institutions." [1]

It is reported that "Massachusetts established the first state welfare board in 1864, known as the Massachusetts State Board of Charities. During the decade which followed eight additional states established similar boards. These boards met together on May 20, 1874 in New York City to consider a proposal to establish for themselves a clearinghouse of ideas and experiences." [2] This meeting was the beginning of the National Conference on Social Welfare. Today all states have boards or commissions responsible for a wide array of governmental services. The same pattern prevails for the thousands of voluntary agencies in the field.

The "administrative board by definition is meant to indicate that final administrative authority rests with the board, even though the authority to manage the operation of the agency may be delegated to an executive. . . . Policy-making indicates that actual agency policy is determined by the board and is the policy governing agency operation." [3]

Another term used for this kind of a board is "governing." Martona says the governing board is "a board which is legally charged with the direct control and operation of a single institutional unit." [4]

A long-established board of a major university was said to "have three major legal responsibilities, according to a report issued in 1957. These are to select the president of the university, to manage the institution's funds and 'to oversee and approve the kind of education offered by the university and make certain that its quality meets the highest standards possible.' " [5]

Responsibilities and Functions of Administrative Boards

When one examines the statement of functions and responsibilities ascribed to boards by different agencies there are clear similarities and differences. While the differences are more a matter of emphasis than anything else they are important and do set a tone for the operation of the agency. For example, one national agency stresses the fact that the boards of their local agencies have a vital *community* role. They say, "The board of directors maintains the continuity and identity of the agency in the community. It has a community trust going beyond the immediate concern of the agency. The board . . . is legally responsible for the conduct of the agency's business. This includes: determination of broad policies which guide the work of the organization and periodic review and revision of policies; employment of the executive; obtaining finances, determining the financial plan or budget, annually authorizing and receiving an audit, and maintaining standards through membership in the local and National Federation of Settlements; representing the agency in the community by developing informed interest and support; reviewing the agency program in the light of changing needs; caring for property and funds; supplying personnel of the board." [6]

In a large midwestern state the statutes provide that "the county welfare board . . . shall be charged with the duties of administration of all forms of public assistance and public welfare, both of children and of adults, and shall supervise in cooperation with the Director of Social Welfare, the administration of all forms of public assistance which now are or hereafter may be imposed on the Director of Social Welfare by law, including aid to dependent children, old age assistance, veterans' aid, aid to the blind, and other public assistance or public welfare purposes." [7]

In a membership agency responsibilities of the board are outlined as follows: "The board is the body to which the electors of the YWCA have delegated the responsibility for the management of the affairs of the total Association. It is responsible for determining and executing the policies and program of the Association. And as the legal entity of the corporation, it is directly responsible for carrying out the functions specified in the constitution and the articles of incorporation. With the exception of the functions it must carry as a legal entity, the board delegates to standing and special committees, to staff and to other individuals, the carrying of specified tasks in relation to the program and administration of the Association. These tasks are within the framework of the policies established by the board, and final responsibility rests with the board." [8]

In a penetrating discussion of the governing boards of academic institutions it is observed: "The governing board of an institution of higher education in the United States operates, with a few exceptions as the final institutional authority. . . . One of the governing board's important tasks is to ensure the publication of codified statements that define the over-all policies and procedures of the institution under its jurisdiction. The board plays a central role in relating the likely needs of the future to predictable resources; it has the responsibility for husbanding the endowment; it is responsible for obtaining needed capital and operating funds; and in the broadest sense of the term it should pay attention to personnel policy. In order to fulfill these duties, the board should be aided by, and may insist upon, the development of long-range planning by the administration and faculty. When ignorance or ill-will threatens the institution or any part of it, the governing board must be available for support. In grave crises it will be expected to serve as a champion." [9]

Spencer has listed six tasks for the board. She says, "The task of the board . . . is, with the help of staff: 1) To develop the focus of the agency program within . . . broad objectives; 2) To determine the scope of program and select the program activities; 3) To determine the level, quantitative and qualitative, at which the services will be offered; 4) To establish long-range plans and timetables for agency development and program modification; 5) To secure and maintain an adequate flow of resources to support the projected program; 6) To maintain evaluation procedures and to use evaluation results in agency structuring and programming." [10]

A clear-cut definition of board function will prevent confusion and overlapping of responsibilities between board and staff.

In an earlier publication the author summed up the functions of the administrative board in this list: 1) To establish the legal or corporate existence of the agency, whether it be under the auspices of government or voluntary effort. 2) To take responsibility for formulating general objectives, policies, and programs. 3) To inspire community confidence in the program because of the competence and dedication of the board members as active trustees of the agency. 4) To assume responsibility for the provision of adequate finances and to be accountable for the expenditure of funds. 5) To provide conditions of work, personnel policies, and staff. The board is particularly responsible for the selection and evaluation of the executive. 6) To understand and interpret the work of the agency to the community. 7) To study, know, and interpret general community needs to the agency staff. 8) To relate the services of the agency to the work of other agencies and to concentrate upon the improvement of community conditions. 9) To conduct periodic evaluations of agency operations with a view toward improving and strengthening the amount and quality of work that is done. 10) To provide the continuity of experienced leadership so that major staff changes will not weaken the agency.[11]

In contrast to this rather comprehensive list of functions Newland would "restrict the administrative function of boards and . . . rely upon them for broad policy control, public relations, organization of community resources, and advice. In an organization that is structured on an executive leadership model, board members who fail to understand this distribution of functions may seriously disrupt administration." [12]

In his discussion of the basic responsibilities of the corporation board, Koontz echoes many of the things that are applied to the community agency board. "Trusteeship—the safeguarding and husbanding of the company's assets in the long-term interests of the shareholders . . . extends beyond a feeling of immediate obligation to the stockholders. It includes responsibility to the public without whose support a business or a corporation could not endure; to employees of the company whose efforts are necessary for its success; and to customers, who buy its products. . . . Another major function of the board of directors is to determine enterprise objectives. . . . These to be meaningful, must be verifiable and understandable, and the decision-making involved must be channeled through formulation of major policies designed to assure goal achievement . . . [other responsibilities include] assuring that major plans are designed to meet objectives . . . approval of major company decisions, and checking on results." Koontz adds that boards "should insist upon review of performance and plans, . . . force consideration of limiting factors . . . and ask discerning questions." [13]

Burns prescribes a concise and limited role for the board when he says, "If one summarized the historical role of the trustee as defined in most American institutions of higher education at this time, it might appear as follows: hold the charter of the institution, establish the overall policies, select the chief executive officer, raise funds, approve the budget, and represent the institution with its publics." He stresses that "the role of the trustees as members of a board is legislative, not executive . . . [and] the majority of board members mindful of their legislative [rather than executive] functions, scrupulously avoid interfering in the operation of the institution." [14]

In the library field, Young outlines twelve duties and responsibilities of the library board. They are: "1) Employ a competent and qualified librarian; 2) Determine and adopt written policies to govern the operation and program of the library; 3) Determine the purposes of the library and secure adequate funds to carry on the library's program; 4) Know the program and work of the library in relation to the community; keep abreast of standards and library trends; 5) Establish, support, and participate in a planned public relations program; 6) Assist in the preparation of the annual budget; 7) Know local and state laws; actively support library legislation in state and nation; 8) Establish among the library policies those dealing with book and material selection; 9) Attend all board meetings and see that accurate records are kept on file at the library; 10) Attend regional, state, and national trustee meetings and workshops and affiliate with the appropriate professional organization; 11) Be aware of the services of the state library extension agency; 12) Report regularly to the governing officials and the general public." [15] This is a long and comprehensive list and it might be questioned whether or not any board member could possibly measure up to all of the demands as stated. It would be perhaps reasonable to assume that most board members, even the most devoted and dedicated ones, would have difficulty in scoring 100 percent on all of these items.

Writing from his perspective as a social welfare administrator, Schmidt lists nine responsibilities of the board: "1) Attaining the goals or purposes of the agency . . . making certain that the established goals are being pursued and advising when the goals need changing because of changed conditions. . . . 2) Creating the structure . . . the board has the responsibility of seeing to it that the agency's legal structure is proper and that it continues to remain so under all state and federal laws. . . . 3) Providing the necessary facilities . . . needed by an agency to conduct its activities. . . . 4) Employing the executive . . . select, fix compensation, establish duties, delegate to him the necessary authority to administer the work of the agency, evaluate his work, relieve him of his duties if necessary. . . . 5) Fixing the policies . . . it is the duty of the board to prescribe the services to be provided as well as the basic policies for the administration of these services. . . . 6) Setting the budget and providing the finances . . . the obligation rests upon the governing board to set the budget and thereby establish services. . . . 7) Checking the operation . . . the board must check the operations periodically and see to it that all is going well. . . . The trustees of an agency are accountable to the public for their stewardship of the agency. . . . They must know that the services are provided as they have directed. 8) Interpreting the services . . . is a special concern of the members of the governing board. . . . 9)

Participating in community planning . . . the board has a clear duty to participate in his community's efforts to plan and raise funds for health and welfare operations." [16]

All of the above points appear to be important. When one reviews them, it appears evident that only when boards successfully fulfill these responsibilities are they able to meet their primary obligations to provide the best possible services.

As one analyzes the various formulations certain basic ideas seem to stand out without regard to the agency being considered. First, it is a major responsibility of board members to understand and have *conviction* about the purpose and function of their agency. The word *conviction* seems to be the key. Board members must feel deeply about the importance of what their agency is doing and must be willing to express those convictions with courage and steadfastness.

Second, it is the responsibility of the board member to be *thoroughly informed* about the program of the agency and be able and willing to interpret that program widely so that more and more people will understand it.

Third, it is the responsibility of the board member to work hard to guarantee that the agency is provided with the *resources* essential to the rendering of good service. Resources mean adequate budget, adequate staff, adequate facilities, so that the agency will be able to render high-quality service in relation to the best of standards.

Fourth, board members must be ready and able to *evaluate* the work of the agency and their own work also. In so doing, they will be making a conscious and continuous endeavor to be certain that the agency is doing the best possible job.

Fifth, it is important that board members have *vision* and that they plan ahead so that needs will be met before acute problems arise.

Sixth, board members have the responsibility to ally themselves with others in the community in creating an articulate *philosophy of human needs* and how these needs should be met.

Leadership Role of the Board in Time of Change

As one writer remarked, change is the central condition with which all groups must grapple. He said, "Everything, in short, is changing faster than our minds and institutions can adjust. This is the central issue of the age. Change is the nightmare of every separate branch of the government. It baffles the leaders of management and labor. It troubles the universities and the churches. For, the pace of change is now so swift that there is scarcely any human relation—whether of nation to nation, President to Congress, Congress to Supreme Court, labor to management, teacher to student, minister, priest or rabbi to congregation, or every parent to child—that is not caught up in unfamiliar problems without dependable guidelines." [17]

Boards everywhere are trying to understand the changes that are going on and are trying to take a leadership role in these changing times. Curiously, as one reviews the literature on boards, there is little in the way of explicit statements about the leadership role of boards. Perhaps the leadership ideal is implicit in what has been written. Nonetheless boards can be expected to give more attention to the provision of broad leadership and less attention to details of agency operations. As a general term, leadership means the ability to inspire people to work together to accomplish a mutually agreed upon goal. Leaders release and relate the energies of people so that they work together and use all available resources to a common end. Although this notion of leadership is usually thought of in terms of the individual, it applies to the board as a group as well. The board must *give, show,* and *take* leadership at various times. The board *shows* leadership by the way it behaves, especially when under pressure. It *gives* leadership by the way it responds to situations and there are many occasions when it *takes* leadership by moving in a certain direction. The board gives, shows, and takes leadership in at least two broad categories. First, there is the internal category or the giving of the leadership to the internal operating affairs of the agency. Here would be included such matters as policy determination, program development, personnel development, evaluation, and long-range planning. So, within the agency the board should be persistently and consistently giving leadership to these various tasks.

The second broad category would be external leadership or leadership in behalf of the agency within the community. This means taking initiative to help people know about, understand and hopefully be in support of the important work that the agency is doing. It means taking leadership with other organizations that share kindred goals, that have a reasonable congruency of values and convictions about the kind of community it should be.

The board's role in giving leadership to the policy process is a most interesting and demanding job. It is not the kind of work that everyone likes to do because usually many factors have to be weighed in major policy decisions. In national agencies some policies are determined at the top and the local policy-making job flows out of these national determinations. This does not mean that national policies are forced upon the local agency, because usually the local agency has its vote in the representative councils of the nationals. The same situation prevails in local governmental agencies that are providing services in partnership with the state and federal government. Here joint policy making is frequently complicated and guided by legislation which may have been enacted at the several governmental levels. In all cases the board must take into account the changing needs and characteristics of the community. They must also take into account the operating experiences of the agency in terms of critical review and evaluation. If operating experience suggests to the board that a current policy is poor, inadequate, or irrelevant to conditions, then that policy is in need of revision. In the ongoing work of the agency the process of policy determination is continuous. It starts when someone sees the need for a new policy or the review of an established one. Then the decision must be made to work on the matter and usually an assignment is made to a task group, frequently a committee of the board or a joint committee of board and staff. If it is a major policy change, it may have a considerable amount of feeling behind it which can raise many questions and arouse resistance to the change. Here, especially, the board must exercise its leadership responsibility. Sometimes it is necessary to set forth a tentative formulation of the policy and have it reviewed and even tested out before it is actually enacted. In any event, when the board adopts a new policy it has the responsibility to prepare people to understand it and make use of it in the program of the agency. Then comes the matter of evaluating experience with the policy, reformulating it if need be, making changes in it if operations reveal inadequacies. The best policies are those which have come out of facts and experiences carefully evaluated.

Another leadership responsibility of the board is that of goal setting. Broad goals, major targets, are most important to the vitality of any organization. The number of persons to be served, quality of service to be provided, the numbers of personnel that are needed, and the facilities required, all enter into the area of the board's leadership responsibility. Goal setting, even when the goal may seem out of reach for the present, is a way of showing faith in the potential of the agency and is a force for motivating people to do their best. Long-range goals are the very essence of leadership. It is important that the board articulate and demonstrate its deep commitment to the enduring values represented by the agency. Unless board members put their minds and hearts behind these values it is unlikely that they or the others involved will work toward goal realization with the maximum amount of energy. As Hughes has said, "The value of the word divorced from the act is at best debatable. It can even be self-defeating; a good way to damage a principle or idea is to affirm it passionately, then fail to give it true testimony in deed." [18]

The board also has a leadership role in the area of program and services. Even though many organizations are very large and serve many thousands of people, it is still important that the board understand clearly what kind of program of services is being offered and what is needed to make it better.

The board must also look at itself and check constantly to see that its ways of work are productive. The voluntary agency board must take leadership in developing other persons to be ready for board service. One of the board's biggest jobs is to see that this happens. It means spotting people in the community who can take on work assignments and grow into competence as eventual board members.

In his discussion of leadership responsibilities of school board members Tuttle remarks, "School board members are called upon to exercise those qualities of leadership which time and again have raised America to new heights of effort and accomplishment . . . seven qualities of leadership [include] integrity, that quality which attracts the confidence of others; perseverance, that quality which persists in the face of difficulties; faith, the unfaltering belief that something better lies ahead; ability to plan; vision; initiative, the ability to move ahead; courage, inner strength to face whatever lies ahead." [19]

The Coordinating Board

Relatively recent but growing in numbers are the coordinating boards which have some responsibility for a number of institutions, usually in a defined field of service and in a defined geographic area. In the field of higher education, Martona says, "The most recent type of board responsible for higher education is that which has no responsibility for controlling or governing any institution but has instead a duty to coordinate a number of institutions and to guide the overall development of higher education in a state." [20]

Coordinating boards have been established in other fields as well as higher education. Increasingly, they are being formed and utilized in such fields as health, recreation, and social welfare. While their chief function is overall planning and coordination it is evident that they do have a determinative influence over existing institutions and some authorities view the coordinating board as a threat to autonomy.[21]

Commissions and Committees

The terms "commission" or "committee" are frequently used in somewhat the same context as is the term "board." Fesler says the term "commission may refer either to a certificate of office or to a body of men to whom some public function has been entrusted . . . the second usage of commission to denote a group of men jointly performing a public function has not been formulated with precision. Legislatures and chief executives that create and name agencies have not developed a nice discrimination among commissions, boards, and committees." [22]

Dickinson agrees that "the word commission is employed in English speaking countries as the official title of many governmental bodies which consist of a number of members and are otherwise called boards. . . . The term appears at the end of the fifteenth century as a designation of any special body of officials charged by royal commission or warrant with the performance of specified duties." [23]

Mansfield elaborates, "The term 'commission' covers several usages . . . the name of an official agency or institution headed by a collegial body of commissioners . . . an agency called a commission may be otherwise indistinguishable from something called a board, a council, a committee, a tribunal, or a court. . . . Two preliminary distinctions, if not too sharply drawn, are useful in sorting out types of commissions and the various functions they perform. One is temporal, between bodies convened ad hoc to deal with a specific situation and those permanently established to handle a class of business arising regularly or intermittently. . . . The second kind of distinction turns on the overt purposes commissions may be established to serve: 1) an arbitral commission to reach a decision binding on the parties to a dispute . . . 2) a commission of inquiry to investigate, report findings, and perhaps pass judgment on the responsibilities of individuals for an event—often a disaster or a scandal—that has transpired, such as the Warren Commission following the assassination of President Kennedy in 1963; 3) a ceremonial commission to mark an occasion of moment . . . 4) a study commission to make plans or recommendations for future public policy . . . 5) an operating commission to conduct a branch of public enterprise . . . 6) an advisory commission to maintain liaison between a governmental agency and some of its clientele publics . . . 7) a regulatory commission to supervise some field of public or private activity. . . . These categories are suggestive rather than exhaustive. . . . The universe of commissions doing business under that name or another, is too heterogeneous for systematic study as a single category, apart from the initial difficulties of definition and collection in compiling an inventory. Research in the field, accordingly, has generally taken one or another of at least three broad paths, not altogether mutually exclusive: historical, topical, and comparative, all dealing with selected fragments." [24]

In addition to the Warren Commission mentioned above, the National Advisory Commission on Civil Disorders [25] of 1967–68 is perhaps one of the better known commissions appointed by the President of the United States. In an earlier period of history the Commission on the Organization of the Executive Branch of the Government [26] (Hoover Commission) made a significant contribution.

Finer presents a useful differentiation between board, commission, and committee when he writes, "The term committee denotes a body of persons charged with some specific function or functions. There appear to be three qualifying characteristics, namely that: 1) This body should, in some sense, be derivative from, or dependent upon, another, and usually larger body. The etymology of the word itself suggests it is a body to which something has been committed. 2) It is usually smaller than the body from which it derives its status. 3) Usually the procedure of a committee is more informal than procedure in the body from which it derives. . . . A sub-committee is a body standing in much the same relationship to a committee as a committee stands in relation to the parent body." [27]

Advisory Boards, Commissions, and Committees

In addition to the policy-making administrative boards discussed earlier in this chapter there are many boards, commissions, and committees whose role is strictly *advisory*. As Macmahon points out, "Advisory boards have been used in many countries chiefly as a means of corrective expression of opinion by groups of the population representing particular interests. Latterly they have tended increasingly to take on the character of councils of technical experts. They are, indeed, significant notably as a phase of the accommodation of government to the diversity and specialization of a society at once technical and competitive." [28] Prominent during the Johnson administration was the twenty-one-member National Advisory Council on Economic Opportunity with an independent staff director responsible for the supervision of the anti-poverty program.[29]

The social welfare laws of an eastern state provide for the appointment of a Citizens' Advisory Committee on Welfare. "There shall be a citizens' advisory committee on welfare, consisting of seven members, appointed by the governor. The welfare commissioner shall be, ex officio, a member of said committee. . . . Said committee shall choose its chairman, annually, provided the welfare commissioner shall not be appointed as chairman. Said committee shall meet at least eight times annually and at such other times as the welfare commissioner may request. The commissioner shall present to the committee, for its discussion and advice, plans for major or important changes in policy, program or organization of the welfare department, and the committee may make recommendations to the welfare commissioner. The commissioner shall make reports at least quarterly to the committee on the operations of the department. Members of the committee shall receive no compensation but shall be reimbursed for their necessary expenses." [30] In referring to the work of this advisory committee the commissioner remarked that "it has been most helpful and faithful in considering with and advising the Department on program directions and policy issues as well as interpreting the welfare program and goals in the community. . . . [This] highly distinguished group of citizens, appointed by the Governor, meets with the Welfare Commissioner and Executive staff members regularly each month to discuss program planning, to review proposed policy changes and to advise on Department problems." [31]

On the local community level, a recent study of the public schools recommended the formation of "neighborhood advisory school boards within each district . . . to facilitate community-school communications." [32] Recently, the Alumni Federation of a large university advocated the creation of advisory boards of visitors to fulfill an inspection role.[33]

It is important to point out that generally the advisory board, committee, or commission has no legal authority as such for administering the affairs of the agency or institution. It is essentially an *advisory* group and the advice and counsel it offers may or may not be heeded.

When an agency decides that it wishes to create an advisory board, or when an advisory board is created for it, someone has to take responsibility for spelling out the qualifications sought in the members. If it can be assumed that it is the purpose of the advisory group to give professional and technical service to the agency, persons with these qualifications should be sought. They should be persons who would bring a broad understanding of the work of the agency and related experience in the field of service under consideration. In addition, they should bring a breadth of vision and a high degree of community understanding and community-mindedness. Good advisers are persons who learn quickly and are rapidly able to see and appreciate some of the problems of the agency. When advisory personnel are asked to serve they should be given a clear statement about how long their term is, how often they are to meet, and what particular items are likely to be considered by the group.

Advisory boards have worked on various assignments. For example, they have helped an agency develop a public relations plan and program; they have helped to formulate a new program of psychiatric consultation service as something an agency felt to be needed but required outside help; they have made suggestions as to the timing and organization of a capital fund campaign for a new facility; they have made a comprehensive review of agency program and offered advice as to how it might be strengthened; they have helped to plan a community survey as an avenue for compiling fresh factual data for the agency; they have reviewed the agency's investment program and have suggested modifications.

It has been suggested that now and then the advisory committee is a device used to develop support for a predetermined position. In his discussion of the use of power by a prominent mayor, Halberstam says, "Where problems have arisen he has quickly appointed committees, often filled with former business foes, and then subtly moved the committee over to his own position." [34]

The advisory board system presents many advantages for today's complicated community agency. It brings into an organized working relationship expert thinkers who can greatly contribute to the development of agency program. It also makes possible the recruitment of professional expertise for special assignments. These persons would not be available for a continuing administrative board relationship but can give time for less frequent meetings as an advisory group. To some extent, having an advisory board makes it possible for the agency itself to become more representative of the best thinking and best practice in an area of service. It is also possible that a well-organized advisory board can make a considerable contribution in the areas of study and research.

In some cases agencies fail to make use of duly constituted advisory groups. Such failure leads to frustration and an occasional resignation. Referring to his unsatisfactory experience and resignation from an advisory committee a chairman wrote: "As chairman of the Advisory Committee on Older Persons programs of that agency [the federal Office of Economic Opportunity], I felt that in good conscience I could no longer serve on a committee that was advisory in name only and used as 'window dressing.' Over the three years of the committee's existence, it was never consulted on any major program, policy, budget or other significant aspect of the elderly poor." [35]

Inasmuch as it is highly possible that some agencies will have both an administrative board and an advisory board or advisory committees as devices for furthering their work, it is necessary to discuss some of the questions that may arise. In the first place, are these two groups clear as to their purposes in the agency structure? If it can be agreed that the administrative board must necessarily concentrate its attention on the major policy decisions of the agency, then the advisory group will center its attention on the professional and technical aspects of agency service and will not try to make policy but will transmit its findings to the administrative board. In addition, when the agency has both kinds of boards, thought must be given to the role of the executive and the different responsibilities he carries in behalf of each. It is likewise necessary to work out communication lines between the two groups. In some situations, joint meetings are held at periodic intervals.

When an agency has both an administrative and an advisory board it is important to be clear on the specific items to be referred to each group for study, consideration and action. Inasmuch as the advisory board is seen functioning appropriately in the area of studying program problems, it is not proper for this group to concern itself with agency administration in an operating sense. The items to be referred to the advisory board for study, consideration, discussion and recommendations would be primarily major questions of program and services where the agency wants the best thinking of these expert people. This is not to say that the administrative board does not concern itself with program and services. It does, but it does so in the framework of policy making and administrative implementation. Furthermore, it is clearly possible that recommendations from an advisory board with regard to program and services may not be acceptable to the administrative board and may not be followed, or only partially followed.

Evaluation of an Advisory Committee

In an eastern state an advisory committee for the Children's Bureau, a public child-welfare agency, was appointed late in 1960. The Administrative Code of the state specified that this committee had the power and the duty to advise the Children's Bureau regarding standards of eligibility, nature and extent of service, amounts of payments to individuals, standards of approval, certification and licensure of institutions and agencies, ways and means of coordinating public and private welfare activities, and such other matters as may by law require citizen review or may be referred by the Children's Bureau. It also had the power and the duty to arrange for and conduct public hearings, to promote better public understanding, and to make recommendations to the State Board of Welfare on matters referred by them to the committee, or as may be required to promote the effectiveness of the program of the Office of Children and Youth.

In seven years this advisory committee held twenty-eight regular meetings, five special meetings, and fifteen public hearings. After an exhaustive study of the minutes of these meetings and interviews with committee members an evaluator of the work decided that there had been "some significant accomplishments" but there was an "absence of cohesive functioning within well-formulated purposes and goals. . . . The Committee has not examined the needs of the children of the state to establish goals and purposes for the Department's program for children. It has not focused its attention on the extent and quality of services being offered and the accessibility of these services. It has not concerned itself with the organizational and financial structure which delivers these services. It has not addressed itself to the development of services in areas of unmet needs. The Committee should re-examine its responsibility and competence from the perspective of its legislative mandate. Its goals should not be fragmented, but should be related to a purpose encompassing a comprehensive program for children and youth. In achieving these purposes and goals, the Committee should not be limited in its structure. The Committee should increase its use of additional citizens in more specialized committees. Regional units of the Committee might be used effectively. More frequent meetings of the entire Committee might be helpful. The time and energy of the Committee could be enhanced by some plan for orientation of new members, by professional staff assigned to the Committee, and by some regular means of communication to be currently advised on all aspects of the program." [36]

NOTES

1. John A. Fairlee, "Boards, Administrative," by John A. Fairlee. Reprinted with permission of the publisher from the *Encyclopedia of Social Sciences,* Seligman and Johnson, editors (New York: Macmillan, 1930, 1958), Vol. II, pp. 6-7.
2. *Citizen Boards in State Welfare Departments* (New York: Advisory Committee on Citizen Participation, Community Chests and Councils of America, Inc. and the National Social Welfare Assembly. Bulletin No. 154, December 1950), p. 3.
3. *Ibid.,* p. 4.
4. S. V. Martona, *College Boards of Trustees* (New York: The Center for Applied Research in Education, Inc., 1965), p. 15. Reprinted by permission.
5. *New York Times,* January 9, 1968, p. 27. © 1968 by the New York Times Company.
6. *The Board of Directors of a Neighborhood Center* (New York: National Federation of Settlements and Neighborhood Centers, 1960), p. 5.
7. *Handbook for County Welfare Board Members* (St. Paul, Minnesota Division of Social Welfare, State Department of Social Security, 1942), p. 5.
8. *The Role of the Board of Directors in a Community YWCA* (New York: National Board YWCA, 1957), p. 3.
9. *Statement on Government of Colleges and Universities* (Washington, D. C. American Association of University Professors, American Council on Education, Association of Governing Boards of Universities and Colleges, *American Association of University Professors Bulletin,* Winter, 1966), pp. 9-10.
10. Sue Spencer, "Developing Effective Board and Committee Organization and Functioning" in *Building Board Leadership for the Years Ahead* (New York: National Jewish Welfare Board, Proceedings, Advanced Leadership Training Institute, September 7–8, 1963, Nashville, Tennessee), p. 42.
11. Harleigh B. Trecker, *Group Process in Administration—Revised and Enlarged* (New York: Woman's Press, 1950), pp. 97-98.
12. Chester A. Newland, "Current Concepts and Characteristics of Administration," *Child Welfare.* June 1963, p. 276.

13. Harold Koontz, *The Board of Directors and Effective Management* (New York: McGraw-Hill, 1967), pp. 24-28. Used with permission of McGraw-Hill Book Company.
14. Gerald P. Burns, *Trustees in Higher Education—Their Functions and Coordination* (Independent College Funds of America, 1966), pp. 13, 37, 42.
15. Virginia G. Young, *The Library Trustee—A Practical Guidebook* (New York: R. R. Bowker, 1969), p. 10.
16. William D. Schmidt, *The Executive and the Board in Social Welfare* (Cleveland: Howard Allen, Inc., 1959), pp. 39-50.
17. James Reston, *New York Times,* August 23, 1963. © 1968 by the New York Times Company. Reprinted by permission.
18. Emmett Hughes, *The Ordeal of Power* (New York: Atheneum, 1963), p. 276.
19. Reproduced from *School Board Leadership in America,* 1963, pp. 27-30, by special permission of the author and copyright owner, Edward Mobray Tuttle.
20. S. V. Martona, *op. cit.,* p. 21.
21. Logan Wilson, "Changing Patterns in Decision Making," Fourth Quadrennial Convocation of Christian Colleges, June 20, 1966. Mimeo., 11 pages.
22. James W. Fesler, "Commission," in Julius Gould and William L. Kolb (editors), *A Dictionary of the Social Sciences* (The Free Press of Glencoe, 1964), p. 105.
23. John Dickinson, "Commissions," *Encyclopedia of Social Sciences* (New York: Macmillan, 1933), Vol. 4, pp. 36-40.
24. "Commissions, Government" by Harvey C. Mansfield. Reprinted with permission of the publisher from *International Encyclopedia of Social Sciences,* David L. Sills, ed., Volume 3, pp. 12-17. © Crowell, Collier, and Macmillan, Inc.
25. *Report of the National Advisory Commission on Civil Disorders* (New York: Bantam Books, 1968), 608 pages plus Appendix.
26. *The Hoover Commission. Report on the Organization of the Executive Branch of the Government* (New York: McGraw-Hill, 1949), 524 pages.
27. S. E. Finer, "Committee," in Gould and Kolb, *op. cit.,* pp. 106-108.
28. "Boards, Advisory" by Arthur W. Macmahon. Reprinted with the permission of the publisher from *Encyclopedia of Social Sciences,* Seligman and Johnson, editors, Vol. II, pp. 609-611.
29. "Council to Guide Poverty Agency," *New York Times,* March 23, 1967.
30. *Social Welfare Laws of Connecticut—Revised Through 1959,* Sec. 17-18, p. 30.
31. "Report of State Welfare Department," *Digest of Connecticut Administrative Reports to the Governor, 1965–1966,* p. 285.
32. "Neighborhood Boards Urged for Schools," *Hartford Courant,* August 23, 1968.
33. *New York Times,* August 12, 1968, p. 1.

34. David Halberstam, "Daley of Chicago," *Harper's* magazine, August 1968, p. 29.

35. William C. Fitch, *Modern Maturity,* June-July 1968, p. 4. Reprinted with permission of the American Association of Retired Persons. © 1968.

36. Example supplied by Professor Robert Lansdale, School of Social Work, University of Maryland, August 22, 1968.

PART TWO

BOARD, EXECUTIVE, AND STAFF

3 *The Board and the Executive*

The way the agency board and the executive work together is of tremendous importance. This fact holds true in all fields of community service and in all types of agencies, governmental and voluntary. Yet, in many cases working relationships are not harmonious and serious problems frequently arise. Although these problems are usually kept under cover, now and then they are presented in the public press. For example, the vice-president of a local board of education "accused city school administrators of allowing a breakdown of communication between the board and the superintendent's office. In a letter to the board's secretary asking that the matter be included on the agenda for the next meeting she said in several incidents board members have learned of new appointments or programs in the newspaper. She said that this continued procedure on the part of the administration is not only an affront to the position of the board members, but an even more serious disregard of the fact that the ultimate responsibility in the education of children lies in the hands of the elected members of the board, who unlike the administration, must answer to the electorate for the actions of all involved. She accused the superintendent of not wishing to disturb the emerging pattern of a passive board allowing the administration to formulate policy." [1]

In another instance, when a hospital administrator was dismissed by the board he claimed that his efforts to bring about changes in the hospital's program ran into the vested interests of the lay board members who had become "settled in their ways." [2]

It is often pointed out that administrators and boards get into conflict situations because it is difficult to separate policy making from agency leadership. While theoretically the board is the policy-making and fiscal control body, the executive has the professional knowledge fundamental to realizing the basic purposes of the institution.[3]

Undoubtedly, there are many areas for potential conflict between the board and the executive with policy making and policy implementation only one, albeit a major one. Most apparent today is the lack of a clear understanding of roles and responsibilities. And, this has become increasingly true with the growth of professionalism and the rapid rise in the number of paid administrators of the community's health, welfare, and education enterprise. In addition to obvious role confusion there may be a lack of understanding of the basic assumptions which underlie the community agency where a board is ultimately responsible for the service rendered but the executive is responsible for day-to-day operations.

Board and Executive—Some Basic Assumptions

In scores of community agencies work is done by two groups of people. There are the thousands of volunteer board members who enter into or offer themselves for service by their own free will and without financial remuneration. Working along with these volunteers are professional staff members who have acquired special knowledge as a result of professional education and experience. They are engaged in this work as a means of livelihood. They have been hired to guide, advise, and work with the board. There is a general agreement that both groups of workers are needed and have important tasks to do. Certain assumptions underlie the way they must work together if the goals of the enterprises are to be achieved.

A first assumption is that the volunteer board members and professional workers of the agency constitute a leadership *team*. They are partners in a common task. In discussing the concept of partnership and shared responsibility one agency states, "Leadership in the YWCA is both volunteer and employee. Volunteers bring to the Association not only their own individual skills, abilities, and often accumulated YWCA experience but a broad knowledge of the community as well—its resources and organizations, its patterns of life, its feelings, its tensions, its values, its sources of pride. The contributions of the employed leaders include individual skills and experience, knowledge of specialized resources for program and administration, an objective way of looking at the community and the YWCA with understanding and insight, and concentrated time for the work." [4]

Second, it is assumed that professionals and volunteers have specific responsibilities as well as common or shared responsibilities. Both groups are fundamentally motivated by a common interest in and a wish to serve people. As for the professional workers, their primary role is that of carrying on or providing the program of professional services which the agency is set up to offer. For the volunteer workers, their chief responsibility is generally thought of as that of providing the conditions under which the agency may render the best quality of service. To a great extent there is an overlapping of responsibilities between professionals and board members. This will be elaborated upon later in the discussion of policy making.

Third, it can be assumed that communication is of the utmost importance as board, staff, and executive work together. They must be in continuous communication about the major concerns of the agency if they are to define, understand, and carry their separate and combined responsibilities.

Fourth, it is assumed that volunteer board members and professional workers have much to learn from each other. In fact, their learnings are continuous as board members glean insights from the problems faced by the staff and as the staff develops a grasp of the feedback from the community via the board.

If the above assumptions are correct, what is meant by the term "role" when used in connection with either the professional or the board member? In this context role means a set of tasks which the individual is expected to perform in the defined agency situation. In other words, it is a *work* role. A work role is a function allocated to a particular person. In the community agency, role has the dimension of the task or what is expected of the person and it has the further dimension of responsibility as to how the task will be done and in what time span. The concept further assumes that persons so entrusted with tasks will have the competence necessary to fulfill those tasks. Furthermore, to define the role of the professional worker it is necessary to define the role of the volunteer because what they do is so interrelated.

Admitting the fact that there are many variables of agency size, situation, community conditions, purposes, and so on, it is likely that the professional staff member will frame his role by selecting items from the task needs of the organization. Since the professional worker, whether he be librarian, school superintendent, social worker, or health worker, is prepared by education and experience to bring *special* knowledge and skill to the job it is rightfully assumed that he is there to exercise his professional skills in providing service to people. The employing agency has hired him precisely for this reason. Consequently, his major role would seem to be that of doing the work of the agency. The board is the policy-making group which decides what work is to be. Every professional worker, in a sense, commits himself to a predetermined role. But, since the agency is dynamic and changing, purposes, policies, and programs are also in a constant state of flux. This means that the professional worker has the further task of bringing to the policy-making board information needed to arrive at sound policy judgments either in terms of innovation or revision. Thus, the professional worker cannot be removed from the policy-making process because he must carry the role of helping the policy-making group to arrive at the best possible decisions. The way in which the worker fulfills this policy participation role varies with the position in which he finds himself. Obviously, the agency executive has a major responsibility in this realm which would not be so for the beginning junior staff member.

So the role of the volunteer board is policy determination. The board must determine policies regarding purpose, program, personnel, finance, public relations, and the like. But they bring to the agency general life experience rather than specific professional education. Out of their general experience they have the responsibility to study and understand and interpret community needs for service. They must know the history, purpose, programs, policies, and prevailing procedures of the agency. They must seek constantly to evaluate the work of the agency to assure that policies are not only being carried out, but that they are achieving the policy goals. But they cannot do this alone. They must do so in cooperation with the executive and staff. There must be a coming together of insight, experience, wisdom, and professional expertise. Policies are, of course, voted by the board but no board can make wise judgments without the contribution of the staff members who have firsthand experience with the services being rendered and the clientele being served.

Executive Role

A review of selected literature on the role of the executive in his work with the board shows that the following points are frequently discussed. 1) The executive instruments the policies of the board. 2) The executive prepares reports, budgets, personnel recommendations, program plans and other information to keep the board well informed. The executive reports needs in the agency and the community which indicate that changes in services may be required. 3) The executive is the liaison person between the board and the staff and other agencies. 4) The executive is responsible for a program of in-service training to improve services. He helps board members to develop their skills both within agency service and externally in community relations. 5) The executive is a key person in helping the board to understand its job and perform its tasks. However, he does not seek to dominate or control the board. 6) The executive interprets policies and actions of the board in the agency and in the community. 7) The executive helps in the selection of board members but, of course, does not make the final selection.

In an interview study [5] a number of executives were asked to describe their role with the boards as they saw it and tried to carry it out. All of them stated that it was their responsibility to carry out the decisions of the board and to translate the board's policies into action. The majority of them felt that they were suppliers of information to the board as aides to the making of policy decisions. They felt that data such as reports of operating experience, service statistics, and the like were essential to effective board decision making. Approximately three-fourths of the executives interviewed saw the supplying of information as only a subsidiary part of their major role, namely that of supplying leadership for the board to help it develop policies, provide resources and make the agency more valuable and useful to the community. They agreed that it was their continuing task to stimulate the board to devote time and attention to the major problems of the agency. They assumed that it was their job to encourage the board to develop its powers of judgment and discrimination in the always vital area of policy determination. Recognizing the inevitable gap between the board and persons served, these executives stressed the fact that they had a key job in helping the board to understand the program of services being offered. They saw themselves as interpreters of changing conditions in the community and as the initiators of program changes based upon revised policies.

The same executives reported that they carried an important liaison role between board and staff. Frequently this role had dual aspects; helping the board become aware of problems encountered by the staff in providing services and staff problems in general as well as interpreting staff attitudes and thinking; helping the staff to understand board thinking and attitudes. Other executives reported that it was a major responsibility of theirs to work with individual board members to help them to develop their capabilities and to enable them to make the maximum possible contribution to the agency. Some executives stated or implied that it was their role to bring and interpret the values, standards, and principles underlying good practice in their field of service.

As the interviewed executives described their roles, certain verbs appeared again and again. The most frequently used were: to stimulate, to interpret, to guide, to motivate, to integrate, to initiate, to direct, to advise, and to suggest. Two-thirds of these executives used several of these words denoting a philosophy of active leadership insofar as their work with the board is concerned.

In an earlier study [6] the author discovered that administrators saw their role with the board growing out of the ten major areas of executive leadership responsibility they felt they had to exercise in the total work of the agency. They stressed that they took responsibility for: planning and coordination, helping to formulate clear plans and then coordinating the work of various individuals and groups within the structure of the total agency; facilitating communication, keeping the channels open within the organization; presenting knowledge of the total agency so that various groups would develop understanding; providing an organized work environment in which group and individual tasks are defined, carried forward, and coordinated; helping develop clear assignments of responsibilities for board and staff members; analyzing tasks in terms of their relevance to specific aspects of program; studying, understanding, and interpreting the community situation in which the work of the agency takes place; establishing and maintaining effective working relationships with the groups to which defined tasks have been assigned; making continuous and creative use of the purpose of the agency with the board, the staff, and the community; providing opportunities for individuals to experience creative growth in their jobs.

Referring to one field, an authority stresses the high importance of reciprocity by saying, "No reciprocal relationship can be built between librarian and board unless at all times it is remembered that each is charged with responsibility as interpreter of the library world to the lay-man, the board as interpreter of the community to the librarian. The two interpreter roles are of equal importance. Both viewpoints must be weighed in the balance before the library can take its proper place in the community." [7]

From the field of public education, where school board and superin-tendent relationships are obviously of special significance, the observa-tion has been made that "the ideal situation . . . [is] where the board, in consultation with the superintendent, and on the basis of all available facts, establishes the policies by which the schools will be operated, and where the superintendent, with the full approval of the board, exercises his professional skill in administering those policies and in reporting their effectiveness or need for modification to the board." [8] The same writer underlines the fact that good relations between board and superin-tendent are based on an understanding of human relations, the mutual goal of serving children, and complete frankness; and he says that board-superintendent relations are never static but always changing and de-veloping.[9]

From the field of child welfare a strong plea was made to entrust to the executive the running of the agency. As Newbury said, "There is nothing that creates more confusion, misunderstandings and heartaches, with eventual loss of efficiency and failure to achieve objectives, than for board members to inject themselves into the day-by-day operations of a social agency. . . . One of the first tasks of the trustees . . . is to select a compe-tent executive. Having done so, the running of the agency from then on is the proper function of the executive, just as the running of a business cor-poration is the proper function of its chief executive officer." [10]

Young calls for more than merely permitting the executive to run the agency when she says, "The board should at all times give unqualified support in defense of the librarian's administration of its policies. In the controversial area of 'freedom to read' which today produces so many in-cidents between library and public, the board should be prepared to stand firm behind its policy on intellectual freedom, and behind the librarian in carrying out this policy." [11]

A school board association has clear and pointed remarks to make about the importance of harmony between school board and executive, although the same thing applies elsewhere: "There are several prerequi-sites for board-superintendent harmony. First, the board and superinten-dent need to be aware of their separate responsibilities and avoid encroaching on each other's area of activity. Second, there needs to be a clear understanding on the part of both the board and the superintendent that harmony between them is of great importance for the greater welfare of the school system and the better education of the children. Third, honest differences of opinion should be openly acknowledged. . . . Fourth, both the board and the superintendent need to be careful to assign credit where due, and where necessary to admit errors." [12]

Board Chairman and Agency Executive

The way the board chairman and the agency executive work together is a major factor in agency operation. If their relationship is good, one can be fairly sure that they will set a pattern for other relationships through the agency. If it is a poor one this also will be influential.

It is strange, but a search of the literature reveals little that has been written about the chairman-executive relationship. Even though the model of the volunteer board chairman and the employed executive director is commonplace throughout the private and public welfare enterprise here and elsewhere, it has not been studied to any great extent. In fact, there is little in the way of a conceptual scheme or framework within which the relationship can be studied, perhaps because society tends to take it for granted that effective partnerships will inevitably emerge. Yet a conceptual scheme is necessary for, as Culliton points out, "A conceptual scheme is a way of looking at things and is closely akin to a theory or principle or hypothesis, except that these other words have taken on special shades of meaning, especially in philosophy and scientific research. . . . Conceptual schemes, then, furnish the way in which we organize our thoughts and actions about reality. . . ." [13] Our conceptual scheme for understanding the board chairman and the executive as partners must be worked out in relation to the *total* enterprise being administered. Culliton helps again when he observes that "quietly, necessarily, and inevitably we are entering a period that forces man to find more accurate answers to questions involving the 'wholeness' of an operation and that demands entirely new approaches to these questions. The evil of specialization, that is, empire building, lack of coordination of different specialties, specialties working at cross purposes—these and similar issues can no longer be approached if the administrator's job were to decide which protagonist happens to be right. In the age of analysis, men were taking knowledge apart, sorting it into manageable portions, and struggling almost desperately, to keep it in understandable, isolated parts. Now, however, the driving force of actual fact is pulling things back together. Man may resist, but he is powerless to hold back the force which is producing the age of synthesis." [14] So to understand and develop the board chairman-executive relationship it must be viewed in at least the two dimensions of *leadership* and *wholeness*.

Dimock has said, "All organizations need strong, constructive, imaginative leadership to pull together all elements of the program which otherwise tend to fly apart. . . . It is integrated leadership that keeps the parts together and hence leadership is more necessary in large bureaucratic institutions than it is in smaller, more informal ones. . . . There must be some one person at the top to watch over the program so as to keep it together, to keep it responsible, to combat self-centeredness, to promote innovation and vitality, and there must be extensions of leadership on subordinate levels so as to form a kind of network through which the influence of the top man is carried throughout the organization." [15]

The executive and the board chairman are the persons who make up the primary leadership team. To lead effectively the president and executive must have: 1) an understanding and acceptance of and a deep commitment to the basic values of the agency; 2) substantial knowledge of the professional service that the agency is rendering to people; 3) a strong identification with the fundamental purposes of the agency. Executives and chairmen are continuously engaged in establishing effective working relationships with and between people. Getting work done to accomplish agency purposes is primarily a matter of motivating people to their finest and highest levels of achievement.

As one observes effective board chairmen at work they seem to have certain basic characteristics. First, they are well informed about the work of the agency; they have the facts; they know what they are talking about because they have spent long hours studying the work of the agency they represent. Second, they care deeply about the work of the agency; they couple competence and concern with commitment. Third, they see the connection between conditions which exist in the community and the need for the agency to provide services. Fourth, they know how to work within and through their organization and in cooperation with other organizations that have similar goals. Fifth, they have a sense of history and a grasp of the processes of orderly, democratic change. Sixth, the effective chairman is generally aware of what is happening in the field and strives to keep up with new developments and new trends.

What are some of the major responsibilities carried by the leadership team of the executive and the board chairman? A partial list would include: 1) They are responsible for giving leadership to the continuous process of identifying community needs. 2) They are responsible for giving leadership to defining and realizing agency purposes. 3) They are responsible for giving leadership to provisioning the agency in terms of financial resources and other forms of support. 4) They are responsible for giving leadership to the development of program and services. 5) They are responsible for giving leadership to the development of a form of organization and structure which will support the program. 6) They are responsible for giving leadership to the continuing process of policy formulation and reformulation. 7) They are responsible for giving leadership to the evaluation of the agency. 8) They are responsible for giving leadership to the change process. However, in carrying these responsibilities the president and the executive director clearly cannot do everything themselves. They work *with* and *through* many persons in creative and productive ways. The work of the executive and the board chairman is thus seen as a process of working with people in ways that release and relate their energies so that they use all available resources to accomplish the purpose of providing needed community services and programs. People, resources, and purposes are thus brought together by the executive and the chairman in a continuous, dynamic process. The executive and chairman, as the primary leadership team, are seen as working with people to establish and maintain a system of cooperative effort with the *total* agency as the point of focus. Since many people must carry separate and specific tasks if the agency is to do its work, and since they inevitably see only a part of the picture, the job of seeing the *whole* agency and providing overall leadership falls to the executive and the board chairman. It is the release of energy and feeling properly channeled, directed, and *coordinated* by the primary leadership team which makes for goal achievement in the large sense.

The board chairman and the executive are also responsible for community leadership. This means the taking of initiative in helping people know about, understand, and hopefully be in support of the important work that the agency is doing. It also means sharing leadership with other agencies that have like goals and that have a reasonable similarity of values and convictions as to what kind of community it should be.

Of great importance in assessing the relationship between the executive and the board chairman is the extent to which they truly trust one another and have confidence in one another. When trust and confidence prevail it is apt to permeate the institution and be reflected in the other essential team relationships among staff members and committee chairmen and the like. Here it is basic that board chairmen and executives see their leadership as being essentially helping, enabling, and supporting, so that an increasing number of new leaders will be developed year after year. The major mechanism for such leadership development is the committee. Through successful and satisfying committee experience persons not only do the work of the agency but they also grow and develop as they do it. In a later chapter attention will be given to working with board committees because it is of major importance and deserves detailed treatment.

Executives and chairmen face many opportunities and challenges in their leadership jobs. Prior to undertaking such tasks they should ask whether or not they have the personality and the temperament to perform satisfactorily in this kind of work. Since they carry *total* responsibility for the agency, the strains and stresses may become great and the emotional drain may become heavy. They are exposed to more forces, often conflicting, and much of their work has to be done before the public. They must reconcile conflicting points of view and must try to achieve a balance under the many pressures put upon them. The inevitable conflicts between administrator and staff as discussed by Utz are likely to occur for board chairmen as well. Utz says, "A certain amount of conflict is inherent in the relationship between the administrative staff and practicing staff. This is so despite the fact that both are part of a larger organism with an overriding purpose to which they both adhere. Since there is a difference in the amount of authority each has, their very interdependence is a potential source of conflict. Other factors that make conflict inevitable are the differences in job responsibilities that call for different commitments on the part of each and different methods of operation. Since conflict produces a feeling of disequilibrium and leads to discomfort there is a natural tendency to wish to avoid it. One might hope that under sufficiently skilled administrative leadership conflict would be completely resolved—and the common purpose of the larger organism supports this hope. But for either administrative staff or practicing staff to believe that conflict can be avoided is to chase a will-o-the-wisp. Moreover, such a vain hope engenders frustration, self-doubt, and recriminations." [16]

Board chairmen and executives must maintain many relationships simultaneously. They must make more decisions and more complicated decisions. In addition, they must develop expertness in sequential thought. Cousins suggests that sequential thought is "the process by which one frame of ideas is attached to another in workable order so that they stick together without rattling or falling apart the moment they come in contact with a logical object or query. Sequential thought is the most difficult work in the entire range of human effort. Even when undertaken by highly trained intelligence, it can be enormously fatiguing. When attempted by untrained minds, it can produce total exhaustion within a matter of minutes, sometimes seconds. For it requires an almost limitless number of mental operations. The route must be anticipated between the present location of an idea and where it is supposed to go. Memory must be raked for relevant material. Facts or notions must be sorted out, put in their proper places, then supplied with connective tissue. Then comes the problem of weighting and emphasis. Sequential thought, like any other advanced form of human activity, is the result of systematic training." [17]

In addition, board chairmen and executives must decide what priorities to adopt, what choices to make, and what decisions to make first. Frequently they must say "no" and sometimes they must compromise because seldom are there enough resources to meet all of the needs that should be met.

In the light of the above it seems clear that executives and board chairmen must have a considerable amount of self-knowledge and self-insight at the time they assume their burdensome tasks and throughout all of the time they work together.

The authority which goes with leadership posts must be understood by both the executive and the board chairman. It is widely recognized that authority is inherent in every job. It goes with the function, the task, and the position. It is also agreed that the amount of, or degree of authority varies with the position held and is specific to the given position. In every case authority implies knowledge, experience, and a degree of competence. It also implies trust, responsibility, and acceptance by people. If organizations are to be effective, authority must be widely distributed. It must be shared by a large number of people. As Peabody says, "Authority relations are an integral component of organizational behavior. Clarification of the concept of authority would seem to be essential to the development of systematic organization." He then goes on to identify the bases of authority. He indicates that they are four in number: "One, the authority of legitimacy or legally conferred authority. Two, the authority of position, or the authority that is inherent in the office occupied by any person. Three, authority of competence which means the person possesses experience and appropriate technical skills based on professional training. Four, authority of person or personal attributes which seem to consist of a fusion of leadership skills." [18]

Insofar as the executive is concerned, it is necessary for him to make substantial use of his authority based upon his competence. He uses it to design and set limits on individual and group responsibility. He uses it to establish methods, procedures, and policies. He uses it to foster coordination and to create agency unity and wholeness. As Walton says, "Not only is authority necessary for the administration of education; it is also legitimate. Its sources, which are legal, social, and personal, provide the positive power and the sanctions that make it effective. . . . By authority we mean simply the power and the recognized right of the administrator, enforced by whatever sanctions he may employ, to make decisions necessary for the coordination of the activities of persons working within an organization. . . . Persons working in an organization accept the authority of the administrator because it is legal, because it is an accepted part of the culture, and because of certain traits in the administrator himself." [19]

Executives and board chairmen as well may have feelings about authority and may have difficulty in accepting the fact that they must use the authority vested in them and in their position. Problems may arise from misunderstandings, and from the failure on their part to spell out precisely the degree of authority involved in the various positions in the agency.

There can be little doubt that those who lead the agency have difficult and demanding jobs. As a student of institutional change has commented, "The administrator has to live in a multi-dimensional world with a responsibility for taking action in leading people and in dealing with concrete problems. He must constantly seek multi-functional solutions. This forces him into many paradoxical situations. The administrator must constantly strive to maintain a consistency in his own behavior while accepting the fact that his behavior will always appear inconsistent from any simple, one-dimensional frame of reference. He must constantly seek for solutions that resolve conflicts between the interests of several dimensions, but accept the fact that such conflicts are inevitable and never-ending. He must constantly seek to change behavior in the social system as a viable entity. He must seek a perfection of balanced development but accept the inevitability of imperfection. He must place heavy emphasis upon achieving organization purposes and must maintain the perspective of an outside observer, but not lose his impassioned involvement with the results of the system." [20]

The world of the executive, of course, varies greatly in terms of his setting. In summarizing his findings about the federal executive, Warner says, "In general, the federal executive conceives of the external world as highly relevant, capable of exerting strong pressures, demanding and complex. He applies this categorization not only to the world but also to the organization of which he is a part. In most cases he accepts the environmental pressure as a 'given,' at times he attempts to change or modify it when he finds it too constricting; but usually the feedback from his actions becomes threatening, and he gives up such notions and turns to acceptance. The external world is filled with authority figures, structural imperatives, associates, and masses of people with whom he must deal. He sees such an environment not only as a pressure-creating medium, but also as a means of getting things accomplished. It is helpful, it gives direction and cue; it influences, it is beneficial; it provides for security; it is supportive. On the whole, he views authority in a positive way. Authority figures are looked up to as persons of eminence and high status. They support, direct, and set goals. He cooperates with authority and a good relationship is maintained. This is a dominant theme among most federal executives." [21]

While the executive is in no sense "supervised" by the board chairman, the chairman and the board do have the responsibility for evaluating the work of the executive at periodic intervals. Regular evaluation rather than crisis evaluation is of great importance.[22] The executive has a right to know how the board views his work and the board has the responsibility to share its views with him. In discussing how a board of education should evaluate the superintendent, four questions are suggested: "1) How has he strengthened and improved the program of instruction? (curriculum development). 2) How well has he spent the public dollar? (financial management). 3) How skillfully has he recruited competent teachers and supervisors, assigned them appropriate tasks, and retained the best qualified? (personnel selection and training, institutional morale). 4) How much support for the schools has he earned from the community? (public and press relationships)." [23]

The Process of Policy Making

One of the crucial responsibilities of the board and the executive is that of policy making. While there is widespread agreement that it is the job of the board to make policy and the job of the executive to carry it out, there is ample evidence to support the thesis that it is not so simplistic as this sounds. In fact, the process of policy making is so involved and so complicated today that it often looms as an area of conflict and confusion. As reported recently in the press, studies have shown that there is apt to be conflict between advisory groups and professional workers because there is confusion about roles. Policy making and policy carrying out are frequently intertwined.[24] Or, as Stein pointed out, "We have been told in no uncertain terms that policy determination is the responsibility of the board alone, that policy execution is the responsibility of the executive and staff, that the executive is ultimately responsible for the results of agency programs. Nearly everyone understands these points and yet boards and executives have had trouble ever since there were boards and executives. It is not, of course, only in social work that problems arise. Every field has its own version of the same underlying concerns." [25]

Perhaps a part of the problem is caused by the fact that persons are not clear on the meaning of the term "policy." A look at a number of definitions reveals a variety of meanings. One national youth-serving agency declares that "a policy is an established course of action to be followed in recurring situations. . . . Policies serve many purposes. They point the way for developing plans, solving problems, and attaining objectives. They provide the framework for carrying out the work and the means by which the board can delegate authority and still maintain control. They permit uniformity and consistency of action throughout the council. For example, in dealing with a question covered by a policy affecting troops, all personnel concerned are able to handle the question in the same way. They bring about quick and effective decisions. Without a governing policy it would be necessary to refer each case as it occurs to the board for decision. When there is a policy, the decision can be made at the point of occurrence without delay." [26]

In the field of education, one writer defines the role of the board as legislative, that is, the establishing of policies and the role of the superintendent as administrative, or the carrying out of policies. By definition, "policies are principles adopted by the board . . . to chart a course of action for its administrator and to define the limits within which he shall exercise judgment and directions. Essentially, policies are a guide to the what, the why, and the how much of desired educational operations." The same authority goes on to say that "rules and regulations, as distinguished from policies, are the detailed directions necessary to put policies into effect. They are more likely to be formulated by the administrator with the informal approval of the board than to be initiated or formally acted upon by the board itself. Essentially, rules and regulations provide a blueprint as to the how, the who, the when, and the where of actual educational practice. Procedures are working rules or bylaws for the board itself as regards its organization, meetings . . . order of business, minutes and the like." [27]

With brevity and focus, Faatz said agency policies were written statements "which express the purpose, intentions, conditions under which the agency offers and effectuates the service for which it was created." [28]

In the library field, Young states that "library policy has been compared to a road map, and policy, like a map, should be clearly drawn on paper. This written policy should set out the terms of the library's operations; the what, when, where, and how, frequently the who, and sometimes the why. Policy determines the pulse of a community's library service—availability of library service, terms of staff employment, the objectives of the library's program, and the intellectual freedom which the community has a right to expect. . . . Policy is the responsibility of the library board, and except for the employment of a librarian, no other duty of the trustee is more important to the library and its welfare." [29]

A leading state association of school boards maintains that "the major functions of any board are the establishment of policies and procedures and the evaluation of school programs. A policy is a statement of a general principle or rule that the board agrees should apply to the solution of problems of a similar nature. Policy statements are used by the administration or board to decide whether a procedure is appropriate, or whether a complaint is legitimate. . . . Policies adopted by the board . . . should reflect certain convictions about desirable goals for the schools. These convictions, taken together, form a philosophy of education and provide a basis for evaluation. . . . Policies can be determined on a less personal and more rational basis if they are considered, developed, and recorded before a crisis arises. In any event, board members should be objective when determining policy. This is no place for snap judgment. You don't, of course, just sit down at a series of board meetings and determine the policies for the year. A set of board policies is a growing, changing compilation of the results of the board's best thinking. It is never a final and absolute product. Policies are subject to modification with changing needs and conditions, and should be formally reviewed periodically to make sure they reflect best practice." [30]

Reid says, "The board's responsibility includes establishing the basic policies of the agency and constantly re-examining and modifying those policies." [31] And Sher agrees that "the board has a profound responsibility, in partnership with administration, to establish policies dealing with such matters as determining priority in offering service. Equally important, it should join with other enlightened people in the community to determine ways and means of making such service available to the total community on a broader community and governmental level." In addition, Sher observes that "if policies are to be wisely fashioned, they must stem from a basic grasp of the agency's purpose within the community and of the extent to which that purpose is being met by the agency." [32]

Sorenson says "policy *formulation* and planning are the responsibility of both board and committee members and of professional staff . . . policy *determination* is the responsibility of the board alone . . . policy *execution* is the responsibility of the executive and his staff." [33]

The policy-making process is far from simple. Many intangible factors enter into it. As Graff observed in his discussion of how the President of the United States makes foreign policy, "What is the atmosphere in which he pieces together the information, the ideas, the inspiration—and, yes, the criticism—that are the stuff of policy-making? No full answers can ever be constructed out of the documents alone because the process of deciding is intangible and evanescent. Yet the questions remain, and they are central in the estimate Americans make of how they are doing in the world. . . ." [34]

And no matter who makes the policy there are always items about which little or nothing can be done. As Leighton said, "Men and women engaged in making policy, whether the level be high or low, are always subject to determinants not of their own choosing. These include law, protocol, budget, personnel, interlocking with other policies, lack of time, and the opinions of fellow government officials, the legislature and the public. As a result it is not uncommon for matters that really have nothing to do with a particular policy issue to force on it a shape which none of the policy makers concerned thinks wisest or best. Policy making in practice is largely a matter of improvisation, of doing the best you can with what you have and, as in other aspects of life, this is seldom ideal." [35]

There is increasing evidence to support the notion that while the board must determine what a policy is to be, a great many people should be involved in working with the board to help them understand how to make wise policy decisions. Surely the executive and the staff have a great deal to contribute. But what about the persons being served by the program? Some would say that clients, students, patients, should have no part in the policy process; yet how can the policy be in tune with the views of the constituency unless they too are involved? Recently it was front-page news when two state commissioners of education "urged that *high-school* [italics added] students be given some control over school policies on curriculum, class scheduling, and after-school activities." [36] While this position may be a distinctly minority one, there is a rising tide of feeling that policies should not be made by remote boards and then simply imposed upon persons on a "take it or leave it" basis. As Jennrich declared, "All persons affected by policy should have some part in creating it, and any social agency that operates under the hoary concept that the board alone makes policies and the staff alone carries them out, should be well on the road to extinction. Ideally, on major policies, neither the executive nor his board nor staff should make final decisions, since the community that picks up the check for these costly services should be involved. Only as we work toward responsible participation and integration of policy-making and operations can we have a dynamic agency." [37]

The president of a national youth-serving agency asked, "How can the volunteers in their policy-making groups come to an intelligent final decision about anything unless they have the information they need on which to make it? And who has the bulk of that information? You [the staff] do. Your part in policy making is to supply the grist for the mill. It is your job to get the information, to sift and sort it. Further, it is your job to pass that information along to those who plan to use it for policy making." [38]

In the field of government administration, policy making and planning are closely linked. Reagon sees planning as a prerequisite to policy making and calls planning a four-factor process: "1) Establishing goals, and priorities among them, in relation to resources (those currently available plus those whose future availability may itself be a planning goal); 2) The measurement of the distance and difficulties between the present situation and the desired objectives (including projections of how far and fast already existing programs would go toward accomplishment of the objectives); 3) The formulation of programs (timing, assignment of specific tasks to specific agencies, estimating required resources in detail, budgeting yearly increments) by which it is hoped the objectives can be reached; and 4) Periodic modification of both objectives and programs in the light of experience with incremental actions." [39]

Tradition enters into the amount of responsibility granted to various groups in the policy-making process. In referring to the university, Woodring remarks that "by a tradition that dates from the Middle Ages, the faculty is the policy-making body. But the faculty of a contemporary American university shares its responsibility for policy with a board of trustees or regents which, in most cases, holds the final legal authority. The fact that a university president stands midway between these two policy-making bodies, each of which frequently wants more power at the expense of the other, makes his task far more difficult than that of the head of an industrial, governmental, or military organization in which power flows from the top downward. . . . Policy in most of America's great universities, as well as in the better small colleges, both public and private, is not made by the administrators. Only in the broadest sense is it made by the board; it results from the interaction of countervailing forces. The board reflects the public conscience and acts as a buffer between the university and the larger community that supports it. The faculty, through its elected representatives—a faculty senate, council or committees—has the primary responsibility for academic policy. . . . The administration clarifies and enunciates policy, reconciles conflicting points of view, mediates disputes, protects students and faculty from threats from outside the institution, and tries to keep the institution solvent." [40]

In his study of voluntary social welfare agencies, Kramer isolated four variables which influence the extent to which the will of the board or the executive would predominate in the policy process. "1) The organizational structure of the agency; its size, complexity, and degree of bureaucracy. 2) The character of the agency's services or program, whether they are technical or highly professionalized in content or conceived as residual or institutional in nature. 3) The type of policy issues, e.g., programmatic, housekeeping, professional, ideological, or fiscal. 4) Aspects of the board member's status and relationship to the agency such as the duration of his membership, degree of financial responsibility and contributions, role as a consumer of agency services, or participant in its program; the number of his other organizational affiliations and his social status in the community. 5) The executive's professional status and duration of employment. . . . The executive exerts a greater influence than the board member in the policy process to the extent that these variables are maximized." [41]

In an earlier work the author [42] listed the factors that must be taken into account in policy making. What are the sources of data, information, opinion, thinking, and feeling which must be considered in this important task? Beyond the defined purpose of the agency it seems necessary to recognize that other things enter into policy making. First, there is the matter of specific community characteristics and conditions which will influence what services should be provided, to whom they are to be given, and how they should be conducted. Second, there is the major source of policy in the operating experience of the agency critically reviewed and evaluated. Third, suggestions from persons served, agency members, clientele and general constituency represent a vital source of data and expression both regarding need for policies and how they should be stated. Fourth, current best practice as revealed by study and research in the field should be considered. Fifth, interagency cooperative projects often provide useful material for policy determination. Sixth, special committees such as professional advisory groups may offer experience particularly pertinent to a given policy problem. Seventh, agencies that are a part of a national organization may receive much help from communicating with their parent body.

The author has described the process of policy determination as a series of steps or phases in which many persons play a part. The board, the executive, the staff, the constituency, and the community must all become involved. Any one of these groups or individuals within them may feel, recognize, and express the need for a stated policy to guide some phase of the work of the agency. The policy process thus can begin at any point. When the need is recognized and accepted by the board, responsibility for fact gathering and preliminary formulation of tentative policy must be assigned. The assignment can be made to the executive and the staff, or it can be made to a board committee, or it can be made to a joint committee of board, staff, and constituency. In any event, as a matter of principle those persons to be affected by the policy should participate in the presentation of facts, suggestions, and ideas prior to the first formulation. Although they may not be *legally* responsible for the ultimate decision, their views are important if the final policy is to be understood and followed. Ordinarily, it is wise and helpful to prepare a trial formulation of a new policy and give consideration to the implications of it before it is enacted. Thought must be given to the effect of the policy on persons served, program, budget, staff work load, and community relations. It is time well spent to check up on the impact of the policy in advance of adoption. In some situations a new policy may be tried out on a time-limited basis before it is enacted as a permanent one. When a policy has been adopted it is vital that a timetable be established for its review and a decision made as to who will be responsible for the review. When major policy changes are to be made, time must be devoted to advance interpretation of them as a way of preparing the persons affected by them. As a general rule, policy making should proceed in an atmosphere of openness and sharing with maximum participation on the part of the people involved. New policies should never be "sprung" on people. While it is true that the board must make the final decision, it is both impossible and unwise to carry on the policy-making process in secrecy. The board cannot do the job alone.

Good policies grow out of a process of participation on the part of many individuals and groups. They are evolutionary and flow out of operations to a great extent. Policies are tools for the board, the executive, the staff, and the constituency to use. Policies should be positive statements clearly offered as helpful tools for those who follow and implement them. Hodgson states the case emphatically when she says, "The application of a policy to a field of practice calls for the exercise of initiative, judgment, and imagination, as well as administrative skill, on the part of various members of the organization. Contrary to a widespread impression policies are intended not to restrict initiative but to provide automatic safeguards to functioning so that the interests of both the organization and the public are served to best advantage." [43]

In summary, good policies should be based upon and develop out of the agency purpose. Adequately evaluated facts are the essential ingredients in policy formulation and reformulation. Persons affected by policy should share in the creation of it. There must be an organic unity and consistency among the various policies of the agency and the relationship between policies and purposes should be apparent. Although the board has the legal responsibility for the final determination of policy, the entire agency should participate in the process leading up to the final decision. Policy making, planning, and operations are integrally related and cannot be dissociated. New policies should grow out of an evaluation of the effectiveness of old policies. The carrying out of policies in the spirit of their intent is an integral part of the administrative responsibility of the executive and the staff.

NOTES

1. *Hartford Courant,* August 4, 1968.
2. *Hartford Courant,* November 30, 1966.
3. Fred M. Hechinger, "Administration vs. Board," *New York Times,* November 28, 1965.
4. *The Board and the Executive Director* (New York: National Board, YWCA, 1953), p. 6.
5. Harleigh B. Trecker, *Social Agency Boards—An Exploratory Study* (School of Social Work, University of Connecticut, 1958).
6. Harleigh B. Trecker, "Understandings of Administration," YWCA *Magazine,* June, 1960.
7. Virginia G. Young, *The Library Trustee—A Practical Guidebook* (New York: R. R. Bowker, 1969), p. 40.
8. Reproduced from *School Board Leadership in America,* 1963, p. 107, by special permission of the author and copyright owner, Edward Mowbray Tuttle.
9. *Ibid.,* p. 108.
10. George Newbury, "The Two R's—Responsibility and Representation," in *The Board Member of a Social Agency* (New York: Child Welfare League of America, Inc., 1957), p. 34.
11. Young, *op. cit.,* p. 37.
12. *Boardsmanship—A Guide for the School Board Member,* Fourth Edition, 1969, p. 47. Revised by the staff of the California School Boards Association, Sacramento, California. Used by permission.
13. James W. Culliton, "Age of Synthesis," *Harvard Business Review,* September-October, 1962.
14. *Ibid.*
15. Marshall Dimock, *Administrative Vitality* (New York: Harper, 1959), p. 175.
16. Cornelius Utz, "The Responsibility of Administration for Maximizing the Contribution of the Casework Staff," *Social Casework,* March, 1964.
17. Norman Cousins, "Not So Fast," *Saturday Review,* July 6, 1963. © 1963, Saturday Review, Inc.
18. Robert L. Peabody, "Perceptions of Organizational Authority: A Comparative Analysis," *Administrative Science Quarterly,* March 1962.
19. John Walton, *Administration and Policy Making in Education* (Baltimore: Johns Hopkins Press, 1959), pp. 104-106.
20. Paul R. Lawrence, *The Changing of Organizational Behavior Patterns* (Cambridge: Harvard University Graduate School of Business Administration, 1958), pp. 225-226.

21. W. Lloyd Warner, *The American Federal Executive* (New Haven: Yale University Press, 1963), p. 193.
22. E. Elizabeth Glover, *Crises in Board-Executive Relationships in Social Agencies* (Unpublished Doctoral Dissertation, The School of Social Work, University of Pennsylvania, 1964).
23. *Boardsmanship, op. cit.,* p. 49.
24. "Study Confirms Head Start's Ills," *New York Times,* August 9, 1968, p. 9.
25. Herman D. Stein, "Board, Executive, and Staff," *Social Welfare Forum, 1962* (Published 1962 for the National Conference on Social Welfare by Columbia University Press), p. 217.
26. *The Council Manual,* p. 33. © 1960, 1969 Girl Scouts of the U.S.A. Used by permission.
27. Tuttle, *op. cit.,* pp. 49-50.
28. Anita J. Faatz, *The Nature of Policy in the Administration of Public Assistance* (Pennsylvania School of Social Work, University of Pennsylvania, Philadelphia, 1943).
29. Young, *op. cit.,* p. 24.
30. *Boardsmanship, op. cit.,* pp. 8-9.
31. Joseph H. Reid, "The Board's Responsibility," in *The Board Member of a Social Agency* (New York: Child Welfare League of America, Inc., 1957), p. 26.
32. David Sher, "Boards Must Do More Than Manage," in *Making Yours a Better Board* (New York: Family Service Association of America, 1954), pp. 36-38.
33. Roy Sorenson, *The Art of Board Membership* (New York: Association Press, 1950), p. 30.
34. Henry F. Graff, "How Johnson Makes Foreign Policy," *The New York Times Magazine,* July 4, 1965, p. 4. © 1954 by the New York Times Company. Reprinted by permission.
35. Alexander H. Leighton, *Human Relations in a Changing World* (New York: E. P. Dutton, 1949), p. 147. © 1949 by Alexander H. Leighton.
36. *New York Times,* September 3, 1968, p. 1. © 1968 by the New York Times Company. Reprinted by permission.
37. Lorraine H. Jennrich, "Social Policy Comes from Knowing Families," in *Making Yours a Better Board* (New York: Family Service Association of America, 1954), p. 34.
38. Mrs. Holton R. Price, Jr., "A Promise and a Partnership in Action." A speech, October 15, 1964, Association of Girl Scout Professional Workers Meeting, Region I, Boston, Mass.
39. Michael D. Reagon, "Toward Improved National Policy Planning," *Public Administration Review,* March 1963.
40. Paul Woodring, "Who Makes University Policy?" *Saturday Review,* April 17, 1965, pp. 65–66. © 1965 Saturday Review, Inc.
41. Ralph M. Kramer, "Ideology, Status, and Power in Board-Executive Relationships," *Social Work,* October 1965, p. 114. Reprinted with permission of the National Association of Social Workers.

42. Harleigh B. Trecker, *Group Process in Administration—Revised and Enlarged* (New York: Woman's Press, 1950), pp. 260-275.
43. Violet H. Hodgson, *Supervision in Public Health Nursing* (New York: The Commonwealth Fund, 1939), p. 63.

4 *The Board and the Staff*

As has been pointed out earlier, the board and the staff of the community agency should form and represent a partnership of persons who share in the common goals of service provision. While each group has specific duties and responsibilities there is still a wide area of overlap and common concern. This is particularly true in terms of objectives to be achieved and the provision and utilization of means to make such achievement possible. Board and staff must be thought of and seen as *working together* because they are *jointly responsible* to the community for the satisfactory operation of the agency.

It is evident that the effectiveness of the agency is related to the way the board and the staff view one another and the extent to which they are in harmony. An exploration of factors that go into the creation and maintenance of effective working relationships between board and staff indicates that several elements are involved. There must be a clear and deepening understanding of what goes into any good working relationship between people. What kinds of attitudes, feelings, and responses will we get when staff and board are positively related in their endeavors? Undoubtedly, there will be a feeling of mutual respect, trust, and confidence in one another. This is a feeling tone or quality which one can sense even though the measurement of it may be difficult. Also, board and staff members will be friendly, relaxed, open, free, and frank with one another. They will show respect for and trust in each other as working partners. People who are working together are in *communica-*

tion with one another. There is much planful conferring, sharing, and evaluating. When working relationships are good, people behave responsibly toward each other. They count on each other to do their work and have a high degree of expectancy that they will fulfill their assignments with competence. People who work together well express pride in the quality of work done. Standards are high. There is a tendency to seek for higher levels of attainment. Under conditions of good working relationships people feel a conviction about the worthwhileness of their efforts and this conviction becomes a sustaining force, especially in times of trouble or stress.

Falck underlines the importance of good working relationships when he observes that "these relationships are engaged in by human beings who have feelings, who have sensitivities, who have intelligence and who have blind spots. While I would not depreciate the importance of a clear delineation of board and staff functions, I think it is important to see a balance between the usefulness of such delineation on one hand and the crucial importance of kindness, forbearance, and human charity on the other. I can think of no more difficult work in this universe than to try to render in an effective manner services to people in our community who need and desire them. For these kinds of services which we render are services which deal essentially not with sentences written on paper but with the problems of living and growing in a confused and confusing world in which conflict is rampant. We are all dedicated to the goal of bringing more harmony, more peace and greater happiness to all people. All that this means is, that these kinds of goals and these kinds of aims need to be demonstrated not only by those who are our members and clients in our activities but must be demonstrated first of all by those of us who are privileged to play key and major parts in the administration of social welfare agencies. Such people are members of the board of directors and members of the staff. While policy is certainly useful and absolutely necessary for the guidance of all, the lubricating fluid, in other words that which makes policy a reality is the good will, the ability and the kindness of human beings who live together, work together and bring happiness to others." [1]

Problems of Board and Staff Relationships

The partnership philosophy and the relationship theory introduced above, while classical in origin and useful to those who achieve it, is not necessarily easy to come by. From studies, and from numerous conferences with both board and staff members, it is evident that there are always problems which board and staff must face together. While the following list is not arranged in terms of priority, there is evidence of concern on the part of many agencies.

First, there is the problem of confusion between board and staff members as to their roles and responsibilities. In some situations the board and staff seem to be getting in the way of each other rather than working with one another. There are feelings that both board and staff on occasion take over tasks that do not belong to them. The most serious problem seems to center around the difference between policy determination which is the primary legal responsibility of the board, administration which is the job of the executive and the staff, and direct service which is essentially a professional responsibility. When clarity is lacking with reference to these functions, there are bound to be many situations where major difficulties arise.

Second, in far too many agencies, particularly the large ones, there is inadequate communication, slow communication, or even breakdown in the communication system. Under these circumstances, board and staff members are not fully informed as to what is going on and as a result they are out of touch with current policies, programs, and procedures. Consequently, they may work at cross purposes and with a considerable waste of energy.

Third, too frequently staff members feel that board members are not doing a good interpretation job in the community. They feel that they are not utilizing their normal and natural community contacts to tell the story of the agency effectively and to build growing public understanding. This same charge is sometimes stated by board members who feel that staff as the first-line representative in the community fails to capitalize on opportunities for good public relations.

Fourth, in some cases the board fails in its responsibility to do a regular, comprehensive evaluation of the work of the executive. The executive does not know where he stands. The staff, usually much closer to the executive than to the board, wants to know how the executive is regarded and what his future is with the agency. In some instances the failure to evaluate periodically has resulted in the sudden and unforeseen dismissal of the executive. Such action always sends ripples of anxiety through the staff.

Fifth, some staff members, and some board members as well, complain about the limited and even insufficient motivation for service shown by some board members. These board members want their names to appear on the roster and want the status accorded by the community for board service but their attendance at board meetings is poor and their real contribution to the agency amounts to little. When this is allowed to continue over a period of time it tends to be a drain on the entire board and a hampering condition insofar as good board and staff relationships are concerned.

Sixth, a very real problem results when the board fails to take leadership in providing the conditions essential for good professional work. If the board does not work to secure a sufficient budget, if working quarters are inadequate, frustration mounts, morale declines, and it is unreasonable to presume that staff and board can mount a posture of harmony.

Seventh, a mutual complaint on the part of both board and staff members is the cumbersome, complicated, and often outmoded structure of the agency. There is the feeling that because of an outdated structure undue amounts of time are required to carry forward the business of the agency. Under these conditions, the board, the executive, and the staff have a real responsibility to do a thoughtful review of the structure and streamline it if need be.

Eighth, not enough planning goes into the actual board meeting itself. Far too often board members feel that there is a waste of time and that meetings could be expedited more and that more important items could constitute the agenda of the meeting.

Ninth, staff members often feel that the board meeting is "top secret" and that they are not informed promptly and completely as to what business was transacted and what actions taken. There is much to be said for open board meetings, open to the staff, to the public, and to the press. There is likewise much to be said for prompt distribution of board meeting minutes, edited only to omit personal and confidential material.

Tenth, it is interesting to observe, and in a sense regrettable, that many staff members and many board members feel that they do not know one another and have little prospect of getting to know one another. They are not given opportunities to get acquainted and without these opportunities it is hard to see how partnership can develop.

Eleventh, elusive, but nonetheless real, is the fact that some staff members hold to unfortunate stereotypes when thinking about the board. They see the board as always "conservative," always "materialistic," and oftentimes deliberately blocking progressive actions on the part of the agency. Unfair as these feelings are, they do exist and can only be modified if efforts are made to bring the two groups together.

Strengthening Relationships Between Board and Staff

Problems of the kind listed above are in no way new, unusual or universal. Every situation is different and no one situation will have all of these problems but most situations have a chance of having some of them. When these problems exist they result from reasons which can be enumerated. For example, agencies have not given enough thought and study to the matter of board and staff relationships. They have tended to assume that good relationships develop without any particular planned effort. This is not true. Also, agencies have not done enough evaluating of procedures and have not reviewed ways of work with sufficient regularity. Unfortunately, some agencies have not developed good orientation programs for new board members or new staff members. In many cases there is an absence of up-to-date written material outlining in specific detail the job responsibilities of the board, executive and staff. In spite of their universal use, committees are not properly staffed and committee experience is frequently negative. If committee procedures would but reflect what is known about productive group procedures the overall experience of participants would be greatly enhanced.

Yet, there are a number of steps that are being taken to strengthen board and staff relationships. The list which is offered below includes but a few of the practical moves that are being made with success in numerous agencies.

First, more and more agencies are using a common orientation program for new board members and new staff members. By bringing newcomers together they learn not only about the work of the agency and their responsibilities within it but are given a needed opportunity to become acquainted with each other.

Second, a number of agencies are exchanging the minutes of board and staff meetings so that both groups may be familiar with the actions taken. In some cases, special bulletins or newsletters are prepared in which are summarized the major decisions made at meetings.

Third, more use is being made of informal social events which give board members and staff members a chance to become acquainted in a friendly way.

Fourth, some agencies are finding that an annual planning conference, usually held in the fall, provides an opportunity for board and staff to review agency goals and objectives and to develop appropriate programs.

Fifth, in addition to the above event, the annual agency evaluation conference at the end of the year often makes a distinctive contribution to closer cooperative patterns.

Sixth, another way of bringing board and staff together is the use of special project committees where representatives have a chance to work together on important agency problems.

Specific Responsibilities of Staff

Since a major problem which confronts all agencies is the clarification of roles and responsibilities, a review of staff responsibilities may give guidance.[2] The professional staff member is: 1) employed to carry out the work authorized by the policy-making body; 2) prepared by specific education and/or experience to bring special skills to the doing of the service job of the agency; 3) responsible for understanding the job to which he is assigned and when in doubt seeking clarification; 4) responsible for learning about the community, the agency and the clientele being served; 5) responsible for making the day-to-day decisions required to do the work of the agency in keeping with its purposes and policies; 6) responsible for consulting with other professionals inside and outside the agency in order to make wise professional decisions; 7) responsible for bringing to the policy-making board the information needed for sound policy decisions; 8) responsible for directing the work of other staff members assigned to him, defining their duties and the degree of freedom they have, and giving support for what they do as long as it is in line with agency policy; 9) responsible for helping the policy-making board to make the best decisions possible.

Specific Responsibilities of the Board

If the board understands what it expects of the staff it follows that the staff has the right to expect certain things of the board. Board members are: 1) responsible for the final decision on all policies related to personnel, finance, public relations, and services; 2) prepared by general experience and interest in the work of the agency to represent the community; 3) expected to know the history, purpose, program, policies, and practices of the agency; 4) expected to know the duties delegated to the staff; 5) responsible for interpreting informally the work of the agency in day-to-day contacts and formally when requested; 6) available to the staff for consultation on matters of common concern; 7) responsible for insuring financial support for the agency's operations; 8) responsible for evaluating the work of the agency with the assistance of the professional staff; 9) responsible for their own self-education and growth in cooperation with their colleagues.

Common Responsibilities for Committee Work

Much of the work done by the agency board and by the staff is done in committees. Some of these committees are made up of staff members; some are composed of representatives of both groups. No matter what the composition, the agency must have an organized approach to working with committees because these committees are the primary tools for agency development and progress.

By "organized approach" is meant a thoughtful, logical, systematic, and planned attack on the work to be done; it further implies an orderly or sequential way of moving from one phase of the work to the next. The common definition of *organize,* when used in referring to people, is to cause to unite and to work together in an orderly manner. Committee organization implies that the committee members will join together in such a fashion that their energies will be pooled and the product of their work will be superior to what one person could do alone.

The concept of organization has several elements which must be understood. First, the element of the worker's self-organization and self-discipline is important. The way a person goes about his work, thinks, plans, and evaluates or "sizes up" the situation is all a part of self-organization. The way the worker regards and uses time, the manner in which he expends energy, and the extent to which he regularly assesses his productivity are important also. Self-organization is a combination of technical and social skill and the person who works well with committees combines these two factors. As Mayo said, "Technical skill manifests itself as a capacity to manipulate things in the service of human purposes. Social skill shows itself as a capacity to receive communications from others, to respond to attitudes and ideas of others in such a fashion as to promote congenial participation in a common task." [3] The well-organized person, responsible for giving leadership to people, integrates his technical and his social skills.

A second element is the organization of the job. The problem here is one of definition and comprehension. The way the worker views the job, the way the worker, staff, board and others define the job, the way the job description states the job, are in a sense crucial. If people are to work well together there must be general agreement at the point of job definition. Beyond the matter of definition is the problem of the way the worker comes to grips with the job, the extent to which he really accepts it and puts himself into it.

A third element, closely related to the second if not a part of it, is that of organizing the efforts of other people. Community service agencies, possibly more than others, require that there be trained professionals who will devote considerable amounts of time to helping other people organize their work as contributing individuals in responsible work groups. Frequently the professional worker is engaged with a number of work groups (committees) at the same time. Then it is necessary for him to relate and coordinate these many efforts in terms of the total operation of the agency. However, no matter how well one organizes, it is necessary to have competent people to organize. As Barnard observed, "It is the individuals who are being organized, and the effectiveness of the group depends not only upon the scheme of grouping and function, but upon the quality of the elementary unit." [4]

Self-organization, job organization, and helping others to become organized are thus essential elements in the staff portfolio of responsibilities. Unless staff members are well organized and have an organized approach to their jobs, it is to be doubted that they can help boards and committees to do their jobs well.

Staff Help to Committees

What are some of the ways staff can be of help to committees? How can committees be helped to be more effective? 1) Staff can help committees to choose effective members. 2) Staff can help committees to define their purposes and goals. 3) Staff can help committees to organize for effective work. 4) Staff can help committees to learn how to work within the policies of the particular agency. 5) Staff can help committees to develop good procedures and good methods of work. 6) Staff can help committees to work within the community setting. 7) Staff can help committee chairmen to develop their skills. 8) Staff can help committee members learn how to carry their assignments. 9) Staff can help committees to understand and evaluate their work.

Perhaps the staff member's greatest responsibility is to help the committee organize its work in relation to a clear set of purposes and goals. This calls for skill in distinguishing between immediate and short-range goals and long-range basic purposes. Here it is important that the staff member take sufficient time to help committee members reach an understanding and consensus as to the major objectives of their efforts.

In addition, staff members must help each committee see its work in relation to all of the work that is being carried on by other committees. In other words, staff members must organize committee tasks with a comprehension of the total job that is being done by the agency. Few persons have exactly the same comprehension of the agency and its wholeness because most people see more closely that part of the agency work which concerns them directly. Since the staff member has an overview he can help people to broaden their grasp of agency totality.

A related task of the staff member is to serve as a channel for communication between the committee and other committees that may be working on other matters. Here he performs his role of an integrator or person able to facilitate the growing unity of the agency.

Furthermore, the professional worker must help committees to organize their tasks with priorities in mind so that the more significant and important jobs will be undertaken first.

Another responsibility of the staff member is to help the committee organize its work and divide large assignments into manageable units, related to the capacities and capibilities of the individual members. (Committee members need jobs that are challenging to them, but at the same time they should not be asked to undertake jobs that will be overwhelming to them.) This will make for a greater sense of progress and productivity as parts of the task become completed. Naturally, this kind of division of labor must be followed by regular attention to coordination and the relating of the various partial assignments.

As Johns has put it so well, "Helping the board of directors and committees of an organization is a professional skill of highest order. It is one of the key lay-professional relationships. The staff service provided is one of the critical factors in determining board and committee effectiveness. Executives and other staff members can assist the board and the organization's committees in a number of ways; they can help in the wise selection of board and committee personnel, they can help to clarify the assignments given to committees, they can help to develop meeting agendas which aid boards to get their work done, they can help in the in-between meeting work done, they can help the president or committee chairman to develop skill in getting participation." [5]

Principles of Committee Work

In an earlier publication [6] the author summarized the principles of good committee work as follows:

1. *The Principle of Democratic Values:* Effective committees are guided in their work by their belief in and respect for democratic values.

2. *The Principle of Purpose:* Effective committees have a clear statement of and a clear understanding of their purpose and job assignment.

3. *The Principle of Constructive Creative Leadership:* Effective committees have responsible, creative, constructive leaders who give continuous guidance to the committee process.

4. *The Principle of Proper Personnel:* Effective committees are made up of carefully selected members who are interested in and qualified to do the work.

5. *The Principle of Planning:* Effective committees approach and conduct their work planfully by outlining in advance the logical steps to be taken.

6. *The Principle of Preparation:* Effective committees prepare carefully for each meeting and have needed material at hand.

7. *The Principle of Setting and Atmosphere:* Effective committees have a good meeting place and develop an atmosphere of freedom and congeniality.

8. *The Principle of Facts First:* Effective committees always begin by asking, "What are the pertinent facts related to our assignment?"

9. *The Principle of Participation:* Effective committees release and utilize the contributions of members who participate actively in discussion, deliberation, and decision making.

10. *The Principle of Teamwork:* Effective committees do their work according to mutually agreed upon rules and functions as a team rather than as individual performers.

11. *The Principle of Progressive Process:* Effective committees move through their work assignment in an orderly and progressive manner taking one step at a time.

12. *The Principle of Time and Timing:* Effective committees develop a good sense of time and timing and function realistically in relation to their time needs and demands.

13. *The Principle of Reporting:* Effective committees keep adequate records which are used in preparing the final report to the organization.

14. *The Principle of Evaluation:* Effective committees look at themselves from time to time and endeavor to improve upon their work by means of systematic evaluation.

15. *The Principle of Member Satisfaction:* Effective committees provide for their members the basic human satisfactions which come when work is well done.

Challenges to and Tests of Boards-Staff Relationships

In recent years, as a part of a national unrest and dissatisfaction, board and staff relationships have been challenged and tested. While for the most part the community service enterprise has functioned effectively with an underlying spirit of cooperation between board and staff, there have been instances of conflict which have sometimes crippled services.

Two principal matters of conflict have emerged. They are, first, salaries and working conditions, and second, lack of inclusion of staff in the area of policy making. Teachers, nurses, and to some extent social workers have been engaged in activist programs aimed at improving their economic status and at getting a greater voice in determining agency policies. There has been a growth in the union movement among professional workers, and the nonunion professional societies have taken vigorous stands in behalf of their members. Some boards have been taken aback by this turn of events and have reacted with feelings of dismay. The newspapers and magazines have been discussing "Our Angry Teachers," [7] "What's Bugging Our Teachers," [8] "Teachers vs. School Board," [9] and "Mr. Chips Is Dead!" [10] Even though strikes of public employees such as teachers and nurses are usually unlawful, one journal predicted three hundred to four hundred teacher strikes for the 1968–69 academic year.[11] Clearly the situation calls for a thoughtful reassessment on the part of boards, staffs, and the community. New patterns of negotiation and reconciliation must be developed. New definitions of roles and responsibilities must be stated. Up to now the community has suffered from stoppages of service and from huge wastes of energy on the part of both groups as they strive to grapple with the new problems which have developed.

Under the headline "Teachers Must Help Make Decisions," a local school superintendent said, ". . . teachers must become more involved in the decision making process . . . with the policies of the Board of Education and the scope of the curriculum; each school should develop its own model of teacher-administrator relationships. It should be a collaborative leadership, designed to be an amalgam of minds touching all phases of the school's work, including policy formulation." [12]

The above declaration would seem to apply to all areas of community service. If administrators and boards would adopt it as a guiding principle much of the conflict of today would be resolved.

The impersonal bigness of the health, education, and welfare enterprise has undoubtedly been a major factor in the discontent of staff members. In a nation which is growing rapidly, and which is becoming increasingly urbanized, it is difficult for the individual to feel that his efforts count. He does not feel that he is a person of power and significance. Hook discusses this problem when he asks, "What does it mean to be a *person* in a bureaucratic age as distinct from being a number, a unit, a member of a crowd, a working bee in a communal hive? It means to have knowledge—knowledge of the world we live in, physical and social, its possibilities and its dangers. It means to have knowledge of ourselves, what we really want in the light of our capacities and limitations. It means the courage to make our own choices in the basic decisions of love, vocation, friendship, political life, and religious communion. Although the alternatives are not open to us, the more we seek them the more often we will find them. It means a willingness to risk something in behalf of our ideals and our sense of justice. It means a refusal to play it so safe that personal experience loses its zest and tang; a refusal to make mere survival the be all and the end all of life and politics. It means a commitment to a social order whose institutions make it possible for more and more *people to become persons.* It means, finally, the absence of fanaticism—the recognition that good often conflicts with good, that *there are no total solutions,* that the test of ends is to be found in the actual or probable consequences of the means used to achieve them. This entails the view that the ultimate authority in resolving all conflicts among men is not the authority of institutions, traditions, or men, but the authority of rational methods, of intelligence which must not be confused with a sweet reasonableness or posture of appeasement unable to see the face of evil. No one can be a complete person except perhaps a divine Being. But although we cannot be gods, we can still live like men in a community of *persons,* and when we put organizations, administrations, or bureaucracies on trial, our verdict ultimately must rest on whether or not they help or hurt persons." [13]

NOTES

1. Hans S. Falck, "On the Administration of the Voluntary Social Agency: Board and Staff—Separate and Together." Mimeo., 14 pages, undated.
2. David M. Austin, "Volunteer-Staff Relations," *YWCA Magazine,* February 1959.
3. Elton Mayo, *The Social Problems of an Industrial Civilization* (Cambridge: Harvard University Graduate School of Business Administration, 1946), p. 13.
4. Chester I. Barnard, *Organization and Management* (Cambridge: Harvard University Press, 1948), p. 5.
5. Ray Johns, *Executive Responsibility* (New York: Association Press, 1954), p. 73.
6. Harleigh B. and Audrey R. Trecker, *Committee Common Sense* (New York: Whiteside, William Morrow Co., 1954), pp. 145-153.
7. "Our Angry Teachers," *Look,* September 3, 1968, p. 64.
8. "What's Bugging Our Teachers," *Saturday Review,* October 16, 1965, p. 88.
9. "Teachers vs. School Board: Continual Attitudes of War," *New York Herald Tribune,* June 9, 1965, p. 16.
10. "Mr. Chips Is Dead," *Connecticut Life,* February 1968, p. 4.
11. "Our Angry Teachers," *op. cit.*
12. *Hartford Courant,* September 5, 1968.
13. Sidney Hook, "Bureaucrats Are Human," *Saturday Review,* May 17, 1958, p. 41. © 1958 Saturday Review, Inc.

PART THREE

WORKING WITH THE BOARD

5 *Building the Board*

Boards as instruments of and architects of community policy play a vital role in determining the quality of community life that the people will enjoy. The need for a planned approach to building the board and keeping it viable is evident, but thus far, not enough attention has been devoted to this subject. It seems in many cases that only a minimum amount of thinking has gone into the consideration of such questions as: What kinds of qualifications are needed by board members? How should board members be chosen? What about better ways of recruiting highly motivated people to serve on boards? How should new board members be helped to make a good start? What are the trends in board composition and development? Answers to these questions, along with others, might do much to improve the quality of board functioning.

Thousands of New Board Members Needed Each Year

There is no accurate information on exactly how many new board members are needed each year to carry forward the work of the community service enterprise but it must run into the thousands. In one field alone, public education, Robinson pointed out that "every year in the United States, 50,000 newly elected members take their places on local school boards. As a rule they know little about the mechanics of their jobs and nothing about the history and philosophy of public education in this country. Consider what happened to one of them. I joined my board of five members on the first of July, 1962, and by August 10 had to accept responsibility for a $15,000,000 budget. Within the last three years, our board has campaigned for a tax election for operating expenses; dealt with a group that opposed discussion of controversial issues in school; is currently working to pass a bond election for new buildings; struggling with merit pay for teachers; and last and most important, making daily decisions on what kind of curriculum to offer to whom under what circumstances." [1] While this comment from one person may not be representative of all, it is certain that more likely than not the new board member is plunged into his work with little preparation.

In addition to securing board members for existing institutions it is necessary to develop completely new boards for new agencies. For example, "during this decade, an average of 50 new colleges opened each year, bringing the total to nearly 2,400 in July, 1967—sixty percent of the new colleges are junior colleges." [2] Obviously more college board members are going to be needed each year as the offerings in higher education increase.

When one thinks of the money that is involved in the public sector of social welfare programs it becomes increasingly evident that board members of a very high caliber are needed. According to the U.S. Social Security Administration, "combined federal, state, and local spending for social welfare programs in 1965, totalled a staggering $77,726 million. Included were $27,726 million for education, $28,098 million for social insurance benefits, $6,651 million for health and medical services, and $6,259 million for income maintenance and related aid to low-income people. The rest went for veterans' program, public housing and other welfare services." [3] In addition, it is estimated that the private health and welfare agencies provide services at a cost "now approaching $3,500 million annually" [4] and that "approximately 400,000 organizations in America serve philanthropic purposes," [5] and that "50 million Americans give some of their spare time to doing unpaid work for causes in which they believe." [6] Certainly, from a national standpoint the task of providing the services that people need is a growing task calling for ever better leadership.

But persons may not comprehend clearly the national picture. They may see it from the viewpoint of their local community. Even there the need for board members is great. For example, in a northeastern city of approximately 70,000 there were 28 public boards and commissions requiring the services of 148 citizens to man them in 1967. [7] In a county located in the southeast, 84 citizens served on 18 different boards of the county government. In referring to their service the County Commission Chairman said, "The efforts of these various boards are of invaluable assistance to the Commission and their recommendations are held in the highest regard and respect." [8] The newspaper account went on to explain, "The Boards have very strong recommending powers which range from county insurance needs to water control and conservation, zoning, and even history. None of the members receive any compensation for their work as advisors." [9] When one includes all of the private agency board positions which are to be filled annually the total is enormous. For example, in one northeastern city it was reported that 24 private agencies needed 650 board members.[10] So, it is clear that many thousands of citizens are now serving as board members and many thousands will serve in the future. There can be little doubt that the number of agencies, programs, and services will increase to meet the needs of a growing population. These agencies and programs and services will need boards of directors and these boards will need manpower as never before. Even more important, they will need a different pattern of manpower, if they are to truly involve a more representative group of people than has been the case in the past.

Some Characteristics of Boards

Before offering suggestions as to how to build or create the kind of board that will be able to deal with today's business and tomorrow's changes, it is important that a look be taken at the board as it tended to exist in the decade just concluded. In an exploratory study [11] of the boards of private social agencies the author sought answers to such questions as: Who are the board members? How old are they? What is their occupation? What is their level of income? How are they chosen? How long have they served? How much time do they give to their jobs as board members? Some of the findings were interesting, even disturbing. In the private social agency field, six out of ten board members were women; only four were men. The average age of the board members was forty-seven. Seven out of ten were between the ages of thirty-six and fifty-five. Six out of ten were forty-five years of age. There were few young persons on boards. Only 5 percent of the board members reporting were less than thirty years of age. On the other hand, 15 percent were over fifty-five. Eight out of ten came from the employer, executive, or professional group. Only one out of ten was a salaried worker or wage earner. The other one was likely to be a housewife from a professional or executive family. On the basis of income it was found that the average family income of board members was more than twice the average family income in the United States. In eight out of ten agencies, board members were chosen by a nominating committee and their election to the board was a mere formality; in fact, usually an act of ratification by the board which perpetuated itself. In two out of ten agencies, board members were elected by the people served. These agencies were membership agencies. Over 80 percent of the organizations studied had no written statements of qualifications sought in board members. The best that could be found was a very general statement of qualification and it was rare when any agency had spelled out in precise written terms exactly what kind of persons were wanted to perform the important tasks of board service.

How long had these board members served? Seven percent in the sample had served more than ten years; 18 percent had served at least ten years; 21 percent had served up to five years; 54 percent had served three years or less. There seemed to be a trend toward planned rotation which placed definite limits on the number of years a person might serve continuously. Sixty-four percent of the agencies studied had adopted a plan of rotation; the remaining 36 percent tended to follow the self-perpetuating pattern. In addition, it was interesting to note that 72 percent of all board members reporting served on more than one board and 25 percent served on as many as five boards. On the average, a board member gave ten hours per month to meetings, preparation, and so on. Yet, 11 percent of all board members gave twenty-five hours per month to board service for a single agency. One can imagine what it was like in the way of a time investment when a board member served on two, three, four, or even five boards!

How well were board members introduced to their new responsibilities? On the whole, the orientation process was poorly handled and there was a lack of planful and thoughtful beginning experiences for the new board member.

It was found that the average size of the boards studied was thirty-three members. They met on the average of once each month for a period of about two hours. Half of the agencies indicated that the average attendance at board meetings was 50 percent.

The average number of board committees was eleven; the range was from three to fifty-five committees. Eight out of ten agencies had an executive committee of the board and in most of these situations the executive committee was authorized to make important policy decisions.

Naturally, most of the time in board meetings was spent on the business of the agency. Only a small amount of time was spent on consideration of matters of social legislation, and in two-thirds of the agencies studied, no time whatsoever was spent on legislative items.

In only a few cases was time spent on evaluating the services of the agency. Even more rare was the board that spent any time on problems of long-range planning and development.

When an effort was made to discover the extent to which board members were growing on the job, little in the way of a planned program of board member education and development was found. Even more disconcerting was the fact that many board members were far from clear on the purpose of their agency and seemed utterly unable to do a thoughtful job of interpreting the agency to the community. In addition, a substantial number of board members felt that their experience was not as productive as it might have been and that a substantial amount of time was being wasted on trivial matters.

In reviewing the findings of this study it would appear that some, perhaps many, board members were quite casually chosen without regard for clearly defined qualifications. Despite counterclaims it would appear that boards were not broadly representative of the community. They were not well prepared for their work, and orientation to help them work together effectively was at a minimum. Unfortunately, it appeared that social welfare services tended to be dominated by a small minority of people who carried multiple board assignments and might be assumed to have interlocking control of a number of agencies. Boards were not sufficiently clear as to their primary functions and were particularly confused about their policy-making responsibilities in relation to administration of services. In many cases the board structure was cumbersome and overorganized with more committees than were really needed. Most boards were narrowly oriented to the agency they represented and failed to direct their thinking toward the larger community. Boards did not seem to be reaching their fullest potential. Their effort had become routinized and they were failing to see the challenge of unmet community needs.

In another study it was reported that "one of every six trustees in New York State's public and private colleges and universities is over seventy, and almost half of them don't even know what is on the agenda before they hold meetings. More than half of them admit the meetings are in effect, rubber stamping of matters previously decided by the president, the board chairman and committees and that, as a rule, trustees are not involved in 'significant decision making.' The 'overwhelming majority' of their important decisions are concerned with fund raising and other financial activities, as contrasted with curriculum and the educational program. . . . The [study] committee urged that the colleges and universities seek out more persons under fifty years of age—only eighteen percent of the trustees now are; more women—more than three of every four trustees are men; as well as educators now seven percent and public officials now six percent. At present, about half the trustees are in industry, law, banking, sales and medicine, and about half have not rendered any service to education before election or appointment . . . the committee suggested adoption or continuation of a compulsory retirement age between sixty-eight and eighty-two (two percent of the trustees are now over eighty); and also the creation of a procedure to get rid of ineffective members. One suggestion called for a year's lapse in membership after a person has served two consecutive five year terms. The committee also recommended establishment of a standing nominating committee, consisting of experienced and new members to find new trustees. The nominating committees would develop criteria for trusteeship specific to the needs of the college." [12]

A national study [13] of local boards of education found that they usually consisted of five or seven members; three- to six-year terms were most common; there were practically no legal limitations on the number of terms a board member may serve; more than 95 percent of all local school boards were elected by popular vote; any qualified voter was eligible for board membership.

A study [14] of boards of local voluntary and public agencies in three hundred and twenty-one cities showed that the voluntary agency boards averaged twenty-three members while public boards averaged eight members. Most boards met at least ten times a year although almost one-third held less than six meetings a year. More than half of the voluntary agency boards had three-year terms of office; public agency boards tended to have longer terms of office. Thirty-five percent of the voluntary agency boards placed a limit on the number of successive terms their members could serve but only 9 percent of the public agency boards did so. Attendance at meetings of public agency boards was better than the voluntary agency boards, with 7 percent of the latter not attending any meetings during the year compared with 3 percent of the former. A little less than half of all board members had served less than three years. Men were much more numerous on boards of all categories. Two-thirds of the board members were forty-five years of age or over. About two-thirds came from employer, executive and professional groups. Five percent of the voluntary agency boards were nonwhite. Most voluntary agency boards were governing while public agency boards were about equally divided between governing and advisory. Responsibility for approval of policy, for budget preparation and presentation, was retained by more than half of the public agency boards while personnel actions, decisions on case situations, and interpretation of programs were more likely to be delegated to the director.

In a more recent study of school boards, "extensive variations in organizations and practice were found . . . in different sized districts and in different regions . . . election by popular vote as the primary method of selecting board members . . . more than half of the boards had five members . . . almost half of the board members were college graduates; about ninety percent were men; over one-half were business owners, officials, or managers; and nearly forty-seven percent had been in office for five years or more . . . a large majority of the boards held twelve regular meetings during the year, and more than half held from one to six special meetings . . . nearly a third of the boards had standing committees . . . ninety percent of the boards always held open meetings; generally citizens did not attend board meetings in large numbers . . . about three fifths of the boards had a policy manual . . . expense reimbursements were provided for most board members . . . school board policy development was reported as a major problem by a large number of systems . . . other problem areas were selection of board members, board-superintendent relationships, board meetings, orientation and in-service training of board members, relation of individual members to the board, and keeping board members informed." [15]

A national study [16] of boards of Community Chests, United Funds, and Community Councils revealed that they were governing, rather than advisory boards, usually selected by agency members through the channel of an appointed nominating committee and usually as a single slate of nominees. Over half of the boards met ten or more times during the year and most had a legal provision for meeting a minimum number of times per year. The most common term was three years; half had a limitation on the number of successive terms members might serve. Seven percent attended no meetings during the previous twelve months. Seventy-eight percent were male and 22 percent female. Two percent were non-whites. The distribution of religious faiths follows that for the United States as a whole. Employers, executives, and professionals occupied two-thirds of the board positions. Nearly all board members were thirty years or older with about a third between thirty and forty-four, one-half forty-five to fifty-nine, and the balance sixty or over.

Every study indicates that boards are made up of people who, for the most part, have a better than average income. This is also true when one studies the income of delegates to national political conventions. In a study of the costs of political participation sponsored by the Citizens Research Council it was found that the median income of the 1964 Republican delegates was $20,192 while it was $18,223 for the Democrats. Fewer than 15 percent of the delegates to each convention had incomes of under $10,000 per year. The study concluded: "Clearly those who participate in the electoral process as national convention delegates are sharply differentiated from the mass electorate by their high incomes." [17]

It would appear that boards are made up of citizens who are far from representative of the population as a whole. They tend to have higher incomes, professional and managerial jobs, flexible time schedules, successful achievement patterns in their chosen fields, and a leadership voice in the affairs of the community. Their qualifications are seldom spelled out in detail and the process through which they arrive at board status is one that is defined largely by their life situation in general. None of this is to say that the current system is wrong, but there is a mounting evidence that the system needs a thorough review and that during the decade ahead a change which is already underway will likely be accelerated.

Qualifications of Board Members

When the author queried a number of agency executives as to what they looked for in the way of qualifications for board members, they placed "interest in the work of the agency" at the head of the list. In order, they advocated "time and willingness to work"; "representativeness"; "skills or professional backgrounds"; "previous service or experience"; "status in the community"; and lastly, "ability to work with people." [18]

Hollander, with characteristic bluntness, said, "Board membership is now entered upon too casually. The factors involved are so numerous and so intricate that at best, board members can achieve but a superficial understanding. Helping people in trouble involves more than an understanding of financial needs. It is concerned with industry and sociology, with politics and economics, with health and employment, with almost every phase of modern life. Yet decisions affecting the lives and behavior of thousands are regularly made by boards whose only qualifications are a listing in the social register or an enviable rating in Dun and Bradstreet. Isn't there something peculiar here? If training is needed for social workers, why not for those who plan their programs and direct their agencies? . . . What we want are board members—Who will keep far enough ahead of the community to be progressive, and close enough to be practical. Who will accept decisions democratically reached, or resign if they find themselves out of step. Who will face budgets with courage, endowments with doubts, deficits without dismay—and recover quickly from a surplus. Who will multiply the agency's and their own usefulness by standing squarely back of the public services and supporting their demands for adequate budgets and decent standards. . . . What's your score? 1) Is your first interest in people and their problems? 2) Have you made it your business to understand thoroughly your agency's program? 3) Do you endeavor to represent the agency to important groups in the community? 4) Do you attend board meetings regularly? 5) Do you speak up courageously where important issues are involved? 6) Do you deal with staff as partners? 7) Are you receptive to new ideas? 8) Will you allow another to replace you on the board after you have made your best contribution? 9) Do you assume responsibility for the well-being of families outside your case load? 10) Are you active in support of good public welfare programs?" [19]

Young lists desirable qualifications for a library trustee as: "1) Interest in the library, in the community, and in the library's relationship to the community. 2) Readiness to devote time and effort to carrying out the duties of trusteeship. 3) Recognition of the library's importance as a center of community culture, recreation, and continuing education. 4) Close acquaintance with the community social and economic conditions, and with groups within the community. 5) Ability to work well with others: board members, librarian and staff members, and the public served by the library. 6) An open mind, intellectual curiosity, and respect for the opinions of others. 7) Initiative and ability to establish policies for successful operation of the library and impartial service to all its patrons. 8) Courage: to plan creatively, to carry out plans effectively, and to withstand pressures and prejudices. 9) Devotion to the library, its welfare and progress." [20]

Martona observes that "in view of the deep public trust placed in persons who serve on boards of trustees, one would expect that they as persons and as groups would be the subject of many scholarly studies. Contrary to this expectation, relatively few definite studies of characteristics of boards of trustees are to be found in the published writings on higher education. This remains an area in which research is yet in the pioneering stages, despite the fact that colleges and universities have been operating for over three hundred years." [21]

Koontz gives attention to the qualifications sought in board members of business corporations. He lists "business experience, knowledge and capability . . . ability to contribute board balance . . . success in principal field of endeavor . . . stature in the community . . . maturity . . . interest in the company . . . willingness to spend time." [22]

It is interesting to note that none of the authorities lists as an important qualification experience as a consumer or recipient of the service being offered. Doubtless some board members have received services from the agencies they represent but for the most part little recognition is given to this important factor.

Jenkins made a strong plea for relating the qualifications of the board member to the job to be done and the purposes to be served. He said, "The major purpose of a board is to forecast, to come to a conclusion as a prelude to action; this purpose may well determine the size and composition of boards, because limits on effective action are set by psychological factors within the conditions beyond the control of the board. . . . The composition of boards is too often determined by considerations having little to do with the central purpose of thinking in order to act. . . . After all, a board is impressive, not by a letterhead, but by the wisdom of its decisions and the results of its actions." [23] Jenkins also questions the role of the specialist on the board: "Unless he can fuse his expert opinion with common sense, he may become a hazard when the other members turn to him for advice on matters where his experience is taken for granted because of his position. However, a strong board is made up of strong people who have clear and tenaciously held opinions, or they would not be influential in the society and in the community. The first-rate board fuses the refractory metals of opinion in the heat of conviction about the supreme value of social and religious purposes, but does not make a fetish of harmony. At its best, a board is composed of persons who have shown by their service in the organization that they understand its purposes, are effective in making these purposes work, and are prepared to influence their friends to widen the circle of participants." [24]

Until a person has served on a board neither he nor anyone else can be sure of how effective he will be. While most students of the board have tended to spell out the ideal traits necessary in the individual and then relate these traits to the success of the individual as a board member, one study *examined the behavior of board members as they carried out their duties.* Stapley summarized this study and listed six "areas of capability, i.e., skills and understandings needed for successful board membership: 1) Board Unity—Acceptance of the principle of board unity and subordination of self interests. 2) Leadership—Ability to initiate or to provide informed leadership in board planning and policy-making. 3) Executive Function—Ability to understand and willingness to respect the executive function of the professional administrator. 4) Staff and Group Relationships—Skill in establishing and maintaining effective relationships with the staff and with community groups. 5) Personal Relationships—Ability to carry on effective personal relationships with staff members and individuals within the community. 6) Courageous Action—Willingness to take courageous action for the good of the schools in spite of outside pressures and influences." [25]

The same study went on to develop a list of critical requirements for board membership derived from the behaviors reported. "Area One: Board Unity—For effective results, a board member should—1) Subordinate personal interests. 2) Adhere to the policy-making and legislative functions of the board. 3) Accept and support majority decisions of the board. 4) Identify self with board policies and actions. 5) Refuse to speak or act on school matters independent of board action. Area Two: Leadership—6) Suspend judgment until the facts are available. 7) Make use of pertinent experience. 8) Help to identify problems. 9) Have the ability to determine satisfactory solutions to problems. 10) Devote time outside of board meetings as board business may require. 11) Be willing to accept ideas from others. 12) Have enthusiastic interest in the welfare of the children. Area Three: Executive Function—13) Understand the desirability of delegating administrative responsibility to the chief executive officer. 14) Support the executive officer in his authorized functions. 15) Encourage teamwork between the executive officer and the board. 16) Recognize problems and conditions that are of executive concern. Area Four: Staff and Group Relationships—17) Have ability to speak effectively in public. 18) Believe firmly in the right of all groups to be heard. 19) Work tactfully and sympathetically with teacher groups and committees. 20) Understand how groups think and act. 21) Assist others in working effectively. 22) Have mature social poise. Area Five: Personal Relationships—23) Be willing to work with fellow board members in spite of personality difference. 24) Display both tact and firmness in relationships with individuals. 25) Treat both persons and teachers fairly and ethically. 26) Foster harmonious relationships. Area Six: Courageous Action—27) Be able to weather criticism. 28) Maintain firm convictions. 29) Be willing to take sides in controversies. 30) Share responsibility for board decisions." Stapley summarized the qualities needed for effective school board membership in these words: "When actual situations are analyzed, superintendents and board members note most highly the exercise of initiative and informed leadership. The effective board member is a person who requires facts to support decisions and considers it a part of his job to secure facts. From his understanding of community attitudes and needs, he makes suggestions that are important in shaping policy. In order to interpret the school program, he is especially active in community affairs. As the need exists, he works with groups of teachers and other school personnel. He is, on the whole, a member of a board which shares the responsibility for educational planning rather than merely reviewing proposals presented by its executive officer." [26]

On a very different level, Gardner stresses the need for people who can help the organization to move forward when he says, "If social action is to occur, certain functions must be performed. The problems facing the group or organization must be clarified, and ideas necessary to their solution formulated. Objectives must be defined. There must be widespread awareness of these objectives, and the will to achieve them. Often those on whom action depends must develop new attitudes and habits. Social machinery must be set in motion. The consequences of social effort must be evaluated and criticized and new goals set. A particular leader may contribute at only one point in the process. He may be gifted in analysis of the problem but limited in his capacity to communicate. He may be superb in communicating, but incapable of managing. He may, in short, be an outstanding leader without being good in every aspect of leadership. If anything significant is to be accomplished, leaders must understand the social institutions and processes through which action is carried out. And in a society as complex as ours, that is no mean achievement. A good leader, whether corporation president, university dean, or labor official, knows his organization, understands what makes it move, comprehends its limitations. Every social system or institution has a logic and dynamic of its own that cannot be ignored. . . . Leaders worthy of the name . . . contribute to the continuing definition and articulation of the most cherished values of our society. They offer, in short, *moral* leadership. The thing that makes a number of individuals a *society* rather than just a population or a crowd is the presence of shared attitudes, habits and values, a shared conception of the enterprise of which they are all a part—shared views of why it is worth while for the enterprise to continue and to flourish. Leaders can help in bringing that about. In fact, it is required that they do so. When leaders lose their credibility or their moral authority, then the society begins to disintegrate. Leaders thus have a significant role in creating the state of mind that is the society. They can express the values that hold society together. Most important, they can conceive and articulate goals that lift people out of their petty preoccupations, carry them above the conflicts that tear a society apart, and unite them in the pursuit of objectives worthy of their best efforts." [27]

In a sharply worded accusation that school board members do not really take education seriously, Wallace and Schneider claim that "a trustee is ideally a person interested in education in the broadest sense of the term. Trustees unwilling or unable to grasp the significance of events occuring outside their narrow area of influence are antiquated. . . . The school board member must come to reconstrue his place in the educational enterprise. The most vital function that he can perform is to engage both the educational establishment and the citizenry in philosophical discussion concerning the nature, value, and direction of contemporary education in our society. Rather than concentrating upon the feeding, transporting, and housing of students, the vital dialogue should center about the learning of children. The school trustee must inquire into what is being taught to children, how it is being taught, and why it is being taught. This in no way implies that the school board member must strive to be an educational specialist nor does it imply that he should issue directives about educational policy to the school superintendent. However, it most certainly implies that [he] must constantly re-examine his own assumptions as well as those of others concerning the educational enterprise and invite others to join him in this endeavor. A properly functioning school board should at all times be devoting some portion of its resources to study of a matter of genuine educational significance." [28]

The Concept of Representation

Basic to the building of an effective board is an understanding of the concept of representation or representativeness. In both public and private agencies one notes that the central idea behind the choice of board members is representation. Board members should be representative of the community; board members should be representative of the agency's constituencies; board members should be representative of the best thinking in the service field. In spite of the wide reliance upon and use of the concept of representation, there is little agreement as to what is meant by it. As Alexander and McCann pointed out, there is at least a dual meaning. They said, "Two distinctively different concepts emanate from the adjective 'representative' or the noun 'representativeness.' The first of these is a socio-political idea and refers to the *authorized functioning or acting by one person in behalf of another or others.* The second comes from a statistical frame of reference and has to do with the *quality of being typical or typifying a group or class.* Both, found in social work practice, need clarification." [29]

As Coker and Rodee observed, "Any corporate group—church, business concern, trade union, fraternal order or state—that is too large or too dispersed in membership to conduct its deliberations in an assembly of all members is confronted with a problem of representation, if it purports to act in any degree in accord with the opinions of its members. The idea of political representation is as old as the state. . . . The literature of democracy, until very recent times, has contained relatively little discussion of the specific question of representation." [30]

Koontz compares the board of the business corporation with the board of the university. He says, "In the business corporation, board members legally stand in the place of the real owners of the corporation, the stockholders. In this position, they are not legal agents in the sense that they must do the individual shareholder's bidding, but are rather representatives of the stockholders as a group. They are in much the same position as government legislators. While these are elected by voters, they are expected to represent them as a group and to use their own judgment in decisions, acting in what they believe to be the best interest of those they represent. The position of corporate boards is quite similar to that of other boards and commissions. In the typical university, the board of trustees or regents are expected to represent the public, alumni, faculty, and students in governing the university and seeing that it is well managed. In government agencies, the typical commission is appointed or elected to represent the public interest." [31]

Since most boards are built on the representational system, Sartori's discussion is valuable. He states, "In order to define a representational system one must first define representation, a many-faceted and elusive concept. The term is associated with three quite different meanings: 1) the idea of mandate or instructions; 2) the idea of representativeness, that is, resemblance and similarity; and 3) the idea of responsibility or accountability. The first meaning is derived from private law and belongs to the context of juristic representation, whereas the second meaning is derived from a sociological or existential context according to which representation is basically a fact of likeness that transcends all voluntary selection and even awareness. . . . What is, and what is not, a representational system? A survey of the literature indicates wide disagreement, for it would seem that any one of the following conditions is either sufficient or necessary: 1) The people freely and periodically elect a body of representatives—the electoral theory of representation; 2) The governors are accountable or responsible to the governed—the responsibility theory of representation; 3) The governors are agents or delegates who carry out the instructions received from their electors—the mandate theory of representation; 4) The people feel the same as the state—the idem sentire, or syntony, theory of representation; 5) The people consent to the decisions of their governors—the consent theory of representation; 6) The people share, in some significant way, in the making of relevant political decisions—the participation theory of representation; 7) The governors are a representative sample of the governed—the resemblance, or the mirroring theory of representation." [32]

When Commons discussed representative advisory committees in labor law administration he stressed that "in order to have real representation with representatives whose word will carry weight, it is necessary that representatives be backed up by an organized group. In practice, a representative must represent somebody. If he is merely a sort of statistical sample of his class he will find himself in the weak position of having to pit his personal opinion against the demands of an organized opposition." [33]

But if a true representative must have a constituency and must voice the opinions and feelings of that constituency, then his behavior would certainly be circumscribed. As Janda points out, "A person's reactions to a situation depend on how he perceives it, and his perceptions do not necessarily accord with reality. It is important to determine the accuracy of the representative's perception of his constituents' opinions on various policy matters. The representative who consciously tried to vote in accordance with his constituents' opinions, but who frequently misreads them, may seem to be ignoring his district when in fact, his behavior is due to a failure in communication instead of a lack of concern for constituency opinions." [34]

With so many meanings for the term it is not surprising that Alexander and McCann said, "There is common misuse of the term 'representativeness' . . . the term is repeatedly applied to designate the role of those persons who are appointed by others to speak for constituencies which have had no part in their selection. These are the persons who are selected as 'representative' of a certain class, ethnic, religious, vocational or special interest group. They are often referred to as 'representative citizens.' The classic example of this point is to be found in the sample constitution for a combined community chest and council, which charges that the nominating committee '. . . shall make every effort to see that the board is at all times representative of the principal civic, commercial and cultural forces in the community. . . .' Representativeness in this context is not reconcilable with the 'authorized functioning' or 'typical criteria.' " [35]

Selection of Board Members

Board members are either elected or appointed to offices they hold. In some fields, notably public education, most board members are elected. In other fields, notably governmental services, they are appointed. In between is the nominating committee recommending process which results in ratification by the existing board or the members of the parent organization. There is no perfect system. And changes are taking place.

In discussing the state university, Heimberger says, "Major responsibility for charting a course into the future will reside in three groups or centers of power. These are the governing board, the president and his principal administrative associates, and the university faculty. Each will play a very significant role, and for real success each must have reason to respect the others. . . . It is not a relationship of master to servant, of employer to employee. Instead, it is essentially a working together as equals, each devoted to a common cause and each having a proper role to play. Governing boards of state universities come in differing shapes and sizes, the personal interests and backgrounds of their members vary widely, and there is little uniformity in the ways by which they are chosen. Among all of these variables, only two or three constants are likely to be found. In almost all cases the prevailing majority will be laymen, and persons with professional knowledge of higher education will be few and far between. . . . This proportionate lack of direct interest and experience in academic affairs poses a delicate problem for the wise governing board, one of judiciously tempering its use of legal powers that appear to be absolute and all-inclusive. This does not mean that the governing board of a state university is powerless in setting goals and shaping methods. It has great power to determine the broad future of the university in all its aspects. But, if wisdom prevails, that power is seldom exercised through direct and authoritative intervention. Instead, it is used slowly but effectively through the choice of those persons, beginning with the president, upon whom a lay board must depend for professional opinions and strong educational leadership. It is difficult to imagine a greater tragedy for a university than having a board that misuses its power and reaches beyond the limits of its knowledge in academic affairs. . . ." [36]

Mills propounded the theory that a power elite tended to develop as the controlling force in most communities and presumably, according to this theory, board members would come from this power group. He said, "In every town and small city of America an upper set of families stands above the middle classes and towers over the underlying population of clerks and wage earners. The members of this set possess more than do others of whatever there is locally to possess; they hold the keys to local decisions; their names and faces are often printed in the local paper; in fact, they own the newspaper as well as the radio station; they also own the three important local plants and most of the commercial properties along the main street; they direct the banks. Mingling closely with one another, they are quite conscious of the fact that they belong to the leading class of leading families." [37] Although one might reject the power elite theory, it is true that many board members are chosen from such a group and, at least into the 1960's, they dominate agencies.

Winser stresses the importance of broad representation when she states,

"For many years, whether by accident or design library boards were invariably drawn from groups of similar background and experience. Today's library has a new and increasing importance to the total community, and a well-balanced board should represent a cross section of the community.

"The outmoded notion that trustee appointments should be made only in a small class of 'cultured' persons is disproved today by the very real interest in libraries evidenced by business, industry, and labor. Every segment of today's society has a stake in the community library, and the needs and desires of every segment of society should be represented in the library's program. The resulting broad diversity of viewpoints will be not only democratic, but conducive to a healthy and living relationship between library and community." [38]

Apart from one's personal point of view, the realities of board selection are apparent. There must be some way of locating qualified people. Even before this can be done the qualifications have to be determined by someone or some group. Having decided upon qualifications, and having located the people, it is then necessary to secure their acceptance. This may be a matter of getting consent to accept an appointment to the board, or it may be a matter of getting consent from a person to run against another person in an election. These are very different circumstances and it is reasonable to assume that persons will be more likely to accept appointment than they will be to engage in a competitive election.

Many organizations, perhaps the vast majority of them in the voluntary field, make use of the nominating committee as the chief mechanism for recommending people to serve on boards. In governmental organizations the nominating committee is seldom used, but there is a tendency to make use of a recommending panel with responsibility for suggesting names to the appointing authority.

A nationwide study of state welfare departments found that "securing the services of citizens who are willing to devote their ability and time to the responsibilities of serving as state board members is not a clearly defined process. The selection of two hundred forty-one individual citizens who serve as state board members was not clearly indicated. Only six states prepare a panel of nominations for submission to the appointing authority. The number of various sources known to be consulted for nominations was negligible. Interested citizens, state agency executives and board members were consulted in only six states. Members of state boards are most commonly appointed either by the Governor of the State or by the Governor with confirmation of the State Senate. The terms of appointment range from one to nine years and are all overlapping, except in four states which have partial or full concurrent terms. In half of the states the appointing authority also has the authority to remove members from office. Almost seventy per cent of the boards have no maximum allowable years of service. In thirty-eight percent of the states the factor most frequently considered in the selection of new board members is 'recognized and demonstrated in interest in public welfare.' In an equal number of states no specific qualifications were indicated in the consideration of appointments. Other factors common to less than fifteen per cent of the states are: not more than 'X number' of the same political party; community interest; sex distribution; geographical representation; citizenship; resident and 'religious and racial representation,' or in contrast, 'without regard to race or religion.' Only one state required that 'prospective appointees must have demonstrated a sincere interest, knowledge, and ability consistent with the responsibility of the office.' Personal conferences and correspondence with state directors suggest that many other implied qualifications were taken into consideration. Wide discretion is allowed the appointing authority, and few limitations or restrictions in the way of specific qualifications are set forth." [39]

The Nominating Committee

As the author pointed out in an earlier work, "The nominating committee has one of the most important tasks in any organization." [40] It is usually the group that has the job of finding good board members. The members it finds will have great influence on the course of the organization. In a recent publication from a national organization the function of the nominating committee was described in this way: "The sole responsibility of the nominating committee is to present a slate of nominees for the officers, board of directors, the delegates to the National Council, and the succeeding nominating committee. It serves no other function. It does not serve the board or any of its committees on a consultative basis. It renders service only to the membership body to which it is accountable, namely, the council." [41] Specific functions were listed as: "to gather information about possible candidates for elective positions from all available sources; to select and secure persons with ability and willingness to serve; to prepare a slate of nominees; to provide the biographical material about each nominee for inclusion in the Call to the Annual Meeting; to approve the report, including the slate, to be presented by the chairman at the annual meeting of the council." [42] Qualifications for members of the nominating committee were spelled out as follows: "Acceptance of the basic philosophy and purpose of the Girl Scout movement and of the principles and policies of the Girl Scout organization; stature in the community and broad acquaintance with community leaders; sensitivity to people, how they act and react; how others relate to them; time to do a thorough job, a willingness to participate actively in fulfilling the responsibilities of the job, and sense of timing to complete the work; ability to approach a prospective nominee with integrity—to define the position, its responsibilities and expectations, and the time needed to carry it out; ability to establish rapport with people; a talent for making them feel needed and honored to be asked to serve Girl Scouting; ability to secure needed information about potential nominees and ability to assess such information without personal prejudice or bias; ability to maintain as completely confidential, information about the nominees and the considerations of the committee." [43] Under the duties of the members of the nominating committee seven items were listed: "To study the council bylaws, especially those parts related to the officers, board of directors, succeeding nominating committee, and the provisions on National Council delegates; to study the Blue Book, especially the sections on the beliefs and principles of the Girl Scout movement, the policies, and the provisions of the National Constitution on delegates to the National Council; to participate actively in all meetings of the nominating committee by sharing fully in its discussions and decision-making; to observe the operations of the board in session to get the feel of what it takes to make the board a cohesive and effective group through attendance at board meetings; to carry out assignments delegated by the chairman of the nominating committee; to attend meetings and events of the council and the communities within the jurisdiction to observe community leaders and to identify individuals with potential for elective positions; to keep the chairman of the nominating committee apprised of progress in making contacts assigned and securing nominees who have been agreed upon by the committee." [44] Under the discussion of the duties of the chairman of the nominating committee the following items are given: "To participate in all board meetings as an elected member or as a member ex-officio; to prepare the agenda for committee meetings; to call and preside at meetings of the committee, or designate another member to serve in her absence; to arrange with the president for non-board members serving on the committee to attend one or more board meetings during the year to observe the board in action; to invite the president and executive director to attend meetings of the committee for consultation; to invite the president designate to confer with the committee on possible nominees for officer jobs in particular; to see that any personnel information maintained by the council is made available to the committee; to extend invitations to serve to those prospective nominees agreed upon by the committee for specific elective positions, to designate a committee member to extend the invitation; to inform persons who are invited to serve as nominees for the succeeding nominating committee that the chairman is chosen according to the method stipulated in the by-laws, from among the members of the committee; therefore, each nominee must be aware of the possibility of becoming chairman; to see that all actions of the committee are properly recorded and accessible for future reference of subsequent nominating committees; to keep the president informed of the schedule of the committee's meetings and general progress of the work; to prepare report of the nominating committee's work for the approval of the committee; to present report of the committee's work and slate of nominees for elective positions to the membership at the council annual meeting." [45]

In a succinct statement the duties of the nominating committee were summarized in these eight points: "1) To set up criteria for board members, based on a clear understanding of the agency's program. 2) To evaluate the eligibility for reelection of persons on the board whose terms are expiring. 3) To maintain a roster of potential board members who satisfy the criteria to serve. 4) To invite selectees to serve. 5) To interpret to nominees their new duties if elected to the board. 6) To present to the board a slate of nominees for election to the board, and a slate of officers for the ensuing year. 7) To fill vacancies which occur during the year. 8) To evaluate procedure followed by the Nominating Committee and recommend to the board needed changes in procedure and structure." [46]

Recruiting Board Members

As has been pointed out earlier, there will always be a need for a large number of board members to keep up with the growth in the number of agencies and the inevitable changes in personnel from year to year. Thus, each agency should have a plan for locating and recruiting into board service, persons who will be able to make a contribution. Responsibility for such locating and recruiting should be lodged in the board or a committee of the board with the assistance of the executive and the staff.

Underlying any planned effort to recruit board members is an understanding of motivation, or why people are willing to give freely of their time and talent to community service. Naylor develops this thought brilliantly when she observes, "No plan for volunteer leadership development can be effective unless it is grounded in realistic recognition of the *particular motives* which bring volunteers into an organization and the satisfactions which keep them going. In no area are we more apt to be misled by false assumptions and superficial impressions. The complex interplay between tangible and intangible factors is part of a balance of altruism and self-interest. A warm welcome to the person, nonjudgmental about his motivation, is the soundest approach. The expressed reasons for volunteering have a way of changing with experience and wider horizons. We have a dual obligation. To the persons offering themselves we owe opportunity for self-development, enjoyment and actualization of ideals and aspirations. To the organization we are responsible for continuity and vitality of the program and progress toward stated goals." [47]

There have been few studies of the motivation of board members; however, one significant one was made of board members in the service of public education in a large eastern state. The report describes the method used and the findings obtained. "Operating on a prediction that board quality depends in some measure on the motivation of board members, we asked two questions in an attempt to obtain a general portrait of the reasons that lead citizens to board service. Of board members themselves we asked, 'What led or prompted you to become a board member?' Recognizing that self-reported motives may differ markedly from the motivations ascribed to board members by close observers, we asked a second question of all our respondents: 'Without identifying individuals, describe the reasons for seeking office of the present board members.' (Current board members were asked to exclude themselves in their answers to this question.) In other words, our first question asked board members to report their own motives. Most, it should be noted, claimed several reasons for deciding to serve. Our second question asked those who were in close contact with our board members—chief school officers, fellow board members, recently retired board members, and parents' and teachers' organization presidents—to describe the motives they felt the board members as a group possessed. Responses to this second question, in other words, indicate the important motivations close observers saw at work among these board members. We are dealing here with varying *perceptions* of the motivations of board members; we cannot vouch that any part of our respondents reported the *true* reasons why men and women choose to serve. An analysis of the responses . . . reveals certain significant patterns. First, board members themselves and their close observers generally agreed that the chief motives of board members were altruistic —they served because they were asked to do so, they served because they had a genuine interest in the community or in the school system. The prestige associated with the office prompted very few. . . . The motivations of board members self-reported and ascribed by close observers were listed in the following order of importance: interest in education, asked to serve by Board or citizens group; interest in community service; had children in school; opposed existing policies; to hold down tax rate; for prestige." [48]

Auerbach, with bluntness and sharpness, points out that the need for prestige and power motivates some people to service. He says, "Two important motivating factors attract lay persons to our agencies. One is the obvious satisfaction of being identified with a social cause and the ability to make a positive contribution to the communiy. The other—less frequently discussed—is the element of recognition, prestige, and power gained through community activity. . . . In the case of our board members, may we not perhaps say that many accept board affiliation not only because they are committed to the agency's social goals, but because they are also searching for such 'unmentionable' values as status, community recognition, social influence, business contacts—or just a safe escape from a nagging wife or dull husband? . . . It is undoubtedly true that very few board members become active in our agencies solely for purposes of prestige, power, or self-aggrandizement. The overwhelming majority are attracted by the goals and accomplishment of the organization. But it is not the social goals alone that attract them. Every board member, to a greater or lesser degree, seeks or appreciates some measure of community recognition, prestige, status, and influence for his community participation. What is more, his identification and participation in agency activity itself acts to channel these power and prestige needs in socially positive directions. The result is often that those who have the strongest need for recognition develop into the most constructive and valuable community leaders." [49]

In addition to understanding the reasons why persons volunteer to serve on boards it is important to know some of the reasons why they do not. The education study cited above found that "the chief deterrent to the recruitment of better talent and the retention of experienced members is the heavy commitment of time demanded by board service. Well over half our respondents indicated that the 'best' people are already too heavily committed to spare fifteen to twenty hours monthly for board service. A second major deterrent is the abuse and criticism to which taxpayers and parents subject board members. Other reasons given were: loss of business due to loss of public favor; feeling that he could accomplish little as a board member; dislike of campaigning and risking public defeat; and would lose income due to demands on time." [50]

These are realistic considerations for the recruitment committee. Their work is far from easy. As has been pointed out again and again, there is a heavy load of community work and often the same people are pressured into service which is really too much for them in terms of time demand. It seems especially evident that large business corporations are expected to contribute more and more leadership, and while they do not complain publicly they do have feelings about it. As one writer of a national newspaper said in his essay, "Lights burn late in executive offices across the land, but in many cases not much company business is being done. Instead, the boss is drafting a budget for the Boy Scouts, dictating letters for a Community Chest drive or composing a report to be delivered to fellow trustees back at his old college . . . the pressures they [the business leaders] are under to engage in public service are felt increasingly throughout the whole business world, and some executives are wondering if the blending of doing good and doing business isn't being carried a bit too far." [51] The message seems to be that business wants to help, always has helped, and will continue to do so, but most communities need a rational plan by way of which leadership tasks are distributed fairly across a broad spectrum of the population. This indicates that the recruiting force of a given agency must have wide sights and look for potential board members in all possible areas of community life.

In addition to using personal contacts and discussion as a way of locating board members, many organizations have developed survey type forms which they mail out to their constituencies and invite them to make nominations. One organization in the mental health field wrote as follows to its members: "A limited number of vacancies exist on the Board of Directors. At the request of the Nominating Committee, I am writing to you for any suggestions you might have of possible candidates for these vacancies. In addition, we would like to develop a resource file of people who might be called upon in the future for both committee and board assignments. We are looking for people who have, or who might develop, an active interest in the field of mental illness and mental health, and who you believe would be willing to participate actively in the program of our association. Some of the particular areas of interest or background from which we would like to draw more board members include: medicine, business and industry, communications (newspaper, television, radio, other media), public health, education, clergy, people with experience in other organizations, such as service clubs, women's clubs, health and welfare organizations. Please let us know people you would like to recommend. For your convenience, a form is enclosed on which you can list your candidates. Thank you for your help. It will be of great help to the Nominating Committee." [52]

Naylor points out that some people are good at recruiting and others are not. She says, "Recruiters must be selected for their qualifications and enthusiasm, and a selection process should be planned . . . our most able people, both staff and volunteer, especially those who have some acquaintance or common interests, can approach the particular people we seek on an individual basis, armed with offers of appropriate and attractive volunteer jobs. These recruiters need help in understanding what the hopes and aspirations of the prospects are so that volunteering will be related immediately to the prospects' own important objectives. Recruiters help prospects to imagine themselves enjoying the work, growing and learning. Good recruiters make sure prospects understand how important their unique abilities would be for the organization and for their community." [53]

Orientation of Board Members

The orientation of new board members can be described as a period during which new members learn about and grow into their responsibilities. The basic purpose of orientation is to help newly chosen board members to establish effective working relationships with their fellow board members and with the agency they serve. The early experiences of new board members have a profound influence upon all of their subsequent experiences; hence the care with which orientation is planned can scarcely be overemphasized. In an earlier study made by the author it was found that 86 percent of the agencies had some kind of orientation program and most of those that did not have such a program were in the process of formulating one.

Among the methods used for orientation were written material to be read by the new board member, special meetings for new members, individual conferences with the new member, the board chairman, and the agency director, board member manuals, board member institutes, audio-visual presentations, committee work, subscriptions to national agency publications, agency visitations, and attendance at special programs.[54]

Among the weaknesses noted in orientation programs by board members themselves is the failure on the part of the agencies to ask the board members what they want to know. In other words, the orientation planners should make inquiry from the new board members and shape the early content of orientation, at least, in terms of the felt needs of the newcomers. Board members want to know about the history, purposes, and aims of the agency. They want to know how the agency fits in with others in the community. They are interested in their job as a working board. They want to know how they relate to and work with staff. They want to know how they are expected to function and what they must do to become a part of the working group. Perhaps the best planning group to develop the board orientation program would consist of *both* experienced and new board members so a balanced program could be created.

A most carefully designed study of school board orientation approached the question with this thought in mind: "Few would deny that to be an effective board member a person must learn a great deal about curriculum, school law, budgeting and a number of other subjects of special concern to the operation of the schools. Our survey attempted to determine the extent and kind of orientation procedures being used, and to gain some notion of their relative value as perceived by board members. We asked the chief school officers to judge, from their long experience with boards, how long it takes the average new board member to 'get into high gear': 'In general, how long does it take a new member to learn to function adequately?' Most chief school officers felt that it takes more than six months; nearly half estimated it takes more than a year; and over a third were sure that it requires at least eighteen months. . . . A few board members . . . remarked that their first year or even their first term was chiefly a learning experience. . . . We asked all current board members and chief school officers: 'What formal and informal procedures exist for the orientation of new board members,' and 'How does one really "learn the ropes"?' Except for the distribution of printed materials and occasional conferences with chief school officers or other board members, little of a formal or organized nature helped new board members to learn the task before them. No boards in our study had held what might be described as full, formal orientation meetings for their new members . . . procedures for the orientation of new board members listed in the order of their frequency included: learn by attending meetings; doing the job; study printed materials (policy statements, handbooks, books); conference with chief school officer; conference with experienced member; attendance at School Board institutes; prior service on citizens' committees, or as officer of parents' organization; attendance at board meetings as Member-Elect; attendance at State School Boards Convention; conference with the Board President. . . . Effective boards employ two orientation techniques not used to any great extent by ineffective boards: 1) members-elect are invited to attend board meetings prior to taking office; and 2) members-elect are often those who have worked closely with the board as members of citizens' committees. Orientation, however, is still chiefly a matter of on-the-job experience, with the result that much of a board member's first term is spent in learning the office." [55]

Imbalance, Weighting, and Partisanship

Studies of board composition and even casual observation of happenings about the community indicate that it is easy for boards to get out of balance, to be weighted, or even highly partisan in a political sense. Such circumstances are rarely, if ever, in the public interest and great care should be taken to avoid them.

Consider, for example, the following newspaper account with reference to an eastern state. While it refers to the legislature and its committees, it can and does happen in other institutions as well. "Whoever it was who set up the committees of the Legislature certainly overloaded some in favor of special pressure groups. For example, of the twenty-two members on the Agriculture Committee, nineteen officially list themselves as professional farmers whose interest is presumably centered around agricultural affairs. The Insurance Committee is overwhelmingly controlled by insurance agents and company representatives and the Judiciary Committee, which handles all matters pertaining to courts, and the legal profession is composed exclusively of lawyers. The Roads, Bridges and Rivers Committee is headed in the Senate by a professional trucker and in the House by a man who has long advocated bigger and broader expressways. . . . The ideal set up in a legislative body is to have all sorts of vocational and professional groups and all sorts of interests represented. . . ." [56] Obviously the above composition of these committees is far from ideal!

In an eastern suburb the membership of advisory boards and commissions was thought to be politically motivated and manipulated. The observer wrote, "It is of course natural for each party to nominate persons who are active in the party to these posts. But today, more than active party membership is considered; the appointments appear to be in some instances based solely on the patronage system, with considerations of merit subjugated to a lesser role. . . . In years past, board and commission members often chose their own chairman, from their ranks. Today, the choice of a chairman appears dictated by political considerations. Thus, a commission can be more or less counted on to follow the party line—which may be good for the party but is not necessarily good for the Town." [57]

While the above illustrations refer to boards and commissions of governmental agencies, similar situations can arise in the voluntary agency field where the "politics" is that of self-perpetuation and deliberate choosing of only the "right" people. But there are many changes taking place in the boards, commissions and committees of the nation's agencies and one of the most compelling changes is in their makeup and composition.

The Changing Composition of Boards

The Secretary of Health, Education and Welfare stated the case in these words: "Throughout our land today there is a great new spirit of involvement and participation. It is part of the social ferment that is transforming our society and its institutions. More people are becoming aware of their rights and responsibilities as citizens. People from all walks of life want a greater voice in solving their own problems and guiding their own destinies. Young people want to belong, to contribute, to have a hand in the decision making process in their schools and jobs. Poor people want a greater role in the systems and institutions that govern their lives. . . . All public agencies need to re-examine their policies and reshape their structures where necessary to make room for genuine, widespread public participation. . . ." [58]

The university has become a center of reevaluation and restructuring efforts as students "want a voice in making the decisions that affect their lives as students in order to be able to press more effectively for new courses, less rigid degree requirements, more freedom of political action on campus, and many other things." [59] Boards and committees of many universities are undergoing change.

Some of the concrete actions taken are now a matter of record.[60] For example, a large eastern university put forward a "plan to create a university senate—consisting of fifty senior faculty members, twenty junior faculty members, ten students, seven administrators, and five alumni." [61] A state welfare department commissioner "consented to an advisory board composed of welfare recipients to meet monthly with district welfare directors to discuss problems and learn of any changes in the Welfare Department." [62] A newly opened school of medicine announced that "two students from each class will be invited to sit in on faculty meetings with full participatory rights." [63] A federal training program for pre-school children made it clear that parents "should actively participate in all aspects of the program . . . these advisory committees, the membership of which is divided between the parents of enrolled children and representatives of the community, must participate in the selection of project directors and no director should be hired who does not receive the specific approval of the committee." [64] A national agency announced the appointment of three youths to its adult board of directors.[65]

The Youth Participation Act of 1968 was introduced into the Congress on July 9, 1968 "to provide opportunities for American youth to serve in policy making positions and to participate in National, State and local programs of social and economic benefit to the country. . . ." The framer of the bill said, "This generation of Americans has displayed an intense desire for involvement." Among the features of the Act is a program of grants in aid to public and private organizations—"especially those run by youth"—that "would give special emphasis to funding organizations which use youth volunteers to plan, administer, and evaluate policy in the programs in which they work." [66] While the fate of this proposed legislation is unknown at this time, it is extremely interesting that it has been introduced.

A leader in an eastern university suggested that the board of trustees be restructured; he recommended that "as vacancies occur, as many as eight of the twenty-four seats go to persons with faculty status, not more than half of whom have deanships or comparable administrative jobs. Faculty members are now excluded from the board. Of the six trustees who must be alumni, two should be under thirty-five. The average age of the board in May 1968 was sixty-two. Two student trustees selected by their peers would discuss and vote on those questions of direct concern to students." [67]

The challenge of changes now underway and forecast for the future will be considered at greater length in the concluding chapter of this book.

NOTES

1. Agnes G. Robinson, "Advice for the Board," *Saturday Review*, September 17, 1966, p. 91. (Review of book by Gloria Dapper and Barbara Carter, *A Guide for School Board Members.*) © 1966 Saturday Review, Inc.
2. *What's Going on in H.E.W.*, July 1968, prepared in the Office of the Secretary, Department of Health, Education, and Welfare, Washington, D.C.
3. *Expanding Social Welfare in the United States,* May 7, 1968 (U.S. Information Service, Washington, D.C.), p. 4.
4, 5, 6. *Ibid.,* p. 4.
7. *Annual Town Report,* West Hartford, Connecticut, June 30, 1967.
8. "Dedicated Citizens Give of Time," Sanford, Florida, *Herald,* August 28, 1968.
9. *Ibid.*
10. *The Report of the Volunteer Board Study Committee,* United Fund of Greater Lowell, Massachusetts, May 14, 1956 (Mimeo.), p. 3.
11. Harleigh B. Trecker, *Social Agency Boards—An Exploratory Study* (School of Social Work, University of Connecticut, 1958), 69 pages.
12. "Rubber-Stamp College Trustees," *New York Herald Tribune,* February 20, 1966.
13. Morrill M. Hall, *Provisions Governing Membership on Local Boards of Education* (Washington, D.C.; U.S. Department of Health, Education, and Welfare, Office of Education, Bulletin No. 13, 1957), 66 pages.
14. *Boards and Board Members of Health and Welfare Agencies* (New York: Community Chests and Councils of America, Bulletin 179, May, 1955), 26 pages.
15. Alpheus L. White, *Local School Boards: Organization and Practices* (Washington, D.C., U.S. Department of Health, Education and Welfare, Office of Education, Bulletin No. 8, 1962), 103 pages.
16. *Boards and Board Members* (New York: Community Chests and Councils of America, Bulletin 178, December, 1954), 9 pages.
17. "Convention Attendance an Expensive Business," editorial, *Hartford Courant,* August 4, 1968.
18. Trecker, *op. cit.*
19. Sidney Hollander, "The Batting Average of Board Members," in *Making Yours a Better Board* (New York: Family Service Association of America, 1954), pp. 3, 5.

20. Virginia Young, *The Library Trustee—A Practical Guidebook* (New York: R. R. Bowker, 1969), pp. 14-15.
21. S. V. Martona, *College Boards of Trustees* (New York: The Center for Applied Research in Education, Inc., 1965), p. 35.
22. Harold Koontz, *The Board of Directors and Effective Management* (New York: McGraw-Hill, 1967), pp. 137-138. Used with permission of McGraw-Hill Book Company.
23. Edward Jenkins, *Philanthrophy in America* (New York: Association Press, 1950), pp. 44-45.
24. *Ibid.*, p. 46.
25. Maurice E. Stapley, "Effectiveness of School Board Members." *Administrator's Notebook,* Vol. 1, No. 2, September 1952, Midwest Administration Center, University of Chicago.
26. *Ibid.*
27. John W. Gardner, "The Antileadership Vaccine," *Annual Report of the Carnegie Corporation of New York,* 1965, pp. 5, 6.
28. John Wallace and Phillip Schneider, "Do School Boards Take Education Seriously?", *Saturday Review,* October 16, 1965, pp. 89, 90-103. © 1965 Saturday Review, Inc.
29. Chauncey A. Alexander and Charles McCann, "The Concept of Representativeness in Community Organization," *Social Work,* January 1956, Vol. 1, No. 1, p. 48. Reprinted with permission of the National Association of Social Workers.
30. "Representation" by Francis W. Coker and Carlton C. Rodee. Reprinted with permission of the publisher from *Encyclopedia of Social Sciences,* Seligman and Johnson, editors, Vol. 13, pp. 309-315. © 1933, 1961 by The Macmillan Company.
31. Koontz, *op. cit.,* p. 19. Used with permission of McGraw-Hill Book Company.
32. "Representational Systems" by Giovanni Sartori. Reprinted by permission of the publisher from *International Encyclopedia of Social Sciences,* David L. Sills, ed., Vol. 13, pp. 465-473. © 1968 Crowell, Collier, and Macmillan, Inc.
33. John R. Commons, "Representative Advisory Committees in Labor Law," *American Labor Legislation Review,* Vol. XIX (1929), pp. 331-335.
34. "Representational Behavior" by Kenneth Janda. Reprinted by permission of the publisher from *International Encyclopedia of Social Sciences,* David L. Sills, ed., Vol. 13, p. 478. © 1968 Crowell, Collier, and Macmillan, Inc.
35. Alexander and McCann, *op. cit.,* p. 51.
36. Frederic Heimberger, "The State Universities," in Robert S. Morrison, editor, *The Contemporary University U.S.A.* (Boston, Houghton Mifflin, The Riverside Press, Cambridge, 1966), pp. 72-73. Reprinted with permission of Daedalus, Journal of the Academy of Arts and Sciences, Boston, Mass.

37. C. Wright Mills, *The Power Elite* (New York: Oxford University Press, 1956), p. 30.
38. Marian M. Winser, *A Handbook for Library Trustees* (New York: R. R. Bowker, 1955), pp. 15-16.
39. *Summary of Replies to a Questionnaire to State Welfare Department Executives Requesting Information on Type of State Board, Qualifications of Board Members and Values of Such Boards,* September 1961. Mimeo., Greater Hartford Community Council, West Hartford, Connecticut.
40. Harleigh B. Trecker, *Building the Board,* (New York: National Publicity Council for Health and Welfare Services, 1954), p. 38.
41. *Nominating for Elective Office in a Girl Scouts Council,* (New York: Girl Scouts of the U.S.A., 1965), p. 2. © 1965 Girls Scouts of the U.S.A. Used by permission.
42. *Ibid.,* p. 2.
43. *Ibid.,* p. 4.
44. *Ibid.,* p. 5.
45. *Ibid.,* p. 6.
46. *Steps Toward Broader Board Leadership* (New York: Federation of Protestant Welfare Agencies, 1955), p. 10.
47. Harriet H. Naylor, *Volunteers Today, Finding, Training and Working with Them* (New York: Association Press, 1967), p. 76.
48. *School Boards and School Board Membership,* Recommendations and Report of a Survey, New York Regents Advisory Committee on Educational Leadership, December 1965, pp. 26-28.
49. Arnold J. Auerbach, "Aspirations of Power People and Agency Goals," *Social Work,* Vol. 6, No. 1, January 1961, pp. 66-68. Reprinted with permission of the National Association of Social Workers.
50. *School Boards and School Board Membership, op. cit., pp.* 31-32.
51. Roger Ricklefs, "Pressure on Executives to Aid Outside Groups Rises, Stirs Complaints," *Wall Street Journal,* September 22, 1965, p. 1.
52. Connecticut Association for Mental Health, May 6, 1960 (form letter).
53. Naylor, *op. cit.,* p. 87.
54. Trecker, *Social Agency Boards—An Exploratory Study, op. cit.,* pp. 57-62.
55. *School Boards and School Board Membership, op. cit.,* pp. 38-39.
56. Keith Schonrock, "Committees 'Weighted' by Special Interests," *Hartford Courant,* March 22, 1953, Part I, p. 7.
57. John G. Sandell, "The Way I See It," *West Hartford News,* October 28, 1965.
58. Wilbur J. Cohen, *The Secretary's Letter,* Vol. 2, No. 2. July 1968, p. 1.
59. "The Universities Look at Student Power," *Hartford Courant,* August 25, 1968, p. 2B.
60. "Teachers College Adds Students to Policy Group for First Time," *New York Times,* September 13, 1968, p. 34; "Princeton Will Add Graduate Trustees," *New York Times,* April 12, 1969, p. 1; H.R. 11132, A Bill to Amend the Charter of Howard University, 91st Congress, 1st Session, May 12, 1969.

61. *New York Times,* September 13, 1968, p. 34. © 1968 by the New York Times Company. Reprinted by permission.

62. *Hartford Times,* August 17, 1968.

63. *Hartford Courant,* September 12, 1968.

64. "Project Head Start Revises Guidelines on Role of Parents," *New York Times,* January 10, 1966. © 1966 by the New York Times Company. Reprinted by permission.

65. "Youths on Board of Urban League," *New York Times,* August 30, 1968.

66. *Congressional Record,* Washington, D.C., July 9, 1968, Vol. 114, No. 117.

67. *New York Times,* August 3, 1968. © 1968 by the New York Times Company. Reprinted by permission.

6 Officers of the Board—The Leadership Team

The importance of carefully chosen officers cannot be overstated. The board chairman, vice-chairman, secretary, treasurer, and key committee personnel constitute the leadership corps of the board. Anyone who has served in such offices will readily testify to the fact that "there is more than meets the eye!" There is always more work than one imagines there will be! Also, anyone who has served on a board or a committee will assert that much of the success of the group depends upon the kind of officers that have been chosen. Great care must be taken to select qualified persons for these crucial leadership posts. And persons who agree to accept board chairmanships and other officers must do some soul-searching of their own before they agree to undertake the heavy tasks called for. While the experience of serving in a leadership capacity can be and is rewarding, it is also demanding and time-consuming.

Officers Are Special People

Although they may be unsung, unrewarded, and unappreciated the officers of any community service enterprise are special people. As Lilienthal puts it, they are "particular and special kinds of human beings. Individuals with a special function: to lead and move and bring out the latent capabilities—and dreams—of other human beings. . . . This I believe, and this my whole life's experience has taught me: the managerial life is the broadest, the most demanding, by all odds the most comprehensive and the most subtle of all human activities. And the most crucial." [1]

Anyone who has had the privilege of working with an outstanding board president soon realizes that he is in the presence of a rare kind of person. Gray wrote about such people when he said, "One of the most gratifying of those minor 'pleasures of life' that Rose Macaulay celebrated so engagingly is to find oneself in the company of an intelligence that one can respect without reserve. The tensions induced by many disappointing past experiences with minds supposedly qualified to instruct drop away; the guards raised unconsciously against pretension, special pleading, or an obvious determination to be beguiling are lowered in delightful surprise; one relaxes in the comforting awareness that here is a temper to be trusted. If it is a learned spirit, one perceives that it is also a courteous, generous, and casual one, up to no bullying tricks. If it is a sober searching guide, it is also capable of humorous as well as earnest insights. I am describing, I hope, the rare but not impossible combination of qualities to be found in high-spirited yet unhysterical adventurers in the realm of ideas." [2]

While there is little in the way of research, it is possible to summarize in a general way, at least, the qualities which seem to stand out in successful officers of any agency. These persons seem to have more energy than do others, or they are better at organizing their time and budgeting their energy. Probably they have more drive than most people; at any rate they seem to enjoy helping other people get things done. They have a clear identification with the values and purposes of the agency they serve and a commitment to the achievement of these purposes. They have moved happily within the community and agency structure and no doubt have more than average status with their fellows.

They are willing to take the responsibility and to exercise the authority that goes with office. They have a willingness to make decisions, sometimes very difficult decisions. They are usually people active in community affairs and probably have a considerable strength in the realm of organizing the efforts of others. They combine a clear sense of the reality of the present with a dream for the unfolding future. As the late Senator Robert F. Kennedy said many times, in many parts of the nation, to those he touched and who sought to touch him, "Some men see things as they are and say why. I dream things that never were and say, why not." [3]

As one reflects on the officers of successful ventures they seem to be quite well informed about the continuing work of the agency and they take the time to "do their homework" and participate in regular briefings to update their knowledge. They have the capacity to see the agency in an overall sense. They focus the time of the board or the committee they head on major matters of issue, policy, problem, and decision. They have a good sense of time and timing. They are clear as to the objectives of their group. They are sensitive to the inevitable power struggles that go in on every organization and they identify with none as they strive to reconcile varying viewpoints. They are aware of the ever-changing scene and spot opportunities to move ahead when the time is right. Most important, they concentrate their attention on the development of people and when their time comes to step aside they can feel that they have left the organization in better shape because a new group of leaders has been located and trained. They delegate matters along the way and through delegation give others the opportunity to serve and to learn.

Responsibilities of the Officers as a Group

If it is correct to assume that the officers constitute the leadership corps of the board and that they along with the executive and key staff are the leadership corps for the whole agency it is perhaps wise to look at what are their overall responsibilities. Spencer does an outstanding job of outlining these tasks when she says, "In planning the *work program* of the board, the officers (particularly the president) and the executive should: a) Select items for board consideration which are appropriate to its function and present them to the board at an appropriate level of sophistication; b) Provide for intensive and successful experience in decision-making at the policy formulation level; c) Provide a committee structure of standing and ad hoc committees to allow for more intensive study of issues and to give board members the opportunity for developmental experience with small groups; d) Provide for a flow of work between the board and its committees; e) Afford some balance in board meetings between the making of relatively easy, clear-cut or short-range decisions and the consideration of more complex or long-range issues; f) Schedule major policy considerations over a long enough span of time: to allow for development of staff and committees of information and possible courses of action; to provide for adequate discussion in board meetings; and to allow for testing of proposed solutions before final action is taken." [4]

The implication of this list and of the thought that the officers constitute a special *work group* for the agency is clear. All *officers* must be chosen with care. Their abilities and talents must be complementary and their special strengths utilized in ways that create an efficient working team. Nominating committees must see the big picture when they are making their recommendations.

As one national agency puts it, the responsibilities and qualifications of the officers must be considered together. "The officers of the board of directors are elected by the board from within its own membership at its first meeting following the annual election of board members. They serve also as the officers of the Association. The officers are listed in the by-laws of the board of directors with a description of their duties. Each Association should have a president, one or more vice presidents, a secretary, and a treasurer. The number of vice presidents is related to the size of the Association and the amount of responsibility that the president may need to delegate to the vice presidents in addition to the presiding and other functions that a vice president assumes in the absence of the president. If the volume of recording and correspondence is heavy the Association may also need more than one secretary, usually a recording and a corresponding secretary. There may also be a need for one or more assistant treasurers in a large Association or as a means of providing continuous coverage of the treasurer's responsibilities without interruption during the absence of the treasurer. . . . Officers of the board of directors should have knowledge of and experience in the total Association in addition to the specific skills required for the offices to which they are elected. Preferably a president should have had committee experience in several phases of the Association program and other administrative experience. Vice presidents should have sufficient experience to discharge the duties of the president in her absence, although election as vice president does not imply subsequent election to the presidency." [5]

It is of great importance that the agency sketch out in detail the jobs that have to be done in relation to the competencies required if these jobs are to be done right.

In an excellent manual for board members, board officers and their functions are presented as follows: "The president gives leadership to the organization and through it should guarantee the democratic functioning of the agency. He represents his agency in the community. He carries out the duties assigned to him by the organization's bylaws. He works in close relationship with members of the board, with committees, and with individuals within and outside the organization. He, with the assistance of the executive, studies the business of the agency and makes up the agenda for board meetings. The vice-president assists the president and may have, and should have specific jobs. He presides at meetings in the absence of the president. The secretary is the board's official recorder and is custodian of the board's records. He handles correspondence upon authorization of the board. He should realize the importance of keeping accurate minutes, since they are the records of the board decision and action and must be kept to give legal sanction to an incorporated body's actions. . . . Minutes should be accurate, as brief as possible, recording action taken with only pertinent facts recorded. They should be reported in the order of business presentation. The secretary signs the minutes; and after reading them at the next meeting, records any corrections and writes 'approved' with the date of approval at the end. The treasurer is the authorized custodian of the agency funds. He carries out duties of the office as prescribed in the bylaws and sits on the finance and budget committees." [6]

The Chairman of the Board

No office carries greater responsibility than that of board chairman or agency president. Sorenson stated it well when he wrote, "The president or chairman is the chosen leader of the board and committee forces of the agency. He is the one most responsible for the agency's policies. The chairman of the board should be a person with standing in the community and one who has a deep sense of social responsibility. He should be neither a dictator nor a figurehead, but one who is tolerant, wise, and active; not an isolationist, but one nevertheless with some degree of devotion to the work of the particular agency of which he is chairman, and one who can speak intelligently about it." [7]

The viewpoint of an agency president and board chairman reveals the great responsibility she felt when in office. She wrote: "The primary job of a president is to lead. That this is done in conjunction with the executive director does not diminish the responsibility or opportunity of either. Joint leadership requires some division of labor; certain areas are the province of the executive, others of the president. But a large middle area must be shared if maximum use is to be made of the two leaders. The president must be qualified for her job, as is the executive, and must add constantly to her knowledge, skill, and insight. How does a president lead? In her Association she constantly presents the triangular relationship between purpose and objective, objective and program, program and purpose. She must preside objectively, but, if she doesn't see that certain knowledge is injected into the meeting, she does a disservice. She appoints chairmen, listens to them and helps them act responsibly. She represents her association in the national movement and helps its members know and use the resources offered. She represents her Association in the community and listens for opportunities for the YWCA to serve and to add to its assets of leadership and money. She finds ways to relate herself and other professional and volunteer leaders to appropriate community groups and individuals." [8]

As pointed out by a national agency, "The board's officers share responsibility with the executive for enabling the board as a whole to carry out its policy-making functions. . . . No one but the president can determine the quality of his own relationships with fellow officers and trustees. His sensitivity, his democratic but firm leadership of Board meetings, his expression of appreciation for the services of Trustees and staff are essential qualities. . . . The quality of leadership given the Board depends in largest measure on the relationship of President and Executive. These constitute the key planning team in determining issues to be brought before the board, and giving overall direction to long-range planning. They must help trustees individually, and as a group, to experience real participation, to contribute to the board's functioning, and to share the satisfaction of agency achievements." [9]

The responsibilities of the board chairman or president are many. Fundamentally, he is responsible to the board and in turn to the community for all actions of the agency. He is expected to preside skillfully at all board meetings. He must confer with the executive about the agenda of regular board meetings, or special meetings as needed. He acts as chairman of the executive committee. He appoints such standing or special committees as are not elected and are authorized by board action for specifically defined purposes. He carries out special assignments delegated to him by board action. He must confer regularly and be in continuous communication with the agency executive and key staff members on any and all phases of the agency program. He must take leadership and initiative in bringing suggestions for any phase of the program to the executive and before the board for the purpose of changing policy or developing new policy. He represents the agency on special public occasions and in community affairs generally.

Serving as board chairman or agency president requires special qualifications and skills. One of the most important is the skill and ability of the chairman to engage the board in real and meaningful participation. As Sikes points out, "The key to meaningful participation is that the ideas of the participants must be given a chance to affect the outcome of the decision. . . . Social scientists have provided a considerable amount of evidence supporting the contention that a management style that encourages participative decision-making can have a favorable effect on organizational productivity and efficiency. The following potential advantages have been indicated. 1) Participation increases identification with the goals of the organization and consequently enhances the motivation of members to produce. People tend to be more enthusiastic about carrying out plans they have helped to develop than about plans handed down by fiat. 2) Participation reduces resistance to change. Change is a constant characteristic of any dynamic organization, and being able to effectively institute changes is a key to organizational success. 3) Participation enhances the personal growth and development of members of the organization through stretching their problem-solving competence and by broadening their understanding of organization problems. 4) Participation brings a wider range of ideas and experience to bear on a problem. The chance of errors caused by lack of relevant information is thus reduced. 5) Participation increases organizational flexibility, strength and growth potential through improving competence at lower levels." [10]

In addition to being able to help each board member engage in meaningful participation, the chairman must direct that participation to a *decision*. Too frequently the board chairman assumes that persons understand the decision-making process when many times it is not so. Persons participate but the board does not seem to get anywhere. Decisions are not reached. Frustration mounts. Talk without decision is indeed the curse of many meetings. Koontz says, "Decision making entails . . . selecting what appears on the basis of the best possible information to be the best way of attaining a given objective. There can be no rational action without 1) a clear goal, 2) a clear understanding of alternatives for reaching this goal, 3) an adequate analysis of alternatives in terms of the goal, and 4) a desire to optimize the use of resources in reaching the goal." [11] Drucker describes the sequence of steps in the decision-making process as being sixfold: "1) The classification of the problem. Is it generic? Is it exceptional and unique? Or is it the first manifestation of a new genus for which a rule has yet to be developed? 2) The definition of the problem. What are we dealing with? 3) The specifications which the answer to the problem must satisfy. What are the 'boundary conditions'? 4) The decision as to what is 'right' rather than what is acceptable, in order to meet the boundary conditions. What will fully satisfy the specifications before attention is given to the compromises, adaptations, and concessions needed to make the decision acceptable? 5) The building into the decision of the action to carry it out. What does the action commitment have to be? Who has to know about it? 6) The feedback which tests the validity and effectiveness of the decision against the actual course of events. How is the decision being carried out? Are the assumptions on which it is based appropriate or obsolete?" [12]

The creative and innovative chairman is in great demand as community service agencies review their functions and revise their programs to keep abreast of rapidly changing times.

Skills of the Board Chairman

In our studies of successful board chairmen [13] a number of primary skills of chairmanship have been identified. They include the capacity of the chairman to think clearly, logically, and creatively. In addition, the skillful board chairman has sound knowledge of the agency and can see the problems and issues of the agency in large perspective. This perspective includes knowledge of the community's problems and the services of other agencies. He must have knowledge of group dynamics and an understanding of the individual personalities that make up the board. He must have self-knowledge and ability to admit his own limitations and deficiencies.

Skill in human relations is perhaps the most essential. It includes skill in working with individuals and groups; skill in creating an atmosphere within which persons may interact productively; skill in enabling his associates to perform their tasks at a high level of performance. Underlying all of this is the skill of developing good working relationships with people.

The skill of planning looms large in the descriptions of successful chairmen. The ability to study cause and effect, to see short-range difficulties in the light of long-range goals, seems to be a key to effectiveness.

In addition, he must be able to organize his work, coordinate the work of others, delegate assignments, and follow up as needed.

Judgment or the ability to interpret important factors in solving problems is most important. This ability to recognize facts, to be able to assemble them, and then to analyze them and make decisions based on them is essential to any leadership role.

Communication skills are obviously important in the art of board chairmanship. These include self-expression—clear, concise, effective oral and written presentation; ability to interpret and reinterpret issues; liaison role in communicating ideas to and from the board, the staff, and the community; ability to share problems; ability to provide flexible channels of communication; ability to present agency problems and suggested solutions to the board.

Basic to all of this is the way the chairman organizes his board with the help of the executive. In the next chapter the organization of the board will be considered.

NOTES

1. David E. Lilienthal, *Management: A Humanist Art* (New York: Columbia University Press, 1967), p. 18.
2. James Gray, review of Frank Kermode's book, *Puzzles and Epiphanies, Saturday Review,* March 2, 1963. © 1963 Saturday Review, Inc.
3. Text of Edward Kennedy's Eulogy of His Brother, *New York Times,* June 9, 1968, p. 56.
4. Sue Spencer, "Developing Effective Board and Committee Organization and Functioning," in *Building Board Leadership for the Years Ahead.* Proceedings Advanced Leadership Training Institute, September 7-8, 1963, Nashville, Tenn. (The University of Tennessee, School of Social Work and National Jewish Welfare Board), pp. 45-46.
5. *The Role of the Board of Directors in a Community YWCA* (New York: Publications Services, National Board, YWCA, Revised Edition, 1957), p. 9.
6. *A Blueprint for Board Members* (Omaha: United Community Services, 1958), pp. 10-11.
7. Roy Sorenson, *The Art of Board Membership* (New York: Association Press, 1950), p. 88.
8. Statement by Mrs. Douglas T. Henderson, *The YWCA Magazine,* June 1960, p. 26.
9. *The Realities of Board-Executive Relationships and Functions* (New York: Federation of Jewish Philanthropies, February 10, 1960), p. 8.
10. Walter W. Sikes, "The Case for Participative Management," *Hospital Administration,* Winter 1965, Vol. X, No. 1, pp. 15-16.

11. Harold Koontz, *The Board of Directors and Effective Management* (New York: McGraw-Hill, 1967), p. 34. Used with permission of McGraw-Hill Book Company.
12. Peter F. Drucker, "The Effective Decision," *Harvard Business Review,* January-February 1967, pp. 92-93.
13. Harleigh B. Trecker, *Executive Role With Boards—An Exploratory Study* (School of Social Work, University of Connecticut, 1960), pp. 76-78.

7 Organization of the Board as a Work Group

The board chairman and the executive have a continuing responsibility to help the board organize itself into an effective, functioning work group. How the board is organized to do its work is of the utmost importance. However, it is rare when the board takes the time to look at its own organization. Usually the pattern of organization that prevails one year continues the next. Only in times of crisis do most boards take a hard look at their own structure. It is rare when one finds a plan of systematic review and modification of the board itself. Although the pace of social change is much more swift many boards continue to function with what seems to be all deliberate slowness! They are trapped in a maze of committees and subcommittees allowed to proliferate to such an extent that efficiency is impossible. The amount of time consumed because of confusion of organization is tremendous. The miracle is that so much work does get done. The unfortunate fact is that it could get done much more expeditiously.

The Meaning of Board Organization

Despite the fact that few boards look critically at their organization and structure it is vital that they understand the place of both in their work. As Houle says so succinctly, "Organization is merely the way by

139

which people relate themselves to one another so as to achieve their common purposes. . . . So far as possible, boards should devote their time to shaping policy and furthering program, but this result can be achieved only if the members of the board are effectively related to each other. A poorly organized board can continue to exist, but it cannot thrive, for it has no way to mobilize or channel the energies of its members. Either systematically or whenever problems of relationship begin to appear, someone—the whole board, a committee, or an individual—must consider whether the structure itself can be at fault." [1]

As stated with clarity by a national youth organization, "To organize is to establish the various parts of an enterprise and to define their functions and relationships. . . . To be effective, organization structure should be a living, dynamic thing and it should be equal to the demands placed upon it. . . . It is important to be constantly aware of the need for structural changes." [2]

In a brilliant presentation of the properties of organization Blake and Mouton list seven essential items which must be understood. They are: "1) *Purpose*—Purpose is the unifying principle around which human energy clusters in the organization. It defines direction. Any decision made can be tested against purpose to see if it makes the organization more effective or less so. . . . To be useful, a statement of purpose must be specific and operational, clearly understandable and able to provide direction. It must be realistic and practical, acceptable and meaningful to those running the organization. It must arouse the motivation to move forward. 2) *Structure*—Every member of the organization is not expected to do all the kinds of work required within it. Instead, there is division of labor. Related work is lumped under organizational units. A way to coordinate efforts between the units is determined. The structure of a large organization is subdivided into regions or functional activities. It may be further subdivided within each of these into departments, divisions, sections, or units of various kinds. These vary widely from one organization to the next and depend to a great extent on purpose. Small organizations are likely to have more simple structures. All organizations of size contain elements of structure. 3) *Financial Resources*—Present in every organization is a financial system enabling it to invest in new efforts or withdraw its investments from less successful activities. Financial resources are important. Without them the organization would not be able to carry out its activities. 4) *Know-how*—To carry out the purposes of the organization its members supply technical skills and competence—know-how. No matter how clearly defined, how realistic, and how sound an organization's purposes may be, if its leaders are not competent to see that the purposes are obtained, the organization will flounder. 5) *Human Interaction*—The human interaction property of the organization exists because the persons manning it must of necessity interact. They must exchange information, implement decisions made, and coordinate their efforts. 6) *Organization Culture*—In any organization, over a period of time, a set of practices builds up. A way of organizational life becomes accepted. A climate is created, established practices become traditional. Everyone in the organization is expected to conform. . . . 7) *Results*—A seventh property of every organization is the generation of results that are in some way measurable in terms of organization purpose. . . . If the conglomeration of persons and equipment is truly an organization it will have a realistic purpose clearly understood by all to provide a direction for their efforts; a structure that provides the necessary coordination of interlocking parts; access to the financial resources needed to support decisions that enable it to obtain its purposes; the necessary technical skill and know-how among its personnel; a human interaction process supporting sound decision-making with a minimum of waste; a culture thoroughly understood and controlled which is an asset not a liability; and, finally, an ability to achieve results so as to be effective within the free enterprise objective of realizing an acceptable return on investments. Results may also be in the form of service that is in the public interest." [3]

Understanding the Agency

Each agency has special characteristics which must be understood if the board is to organize itself within the cultural framework that is provided. When one looks at boards in the fields of health, education, and welfare it becomes apparent that the nature of the agency being administered and the nature of the service being rendered has a strong bearing on the way the board must conceive of itself and organize itself. In discussing the modern university, Truman says, "The university as an organization is unique. Roughly characterized, it is an association of elements—faculties, departments, services, trustees, administrators, students—among which there is little hierarchy, nothing monolithic, and authority is remarkably fractionalized. It is an association which, if its complex function is to be met, rests heavily upon comity, persuasion, restraint and mutual respect. . . . The unique association of elements that is a university involves a subtle division of labor that is not always precise." [4]

As the chairman and the executive think about the board and try to understand its job in the particular agency they need to ask themselves certain questions:

Do the board members understand clearly the reasons why the agency is unique; what its role is and how it effects it; how the agency and the board differ from—and are similar to—other agencies and boards; how the agency and board have been and should be meeting the needs for change; in what areas the agency might reach out for cooperative efforts with other agencies?

Is the board relating the talents and experience of its various members to the special needs and characteristics of the agency? Are these talents and experience being utilized fully in selecting members of board committees?

Criteria of Good Organization and Structure

In our studies of boards [5] and their functioning it has been possible to suggest some of the criteria of good organization and structure. In spite of the wide differences among agencies, when a well-organized board is found the following elements of organization and structure are also found. First, the structure is no more extensive than is needed to support properly the work of the board. Simplicity rather than complexity is an important key to effectiveness. While this thought runs counter to much experience, especially in terms of the number of board committees, when agencies take a look at their structure they improve it most by simplifying it. Second, a good structure is economical to manage from a time, money, and leadership standpoint. While it is rare for an agency to put a monetary value on time spent in board and committee work, it is important to recognize that "time is money" and every effort should be made to keep structure as simple as possible. Third, when structure is well constituted there is an orderly flow of work within the board and an orderly flow between the board and its several committees. The structure allows the chairman and the executive to keep track of the various jobs that are going on simultaneously and there is both coordination and orderly progression as work is completed. Fourth, when the board is well organized it has a structure with clarified areas of responsibility for individuals and groups so that they know what they are to do and how their work relates to the work of others. While an organization chart is only a visual aid to understanding organization it is very important that the board be able to chart its own organization with clear lines of relationship. Fifth, good structure shows the position of the board in the agency and how it relates to other groups within the agency including the staff and the constituency. Sixth, good structure shows the position of the board in relation to other related agencies in the community and if the board is a local affiliate of a national agency, regional and national ties should be shown. Seventh, satisfactory structure provides for an orderly grouping of the various duties which must be performed by the board and provides for the assignment of specialized tasks to designated committees or task groups. Eighth, good structure brings about a free flow of communication and tends to be a force for continuous interaction between all of the board members. Ninth, when structure is well conceived and well formulated it serves to create unity rather than separation or compartmentalization and brings about real coordination and integration of efforts. Tenth, a good structure provides for a reasonably rapid transmittal of information from committees to the board and from the board to the agency staff, constituency and the community. Eleventh, when structure is dynamic provision is made for flexibility and periodic review and evaluation. Twelfth, when it is determined that there is a need for changes in organization and structure the entire board must be given the opportunity to participate in drafting these changes and in devising the new plans.

Board Committees and Their Functions

As the board organizes to do its work, it ordinarily makes use of the committee as a device for assigning or "committing" specific jobs to small groups of its members. Except for very small agencies with equally small boards, it is not possible to do everything with the board functioning as a "committee of the whole." Even though committees are the usual device for getting work done by the board, a school board association states: "Standing committees are of doubtful value. There should be little need for permanent subcommittees if boards concerned themselves only with major policy functions. Details of fact-finding, reporting, and administration ought to be delegated to the superintendent and his staff . . . special committees—those which are appointed for a specific task and for a limited time—may serve a useful function." [6] In spite of this skepticism most agencies in our studies of boards [7] had a number of committees at work the year round. The average number of board committees was eleven. One very large agency had a hundred committees covering responsibility for a statewide program. There was little uniformity as to the size of committees or the number of times they met each year.

In a guide for board members, a community planning agency pointed out that "committees are the working machinery of an organization. They plan and promote the activities in the various areas of program. Each committee, of two or more persons elected or appointed because of their qualifications, has a definite purpose which is controlled and directed by the agency board. Committees divide up the work of the agency, expedite the work by removing routine tasks from monthly board consideration, utilize specific talents and knowledge of people, and permit broader participation. Committees must recognize that the agency board makes decisions on program changes before they are undertaken. This assures the board's keeping its rightful and delegated responsibility for the agency's business. There are four types of committees: *Executive committee,* usually the board officers, acts in emergencies between board meetings but refers any action taken to the board for approval. *Standing Committees* are the permanent commitees which implement the group's program and business. Recommended are: nominating, public relations, education, budget-finance, personnel, and program. *Subcommittees* may be appointed by a committee chairman to do a special part of the work for a standing committee. *Special committees* are organized, usually through appointment by the president, to fill a temporary need and are dissolved when the work is finished. The chairman of each standing committee is a member of the board. There should be some committee organization including a secretary to be responsible for committee minutes and records. Staff members should participate in committee meetings as advisors." [8]

In a detailed discussion of board committees, a national youth agency points out that "the board looks to each of its committees for advice and recommendations on proposed plans, policies, and standards in that committee's assigned area of work. . . . Standing committees are committees with continuing responsibilities. . . . Special committees are organized to fill a temporary need. . . . Subcommittees carry out a part of the work assigned to the parent committee and are responsible to the parent committee. . . . All standing committees of the board have a common set of responsibilities. . . . Each committee: Develops and recommends to the board of directors policies and standards. Assists the board of directors in establshing council-wide objectives and goals. Develops and recommends to the board the plans for projects and services in its particular area of work. Advises and serves as a resource to the board of directors, to other committees, and to others carrying related responsibilities. Evaluates periodically accomplishments in its area of work in terms of council-wide goals. Keeps the board of directors informed of trends and developments in the field of its assigned area of work." [9]

It is highly important that committees be active and functioning. When they have completed their tasks they should be discharged. The function and scope of each committee's authority must be decided by the board and must be put in writing. All standing and special committees not provided for in the bylaws must be created by board action for the specific purpose of fulfilling a need. There should be a clearly stated charge and a definite timetable for reporting back to the board. The usual standing committees are Budget and Finance, Personnel, Services and Program, Public Relations, Nominating and Executive.

In an earlier publication the author pointed out that the committee is "an organizational device for getting work done by a group process" and that "all committees are *task-limited,* that is, they have a job to do, a function to perform. They have a boundary which should be sharp as to problem, charge, or responsibility. Second, committees are *time-limited,* that is, the job they have to do must be done in a defined period of time. They should not go on like the babbling brook but should complete their work in a specified time-span. Third, committees are *tool-limited,* and their chief tool is directed interpersonal communication; language, words, ideas, feelings, opinions, attitudes, experiences are the stuff of committee process. Fourth, committees are *organizationally limited* in that the purpose, policies, and procedures of the parent organization must necessarily influence the way the committee works." [10]

Even with these limits there are many values in the committee system. Committees make it possible for the board to divide up the work so that it will not be too burdensome on the board as a whole. Committees can expedite the work of the board because of the concentrated study a committee can make of a problem. Committees enable the board to utilize the special knowledge and special experience of board members. Committees also serve as training opportunities for new board members who may advance to leadership posts. Of great importance is the fact that the committee is a safeguard against overcentralization and domination of the board by a few persons. When a committee does a good job on its assignment there is every reason to believe that the report produced will be far better than anything one person could achieve. If one is to evaluate the work of the board a good place to start is the committee structure. Usually it is a key to success.

The Executive Committee

In our studies of boards [11] the vast majority make use of the executive committee as the chief instrument of the board for internal planning. In some cases the words "steering committee" or "executive council" are used. No matter what the name, boards need a small group to take responsibility for their work. In one agency, "membership on the executive committee of the board of directors is specified in the bylaws of the board. It includes the officers of the board and preferably not more than three additional members appointed by the president. Its function is to act in the interim between board meetings on matters requiring immediate attention. It may act on matters that are within the established policies of the board and within the budget approved by the board. It may not rescind or go counter to any action of the board, nor may it authorize expenditures outside of the aproved budget. Unless the board of directors has made a specific delegation of authority to the executive committee to act as its agent, all actions of the committees are subject to ratification by the board. The committee does not assume the board function either in decisions that are the prerogative of the board or in exercising judgment on whether policy questions shall be referred to the board." [12]

In practically every case studied the executive committee is provided for in the bylaws and it is appointed by the board chairman with the proviso that all officers and standing committee chairmen should be members. Other members may be appointed at various times, particularly if their presence brings a needed point of expertise not available in the others.

A review of the problems handled by executive committees in order of frequency indicates that matters of budget, finance, and capital improvements came up twice as often as any other item. Next was the matter of program and the administration of services. After them came matters of personnel policies, employment of the executive and approval of presidential appointments. Emergency matters which had to be dealt with in between regular board meetings were next. Community relationships, public relations, interagency matters and legislation were also listed. Agency evaluation was considered only to a limited degree.

Committee Chairmen

Almost any chairman of the board will remark that his work is not only easier but much more satisfying if he succeeds in appointing competent chairmen for board committees. The chairman's job is one of group leadership in planning, carrying out, and evaluating the work assigned to the committee. He must be informed about all aspects of the board's work and must be clear about the job of his committee in relation to the other committees at work at the same time. He must be able to organize his committee and develop with it a plan for accomplishing its tasks. He is responsible for preparing the agenda and seeing to it that copies are made available to the committee members in advance of the meeting. He presides, leads discussion, summarizes and assists the group in formulating conclusions and taking action. He serves as a channel to the board by reporting on the work of his committee and frequently by moving for action on the report.

It is clear that in appointing or selecting committee chairmen the same amount of care that goes into the selection of officers is required.

Effective Work Groups

When the board is well organized, when committees have been carefully created and properly coordinated, the evidence is that the work will get done smoothly and efficiently. Under these circumstances it is possible to observe "the properties and performance characteristics of the ideal highly effective group" as Likert has outlined them: "1) The members are skilled in all the various leadership and membership roles and functions required for interaction between leaders and members and between members and other members. 2) The group has been in existence sufficiently long to have developed a well-established, relaxed working relationship among all its members. 3) The members of the group are attracted to it and are loyal to its members, including the leader. 4) The members and leaders have a high degree of confidence and trust in each other. 5) The values and goals of the group are a satisfactory integration and expression of the relevant values and needs of its members. They have helped shape these values and goals and are satisfied with them. 6) Insofar as members of the group are performing linking functions, they endeavor to have the values and goals of the groups which they link in harmony, one with the other. 7) The more important a value seems to the group, the greater the likelihood that the individual members will accept it. 8) The members of the group are highly motivated to abide by the major values and to achieve the important goals of the group. Each member will do all that he reasonably can—and at times all in his power—to help the group achieve its central objective. He expects every other member to do the same. . . . 9) All the interaction, problem-solving, decision-making activities of the group occur in a supportive atmosphere. Suggestions, comments, ideas, information, criticisms are all offered with a helpful orientation. Similarly, these contributions are received in the same spirit. Respect is shown for the point of view of others both in the way contributions are made and in the way they are received. . . . 10) The superior of each work group exerts a major influence in establishing the tone and atmosphere of that work group by his leadership principles and practices. In the highly effective group, consequently, the leader adheres to those principles of leadership which create a supportive relationship among the members. For example, he shares information fully with the group and creates an atmosphere where the members are stimulated to behave similarly. 11) The group is eager to help each member develop to his full potential. . . . 12) Each member accepts willingly and without resentment the goals and expectations that he and his group establish for themselves. . . . 13) The leader and the members believe that each group member can accomplish "the impossible." These expectations stretch each member to the maximum and accelerate his growth. When necessary, the group tempers the expectation level so that the member is not broken by a feeling of failure or rejection. 14) When necessary or advisable, other members of the group will give a member the help he needs to accomplish successfully the goals set for him. Mutual help is a characteristic of highly effective groups. 15) The supportive atmosphere of the highly effective group stimulates creativity. The group does not demand narrow conformity as do the work groups under authoritarian leaders. . . . The group attaches high value to new, creative approaches and solutions to its problems and to the problems of the organization of which it is a part. The motivation to be creative is high when one's work group prizes creativity. 16)

The group knows the value of 'constructive' conformity and knows when to use it and for what purposes. Although it does not permit conformity to affect adversely the creative efforts of its members, it does expect conformity on mechanical and administrative matters to save the time of members and to facilitate the group's activities. The group agrees, for example, on administrative forms and procedures, and once they have been established, it expects its members to abide by them until there is good reason to change them. 17) There is strong motivation on the part of each member to communicate fully and frankly to the group all the information which is relevant and of value to the group's activity. This stems directly from the member's desire to be valued by the group and to get the job done. The more important to the group a member feels an item of information to be, the greater is his motivation to communicate it. 18) There is high motivation in the group to use the communication process so that it best serves the interests and goals of the group. Every item which a member feels is important, but which for some reason is being ignored, will be repeated until it receives the attention that it deserves. Members strive also to avoid communicating unimportant information so as not to waste the group's time. 19) Just as there is high motivation to communicate, there is correspondingly strong motivation to receive communications. Each member is genuinely interested in any information on any relevant matter that any member of the group can provide. . . . 20) In the highly effective group, there are strong motivations to try to influence other members as well as to be receptive to influence by them. This applies to all the group's activities: technical matters, methods, organizational problems, interpersonal relationships, and group processes. 21) The group processes of the highly effective group enable the members to exert more influence on the leader and to communicate far more information to him, including suggestions as to what needs to be done and how he could do his job better, than is possible in a man-to-man relationship. By 'tossing the ball' back and forth among its members, a group can communicate information to the leader which no single person on a man-to-man basis dare do. . . . 22) The ability of the members of the group to influence each other contributes to the flexibility and adaptability of the group. Ideas, goals, and attitudes do not become frozen if members are able to influence each other continuously. . . . 23) In the highly effective group, individual members feel secure in making decisions which seem appropriate to them because the goals and philosophy of operation are clearly understood by each member and provide him with a solid base for his decision. This unleashes initiative and pushes decisions down while still maintaining a coordinated and directed effort. 24) The leader of a highly effective group is selected carefully. His leadership ability is so evident that he would probably emerge as a leader in any unstructured situation. To increase the likelihood that persons of high leadership competence are selected, the organization is likely to use peer nominations and related methods in selecting group leaders." [13]

Bringing About Change in Board Organization

At periodic intervals, perhaps every two or three years, the board should take a look at its organization and see if it is satisfactory for the changing times. Usually a special study committee on board organization is the best way to make the review. In his discussion of adaptability to change, Stein points out that "the processes of change in large organizations are still not too well understood, but change does occur and often stems from imagination and creative planning rather than being simply accidental. To develop the actuality of change towards well-understood goals requires, of course, that the function of planning be clearly located within the organization. Unless planning is a conscious activity it will not tend simply to happen. There will be changes, but they will be uncontrolled and at the mercy of external factors rather than self-directed, or planned to meet the influences of external pressures in the environment of the organization. The centralization of a planning function does not mean, however, that participation in planning and in policy formulation must be restricted to a specific individual or group of individuals. On the contrary, participation in planning can and should be widespread through an organization." [14]

NOTES

1. Cyril O. Houle, *The Effective Board* (New York: Association Press, 1960), pp. 52-53.
2. *The Council Manual,* pp. 28-29. © 1960, 1969 Girl Scouts of the U.S.A. Used by permission.
3. Robert R. Blake and Jane S. Mouton, "Grid Organization Development," *Personnel Administration,* January-February, 1967, pp. 8-9.
4. David B. Truman, "The University." Reprinted from *Columbia Forum,* Fall 1967, Vol. X, No. 3. © 1967 Trustees of Columbia University in the City of New York.

5. Harleigh B. Trecker, *Social Agency Boards—An Exploratory Study* (School of Social Work, University of Connecticut, 1958), 69 pages.
6. *Boardmanship—A Guide for the School Board Member.* Fourth Edition, 1969, p. 14. Revised by the staff of the California School Boards Association, Sacramento, California. Used by permission.
7. Trecker, *op. cit.*
8. *A Blueprint for Board Members* (Omaha United Community Services, 1958), pp. 11-12.
9. *The Council Manual,* pp. 22-23. © 1960, 1969 Girl Scouts of the U.S.A. Used by permission.
10. Audrey R. and Harleigh B. Trecker, *Committee Common Sense* (New York: Whiteside, William Morrow, 1954), pp. 18-23.
11. Harleigh B. Trecker, *op. cit.,* pp. 38-43.
12. *The Role of the Board of Directors in a Community YWCA.* (New York: National Board YWCA, 1957), pp. 11-12.
13. Rensis Likert, *New Patterns of Management* (New York: McGraw-Hill, 1961), pp. 166-169. Used with permission of McGraw-Hill Book Company.
14. Herman D. Stein, "The Study of Organization Effectiveness," in David Fanshel (editor), *Research in Social Welfare Administration* (New York: National Association of Social Workers, 1962), p. 29. Reprinted with permission of the National Association of Social Workers.

8 *The Board Meeting*

The regular meeting of the board, usually conducted on a monthly time schedule, is essentially a *business meeting*. As defined by one authority, "the term business meeting as here used denotes a meeting in which there is an attempt to act upon current organization matters, as distinguished from a meeting the purpose of which is to present a speaker, a demonstration, a film, an entertainer or other attraction. In some meetings, business is only a part of the proceedings; in others, the order of business is, in effect, suspended after the call to order so that the special feature may be presented." [1]

Board meetings are called for the exercise of corporate responsibilities.[2] The legal frequency of meetings is specified in the constitution or bylaws.[3] Frequently the kind of advance notice required for meetings is likewise specified.[4] It has been consistently recognized in rulings by the courts that a corporation is ordinarily bound only by action taken by directors at a meeting.[5] Although the primary purpose of any formal board meeting is to make and put on record formal action on procedures and policies, secondary or ultimate purposes are also an important consideration. King views the ultimate purpose to be the growth in wisdom and vision of board members so that they can decide more important issues in the future.[6] Matthews also asserts that the meetings of any organization serve both individual as well as group purposes.[7] Ross and Hendry describe the board as a task-oriented group but consider the importance of secondary objectives which have to do with the develop-

153

ment of the individual board member insofar as this development relates to helping further the primary objectives of the board as a whole.[8]

There are many matters to be taken into consideration if board meetings are to be productive. The frequency of meetings and the number of meetings to be held each year have to be decided. The length of time for each meeting as well as the time when it will be held have a bearing on the important matter of attendance. The content, or what is to be considered at board meetings, is of course a major area for decision. Agenda preparation, the assembling and advance mailing of material for study, and the preparation for the meeting loom large in the portfolios of the board chairman and the executive.[9]

In spite of the importance universally placed on the board meeting as a legal happening, as a "means of carrying a large and important part of the business of the democratic world," [10] and as having a "very important place in our social order and way of life," [11] the treatment of the subject of board meetings is usually brief and somewhat general in the literature, although it is almost universally mentioned. Routzahn comments that "so far no one has attempted to calculate the cost of the numerous meetings which fill the days of leaders and staff workers of organizations, even in a single area like social work or public health." [12]

Some Research Findings on Board Meetings

Several studies of board meetings have been made. Their findings yield important clues for improving the effectiveness of such affairs. The author conducted an extensive interview study [13] where board members themselves were queried as to their evaluation of board meetings. These interviews, along with questionnaire data, enable us to get a picture of current practice in the social welfare field. Most of the social agency boards reported that they met once a month with some relaxation of schedule during the summer. A few agencies reported quarterly meetings of the board as a whole with much committee work in the interim. Board meetings lasted from one and one-half hours to two and one-half hours with two hours being the average time spent. Most agencies reported that they found it wise to set and hold to a regular time for the call to order of the meeting and a regular time of adjournment. Since many board members were "fitting the meeting into their full day" they had to have a clear idea of the length of the meeting. One of the greatest deterrents to board service was the lengthy meeting without agreed-upon termination time. In a world where people live by the calendar, the clock, and the time schedule the open-ended or indeterminate meeting is not acceptable to busy board members.

Without exception, members reported that they were notified in advance of meetings, regular or special, and said that advance notification was of great importance. The method of notification differed but most agencies used the written communication, the return card to signify attendance, and the follow-up telephone call to encourage attendance. Even with this approach attendance varied considerably, with some board members present only half of the time.

In general the board members believed that they received sufficient material in advance of board meetings and considered it to be helpful. The degree of value was somewhat dependent upon the nature of the subject to be discussed and upon the kind of information circulated prior to the meeting. Most members said they appreciated having a particularly crucial problem called to their attention prior to the discussion of it and preferred to be armed with pertinent facts.

In no instance did a board member believe that a good meeting just happened. Agendas are planned in advance by the board chairman and the executive and attention is given to arranging the items in terms of priority. Most agencies distributed the agenda in advance of the meeting. Those that did not do so made sure that copies were available at least at the time of the meeting. Board members liked to have agendas "keyed" in the sense that items requiring a vote would be so marked. They liked to know what would be the disposition of the given item and what would be expected of them in terms of formal action.

Over half of the agencies mailed out the minutes of the board meeting so that their approval could be handled thoughtfully and quickly. Few of the agencies went through the formality of reading the minutes of the last meeting. A motion to approve as written, or approve with corrections or changes seemed to suffice. Generally, the elected secretary of the board carried the responsibility for preparing the minutes and circulating them in advance.

Board meetings were held in a number of different places including the agency board or conference room, offices, restaurants, and various community settings. In the case of large agencies with several branches it was now and then the practice to have the board meet at one of the branches. The two most popular times for meetings were the noon or luncheon period and the period after dinner in the evening. There was, however, a trend toward meetings held during business hours * especially for boards of large public agencies. It was considered important that the meeting be held at a regular time so that persons could plan their schedules accordingly.

Physical surroundings were deemed to be important by all of the persons interviewed. A setting conducive to discussion and deliberation and free of distractions was thought to be vital.

In all the agencies studied it was common practice for the executive director to attend board meetings. In many cases key staff members also attended to serve as resource persons. The majority of board members were satisfied with the degree of staff participation at the meetings and felt that staff contributions were essential to the progress of the meeting and the work of the board.

Most board members were clear in their understanding that their function was to make final decisions on policies and that the staff had the task of carrying out these policy decisions in the offering of services and program. In general, the board meeting time was given over to matters of finance and budget, trends in services, personnel matters, community relationships, and legislation. Some board members showed impatience with the fact that much time had to be devoted to financial matters and many hours were given to budget preparation.

In general, board members were impressed with the democratic methods used in the conduct of their meetings. A very small number viewed their activity in the "rubber stamp" class. Persons who wished to comment were encouraged to do so and to speak frankly. Occasionally interviewees noted with pride the skill of the board chairman in involving all members in fruitful discussion.

The major work of most social agency boards is accomplished through the efforts of committees which study the problems falling within the area of function or which are assigned to them by the chairman of the board. The fruits of committee research and study, often with specific recommendations, are presented to the whole board for consideration and action.

Most committee chairmen felt that the board gave full consideration to their reports and that these reports were thoroughly and openly discussed. Many times they were modified and in some cases were referred back to the committee for further work. In a few cases board members

* The time of board meetings might well be changed from "business hours" as boards begin to include more nonexecutive and nonprofessional personnel.

felt that there were too many committee reports and that some of them were not adequately reviewed by the board as a whole. In general, however, board members felt that the committee system was the only one which would allow for detailed development of plans and careful consideration of issues. The board meeting does not provide sufficient time for the entire board to function as a committee of the whole. Board committees were much more active than the board as a whole. They met more often and gave more attention to particular problems. Some board members observed that when they served on several board committees, these meetings along with the board meeting made it difficult for them to find the time to do all of the work required.

Most board members interviewed believed that their meetings were carefully planned and generally productive. There was widespread feeling that ample and free discussion was permitted as a prelude to board action. There was agreement with the proposition that the efficiency of board function is largely dependent upon the forethought given to the agenda and the strength and wisdom of the board president in his role as a presiding officer and discussion leader.

Most people thought that the time-limited meeting with a definite adjournment hour helped board members to keep their discussion in focus and directed to the main matters under consideration. Overly extended meetings tended to bring about a decrease in productivity and irritation on the part of the members.

A study of boards of education showed that "boards meet from ten to twelve hours monthly in regular or executive session and that with an added seven to twelve hours of outside duties, this constitutes a major deterrent to potentially good board members." When the same study looked at how boards spend their time among several functional areas it was found that budgetary matters, curriculum, plant construction and maintenance, pupil services, staff recruitment, review and dismissal, and community requests and grievances were dealt with in this order. Budgetary matters occupied from one-fourth to one-third of the board's time in meetings. Only a little more than one-fourth of board meeting time was devoted to functions directly determining the nature of educational program. Far more was spent on handling budget, construction, maintenance, transportation, lunch and the like. When board members were asked, "How much of total board meeting time is devoted to important policy development?" it was found that only about 39 percent of board meeting time was devoted to what board members felt to be important policy. The rest, apparently, was either not important or not policy, as they saw it. By board members' own count, most of the time was spent on functions not directly related to the educational program itself, and most of it was not devoted to important policy decisions. In substance, board members did not feel that they used their meeting time to the best advantage.[14]

In a study of hospital boards LeRocker and Howard found that "decisions made by hospital boards of trustees are largely concerned with matters of finance, physical plant, and non-medical personnel." In order of frequency the decision subjects were financial, physical plant, personnel, medical staff, patient care policy, hospital organization, public relations, education, research and miscellaneous. After reading the minutes of hospital board meetings the authors declared that "matters concerning finance and physical plant occupy more than half the field of board decisions." [15]

Understanding the Purpose of the Board Meeting

From the studies of what boards actually do during their meetings one would get the impression that they are busily engaged in trying to find the money needed to run the enterprise and in trying to manage funds successfully. While an inordinate amount of time seems to be spent on finances, the main purpose of the board meeting is to *develop the overall policies* needed to guide the agency in providing services. Finance is surely an important part of this but it is not the only job that has to be done.

When one reviews the many responsibilities allocated to the board and discussed in an earlier chapter [16] it should be apparent that the purpose of the board meeting is to bring together the official, legal or corporate body of the agency to transact the business required by the agency as a whole. The board meeting thus becomes a formal setting for decision making in terms of the continuing tasks of providing satisfactory community services. It is not a social gathering, although sociability may be a by-product. It is not an educational meeting, although education does occur. It is not an open forum or informal discussion, although discussion naturally occurs. The board meeting is a formal, carefully planned, legally authorized, regular gathering of the elected or appointed citizens who are responsible for the work of the agency.

Planning the Board Meeting

The chairman of the board and the executive director are primarily responsible for developing the plan for the board meeting. In addition they may ask the executive committee or steering committee of the board to lay out a plan for the board meetings for the entire year. This year-ahead plan, which allows for the consideration of major matters in terms of orderly and calendar requirements, is enormously helpful when one considers that board meeting hours are limited as to number. Each hour should be carefully allocated to *major* matters. Many of these matters are of a cyclical character in that they come up regularly at predetermined times. For example, the budget has to be presented and approved in relation to the fiscal year. The same holds for the report of the nominating committee. Special summer programs have to be considered in the winter or spring if they are to be ready for summer offerings. In addition to these regular meetings which come up every year, the agency always has a number of standing and special committees which are at varying stages in their work. Some committees are ready to report at one board meeting. Others will report at future meetings. To get full and fair consideration of committee reports they should be properly scheduled and no one board meeting should have too many lengthy reports lest time run out before they can be acted upon.

The success of board meetings collectively and individually depends upon the kind of advance planning and preparation that is made. While the board chairman and the executive have the major responsibility for planning, all board members must do their "home work" if meetings are to be productive.

Planning, a national organization says, "involves present decision for future action. . . . Planning is based on the evaluation of past work and the anticipation of future needs. Principles of planning include: 1. Plans should be based on facts concerning past and present conditions and predictions of the future. Facts should be obtained from reliable sources in order to lend stability to plans. 2. Plans should be within a framework of clearly defined objectives and goals. These help everyone to move in the right direction and to focus on the most important needs. 3. Plans should be developed with the help of those concerned. The board relies on committees, associations in the geographic subdivisions, and staff for facts and for suggestions for improving services. People are more willing to accept and carry out plans which they have helped to develop. 4.

Plans should be ambitious, yet realistic. They should strive for continuous progress and should challenge people to put forth their best efforts. Too, they should be within the realm of possibility from the standpoint of available time, money, and people. 5. Plans should be flexible. They should be adaptable to changing conditions and needs. 6. Plans should be clear and simply stated so that every one involved in carrying them out knows what is to be done, when, and by whom." [17]

In planning for each board meeting the chairman and the executive director have several essential tasks to perform. First, they must select the items which are to appear on the agenda for the meeting. Some of these items appear on every agenda such as call to order, action on the minutes of the last meeting and so on. Other items appear as a result of work in process by the several committees of the board. Second, after determining what is to go on the agenda the items must be arranged in sequence. Most boards organize under the heading of old business and new business. Third, in addition to selecting and arranging the items it is wise to indicate alongside of each item the expected disposition. For example, some committee reports are made for "information only." Others are "progress reports." Others require a vote or "action." In connection with the clues as to what is to be done about a given item, the chairman must have some ideas as to the amount of time to be devoted to each item. Fourth, it is necessary to mail out the agenda and enclose with it necessary supporting materials. Ordinarily, the agenda should go out a week or at least several days in advance. Frequently public agency boards publish the agenda in the press so that the community will know what is to come up at the meeting. Fifth, when the agenda has been prepared it is necessary that someone inform or brief the people who are to make reports indicating to them the location of the item on the agenda, the amount of time allocated to them, and the proposed disposition of the report. The above steps are the minimum essentials for a well-planned board meeting. Although it is clear that following them does take time in advance of the meeting it will save much time during the meeting and bring about much better discussion and action.

As was pointed out in an earlier publication, "Good agendas are a guide and stimulus to thoughtful group discussion. They should meet the following criteria: *They are realistic in a time sense.* They are not crowded with items that cannot be dealt with in the available time. It is far better to have a short and completed agenda than a long and partially completed one. *The items require thought* on the part of the group members. If the agenda becomes cluttered up with many informational items which could just as well be covered in a news bulletin, valuable time is wasted. *The items are arranged in a logical sequence.* Such a sequence usually includes preliminary items of lesser importance, then the main or major items come in the body of the agenda to be followed by the closing items. *A good agenda contains suggestions on how the group should deal with each item.* By using simple notations it is possible to indicate needed disposal of each item. For one item it may be, 'Accept or ratify this report.' For another it may read, 'This matter will require full discussion.' For another it may read, 'This item is a continuation of our discussion of last meeting; we should conclude it today.' " [18]

Conducting the Board Meeting

It is important that the board follow a regular plan and order of business. It is also necessary that there be agreement on rules of procedure. The skills of the board chairman are brought to bear most directly while the board is in session. Much of the success of any meeting depends upon how well the chairman presides, leads discussion, keeps the meeting moving along, summarizes, and senses the mood of the group. As Tannenbaum and Schmidt put it, "The successful leader is one who is keenly aware of those forces which are most relevant to his behavior at any given time. He accurately understands himself, the individuals and the group he is dealing with, and the . . . broader social environment in which he operates. . . . The successful leader is one who is able to behave appropriately in the light of these perceptions. If direction is in order, he is able to direct; if considerable participative freedom is called for, he is able to provide such freedom. Thus, the successful manager of men can be primarily characterized neither as a strong leader nor as a permissive one. Rather, he is one who maintains a high batting average in accurately assessing the forces that determine what the most appropriate behavior at any given time should be and in actually being able to behave accordingly." [19] Massarik and Wechsler call this "a talent for sizing up group opinion." [20]

In reviewing the chairman's responsibility, a national agency states that "the chairman has responsibilities that she must carry out before, during, and after the meeting. She must prepare the agenda and make other necessary preparations for the meeting. There are follow-up matters to be attended to after the meeting. But her chief responsibility is to conduct the meeting in a manner that will produce effective results and a feeling of achievement and satisfaction on the part of the members. This requires skill in discussion leadership. A good chairman: Helps to focus the discussion and to keep it on the subject. Encourages all the members to express their ideas. Tactfully interrupts those who tend to dominate the meeting and draws out those who are reticent. Avoids dominating the group, taking sides, or judging opinions expressed. Makes sure that all implications of each question are considered. Helps reconcile differences of opinion. Keeps enthusiasm high; adds a touch of humor when needed. Summarizes during and at the end of the discussion; calls attention to any unanswered questions for future study." [21]

When one has had the experience of participating in a meeting under a really excellent chairman and when one attempts to characterize how that chairman has presided, the following items stand out. He is an encouraging person who makes it easy for people to express themselves. He is a positive person who avoids rejecting or downgrading the contributions of others. He is a quietly questioning person who asks for and solicits opinions from all who are there. He spends time stating, defining, and redefining the problem so that board members will grasp precisely where they are in their discussion. He will help the group to define its position at a given time and will regularly summarize the extent of agreement so that the group can move on. He will give good direction to the meeting and will show evidence of having a planful approach. He will inspire confidence because of his sincere interest in the job at hand and because of his warm regard for the ability of his fellow board members.[22]

A substantial amount of time at all board meetings is devoted to receiving and acting upon reports presented by committee chairmen or staff members. It is important that clear instructions be given to those who are to make reports. Ordinarily, the report should be mailed out in advance and highlighted orally at the meeting by the person responsible for it. It is seldom, if ever, necessary to read lengthy reports. They can be read by the board members in advance of the meeting and they can have their questions ready. As has been pointed out earlier, the agenda should indicate the expected disposition of the report and the chairman should introduce it with instructions as to what action is called for.

Reports calling for a vote should be discussed quite fully so that there will be maximum understanding of the action to be taken. Every report brought to the meeting should become a part of the permanent record of the board and should be appended to the minutes of the meeting.

While most board meetings move along reasonably productively, the chairman can expect that there will be problems of individual member behavior which can impede progress. Lind lists five "problem behaviors" in meetings: "1) People tended to interrupt each other. 2) They didn't listen when others spoke. 3) The meeting frequently broke down into 'cross-talk' and discussion between neighbors. 4) Speakers rambled in the course of their speaking, and freely changed the subject. 5) The chairman was not successful in maintaining control or an ordered flow of discussion." [23] It is obviously clear that such behavior will seriously hamper the board and it is the responsibility of the total board to establish ways of participation which will be fair and satisfying to all members. On rare occasions the board may have upon it a "troublemaker" seemingly bent upon disrupting the work of the group. As Sanford points out, "Trouble-makers, we now see, are usually troubled people, and their difficulties may be attributed in large part to the situation in which they live or work." He distinguishes between the disturbed person and the nonconforming person when he writes, "The creative, non-conformist individual with strong needs for independence finds it very difficult to fit into a pre-set organizational mold." [24] Although difficult, it is sometimes essential that the extremely troublesome person be removed from the board or at least not reappointed when his term expires.

After the Board Meeting

The work that goes on immediately after the board meeting is of great importance. Minutes must be prepared promptly and circulated to the board members. The actions taken by the board should be communicated to the staff, the constituency and the community. In some cases, right after the board meeting the chairman or the executive or both prepare and distribute a newsletter summarizing the highlights of the meeting. This proves to be an excellent way of acquainting everyone concerned with the work that is in process and the actions that have been taken.

Usually the board meeting will refer matters to standing committees or to newly created special committees. Here it is necessary that follow-up be assigned to either the chairman or the executive so that these important matters will be worked upon by the appropriate group and in terms of a time schedule.

Soon after the board meeting the chairman and the executive should have a formal review conference. This conference enables them to assess the work that has been done and begin to plan for the next meeting. When one realizes that board meetings are usually planned on a monthly basis the follow-up cannot be allowed to lag.

Obviously much work goes on in committees between board meetings and it is frequently necessary for the executive or board chairman or both to participate with some of these committees to make sure they are working along the right lines.

Often special assignments of a fact-gathering nature will be allocated to the executive or other staff members. These requests need to be handled promptly so necessary data will be on hand for the subsequent meeting.

Should Board Meetings Be Open to the Public?

Increasingly, board meetings are becoming open to the public. In the case of public agency boards it is frequently a legal requirement that they be open. For example, "California law provides that school board meetings must be open to the public except when boards are dealing with salary or personnel matters. Specifically, the law states that executive sessions may be held when: (1) the board is discussing with its designated representatives salaries, salary schedules and compensation paid in the form of fringe benefits; (2) the board is considering the employment or dismissal of a public officer or employee, or when the board is hearing complaints or charges brought against a public official or employee (unless he requests a public hearing); the board is considering the suspension or expulsion of a pupil. All official action of the board, however, must be taken at meetings open to the public." [25]

Even though board meetings are required to be open to the public, it does not follow that the board will always accept the value of such an arrangement. In one state, school boards were "urged to be more open with the public and press in their deliberations on school policy . . . [a speaker] blasted school boards for concentrating so much 'on trivia, when they should be discussing educational policy. . . . Why is it that boards will have an hour and a half long discussion on whether to purchase a panel truck for school headquarters, and then put off until late in the evening—when most of the public has gone home—discussion on more serious business?' " [26]

It seems clear that the advantages of open board meetings are many if there is a genuine wish to have the agency understood by the public. When one accepts the fact that the agency exists to serve the public, every way should be utilized to bring the public into a relationship with the problems and goals of the agency.

Criteria of Good Board Meetings

When one evaluates board meetings he tends to turn first to the chairman and naturally relegates his own behavior to a role of lesser importance! In looking at the chairman it is necessary to ask such questions as: 1) To what extent did the chairman make adequate preparation prior to the meeting? 2) To what extent did the chairman have a meeting plan in mind and to what extent did he follow it? 3) To what extent did the chairman help the board members to become comfortable with each other by using ways of putting people at ease? 4) To what extent were good physical arrangements provided? 5) To what extent did the chairman offer a clear statement of the purpose of each item on the agenda and state the goal to be achieved in its consideration? 6) To what extent was the chairman skillful in helping board members to express themselves? 7) To what extent did the chairman succeed in keeping the discussion focused on the major issues before the board? 8) To what extent did the chairman give frequent summaries of group thinking so that the group could see and feel the progress being made? 9) To what extent did the chairman help the group arrive at conclusions regarding the various items? 10) To what extent did the chairman sketch out the matters to be held over for further consideration at the next meeting of the board?

The member of the board is also responsible for seeing to it that the meeting is productive. As stated by a national organization, "Some meetings fail to accomplish their purpose because of the false notion that the sole responsibility for the meeting rests with the chairman. It is only when each member assumes her share of responsibility for participation that the group will operate effectively and in a truly democratic fashion. The members should arrive on time and remain until the meeting is adjourned. They should study the agenda and come prepared to participate in the discussion. They should: speak up when they have something to contribute; stick to the point; listen attentively when others are speaking; respect and give thoughtful consideration to the viewpoints of others. They should request further information if they feel that the group has insufficient data on which to make a decision. They, as well as the chairman, can help clarify a point, encourage others to express their views, and summarize ideas. Whether or not the final decisions are valid is as much their responsibility as the chairman's." [27]

Houle sees six major ways of improving board meetings: "First, the patterns and procedures of board meetings should be reduced to routine as far as possible, so that constant decisions do not need to be made about them. . . . Second, the board meeting should be a culmination of a long process of preparation. . . . Third, reports made to the board should be as well presented as possible. . . . Fourth, as much of the time of the meeting should be reserved for discussion as is possible. . . . Fifth, there should be as much informality as possible. . . . Sixth, meetings should be kept brief." [28]

In summary, the productive board meeting is very much like any productive group meeting. Many studies from a variety of fields enable us to single out certain conditions which seem to be essential. First, groups produce more when they are composed of the right people. That is, the members are qualified in terms of competence, skill, and ability to do the assigned job. Second, productive work groups have assignments which are within the realm of their competence. Third, these groups are clear on the overall purposes and goals they are trying to achieve. They are straight on their assignments from the start. Fourth, productive work groups have good advance, overall planning and preparation. Fifth, productive work groups think through the methods they will use in carrying through on their assignment. Sixth, productive work groups divide their total assignment into parts and take one step at a time as they proceed with their work. Seventh, productive work groups develop a time schedule and a time framework and work within both. Eighth, productive work groups have good leadership or chairmanship able to release their thinking, focus discussion, and bring the group along to decisions. Ninth, productive work groups make a periodic assessment of what they have accomplished and what are the next steps. Tenth, productive work groups are given appropriate recognition for their accomplishments as a way of building and sustaining pride in their work.

NOTES

1. Mark S. Matthews, *Guide to Community Action* (New York: Harper, 1954), p. 37.
2. Roy Sorenson, *The Art of Board Membership* (New York: Association Press, 1950), p. 81.
3. Elwood Street, *A Handbook for Social Agency Administrators* (New York: Harper, 1947), p. 27.
4. *Ibid.*, p. 85.
5. Sorenson, *op. cit.*, p. 70.
6. Clarence King, *Social Agency Boards and How to Make Them Effective* (New York: Harper, 1938), p. 13.
7. Matthews, *op. cit.*, p. 37.
8. Murray G. Ross and Charles E. Hendry, *New Understandings of Leadership* (New York: Association Press, 1957), pp. 91-96.
9. Mary Swain Routzahn, *Better Board Meetings* (New York: National Publicity Council for Health and Welfare Services, 1952), pp. 13-14.
10. *Ibid.*, p. 13.
11. Sidney S. Sutherland, *When You Preside* (Danville, Illinois: The Interstate Printers and Publishers, 1952), p. 90.
12. Routzahn, *op. cit.*, p. 13.
13. Harleigh B. Trecker, *Social Agency Boards as Viewed by Board Members* (University of Connecticut, School of Social Work, 1959), 67 pp.
14. *School Boards and School Board Membership—Recommendations and Report of a Survey* (The New York State Regents Advisory Committee on Educational Leadership, 1965), pp. 44-65.
15. Frederic C. LeRocker and S. Kenneth Howard, "What Decisions do Trustees Actually Make?" *Modern Hospital,* April 1960.
16. See Chapter Two, *infra.*
17. *The Council Manual,* p. 37. © 1960, 1969 Girl Scouts of the U.S.A. Used by permission.
18. Audrey and Harleigh Trecker, *How to Work with Groups* (New York: Womans Press, 1952), pp. 51-52.
19. Robert Tannenbaum and Warren H. Schmidt, "How to Choose a Leadership Pattern," *Harvard Business Review,* March-April 1958, p. 101.
20. Fred Massarik and Irving R. Weschler, "Empathy Revisited: The Process of Understanding People," *California Management Review,* Vol. 1, No. 2, Winter 1959, p. 39.
21. *The Council Manual,* p. 52. © 1960, 1969 Girl Scouts of the U.S.A. Used by permission.
22. Audrey R. and Harleigh B. Trecker, *Committee Common Sense* (New York: Whiteside, William Morrow, 1954), p. 72.
23. Roger M. Lind, "Applications of Socio-Behavioral Theory to Administrative Practice," in Edwin J. Thomas (editor), *The Socio-Behavioral Approach and Applications to Social Work* (New York: Council on Social Work Education, 1967), p. 60.

24. R. Nevitt Sanford, "Individual Conflict and Organizational Interaction," in *Conflict Management in Organizations* (Ann Arbor, Michigan: Foundation for Research in Human Behavior, 1961), pp. 3-8.
25. *Boardsmanship—A Guide for the School Board Member,* Fourth Edition, 1969, p. 17. Revised by the staff of the California School Boards Association, Sacramento, California. Used by permission.
26. "Education Units Asked to Open Door," *Hartford Times,* October 22, 1965.
27. *The Council Manual,* p. 52. © 1960, 1969 Girl Scouts of the U.S.A. Used by permission.
28. Cyril O. Houle, *The Effective Board* (New York: Association Press, 1960), pp. 132-137.

PART FOUR

THE BOARD AND THE CHANGING

COMMUNITY

9 *The Board, the Constituency, and the Community*

The board of every agency is fundamentally responsible to and account-able to the constituency it serves and the community it represents. The relationships which are established between the board and the community are increasingly vital. No board can perform its task effectively unless it has a clear policy and program of constructive community relationships.

The work of health, education and social welfare agencies is so closely interrelated in the modern community that to a great extent each depends upon the others. Health services without good housing for people cannot be expected to create an optimum level of community health. Recreational agencies alone cannot solve the leisure time problem; they need to be a part of a broad cultural network. Schools to educate our children can only do so if home and family life are strong. Although as a nation we tend to organize and offer specialized services, each service is but one link in the complete chain of community, state, and national endeavor. To be sure, the first duty of a board is to see to it that the work of its agency is properly done. But its ultimate effectiveness as an agency depends in no small measure on the cooperative relationships it establishes with other agencies and upon the overall community planning that is taking place.

The board today cannot isolate itself from either the constituency or the community. It should see that its work is well known and well understood. Not only is this the right of the community, it is simply good management. As put by one agency, "No good agency or organization is complete without a community dimension. An agency, whether it wishes it or not, is an integral part of community life because those who direct it, those who finance it, and those who receive its services are a part of the community. . . . Part of the board's responsibility lies in community planning, community participation, and community action. Added hours of leisure, the mounting pressure and impact of an increasing population, as well as the constantly changing conditions and needs in an impersonal, metropolitan center, are forcing even reluctant agencies to see that they can no longer be isolated entities. They can no longer be indifferent to other agency work or pull apart from them. . . . Community relations imply the methods in which an agency relates itself to the community. They can be promoted through public relations and agency services, which are easily understood, and also through agency participation in a community council. Such community participation will: 1) Keep the agency related to other important groups in the community. 2) Maintain contacts with new developments. 3) Keep some control over plans for future development in the community. 4) Coordinate services with those of other agencies. 5) Support cooperative planning and development of new services in the community. 6) Prevent, or at least avoid, duplication of services. 7) Emphasize the necessity of constant scrutiny and evaluation of agency services. 8) Promote wiser use of the community tax and welfare dollars. . . . A cooperative status comes only when agencies and people learn to work together, to taste the satisfaction of cooperative endeavor, to enjoy mutual success, to find common values and ways to express those values. . . . It is important, then, that agency boards cultivate ways to make community participation the concern of each board member. Within agency groups, boards can: 1) Study present potential relationships to determine possible areas in which they can cooperate with other agencies and organizations. 2) Review and evaluate, critically, the agency's actual services in relation to community needs and to the services of other groups. In cooperative, integrated community efforts whose emphasis is on services needed rather than on perpetuating individual agencies, could another agency furnish the same service at lower cost to the community? Does the group still fill a vital need? 3) Find out what other agencies are contributing to the community through exchange visits. 4) Set goals for agency plans in relation to community needs, which are in line with agency policies, goals, and plan of work. 5) Develop active and effective lines of communication between the agency, other agencies, and the community council. 6) Guide the board and committees into community relations aspects of agency work, making them community relations conscious. Allow adequate time for the liaison person to report on community council work at board meetings and to lead discussions concerning it. 7) Bring any proposed major changes for the agency to the attention of the community council. 8) Create an awareness in the board of the programs of other civic groups interested in social study and action and bringing about better community living." [1]

The Board and Agency Interpretation

A major responsibility of the board chairman and the board members is to interpret the work of the agency to the community. To do a good job of interpretation, persons must be clear about the purposes of the agency and the clientele it serves. Too often it is taken for granted that board members do know what their agency is doing and with whom it is doing it. Our studies reveal that while a large proportion of the board members interviewed felt that they had a good understanding of the agency purpose and philosophy some did not, and all agreed that it takes time to learn. As one board member put it, "It takes about a year to get a good grasp of agency purpose and philosophy. Those who are already active on the board tend to overlook how much new board members do not understand, do not give them as much help as they should. The activities of the agency are so varied that it takes some time to grasp its purposes and programs fully." Many board members pointed out the importance of full and complete orientation when they are new to the board. While all board members were aware of the fact that they were supposed to fulfill a public relations role, there was much dissatisfaction with the way this role was being carried out. Except for the officers, who could be expected to know more about the agencies, board members generally felt inadequate as interpreters. All felt that special training was required.

While most board members had a general knowledge of the constituency or clientele being served, none felt that they were sufficiently knowledgeable in this area. In fact, there seemed to be an unfortunate gulf or gap between the board and the persons served. Before the board member can be expected to do an intelligent job of acquainting others with the work of the agency, he must know far more than he seems to know today.

In addition, the agency must have a comprehensive, up-to-date public relations program.[2]

Public Relations—The Continuing Task

Public relations is a vast field today. There is a considerable amount of expertise and specialized knowledge and skill to be mastered by those who provide professional leadership in this realm. While no one should expect the board and its members to be specialists in public relations, they should have some idea as to what the term means and how they can contribute to the agency's overall impact upon the community. The term "public relations" has been defined in a variety of ways. Harlow and Scott say, "Public relations is the skilled communication of ideas to the various publics with the object of producing a desired result. Public relations is finding out what people like about you and doing more of it; finding out what they don't like about you and doing less of it. . . . Public relations is the art of making your company liked and respected by its employers, its customers, the people who buy from it and the people who sell it. Public relations is the art of making friends for your organization." [3] Cutlip and Center distinguish between public relations and publicity: *"Public Relations*—The communication and interpretation of information and ideas from an institution *to* its publics and the communication of information, ideas, and opinions *from* those publics to the institution, in a sincere effort to establish a mutuality of interest and thus achieve the harmonious adjustment of the institution to its community. *Publicity*—The dissemination of information, making matters public from the point of view of one who wishes to inform others. Systematic distribution of information about an institution or an individual." [4]

Dapper points out that "good public relations . . . starts with having a good product and makes skillful use of every device available to inform the people about it. The aim is understanding, and the hope is that people will not only think well of the product but be encouraged to suggest ways to improve it. Unless this is done openly and with great faith in the public, there is probably no chance for ultimate success, no matter how skillful one is in manipulating the various communications media." [5] Dapper also points out the public relations values in open board meetings and urges school boards to develop and disseminate a complete public relations policy for their work and the work of the schools.[6]

Every agency has as one of its goals the continuing increase of public understanding of what it is trying to do within its realm of community need-meeting and service. It wants the public to realize that it is doing a good job that is worthy of regular and ever-increasing financial backing. Furthermore, it wants the people who are in need of the services offered to know about the programs that are available and to utilize them. In addition, the way the agency is regarded by the community is a powerful factor in staff recruitment and in soliciting the support of new board members.

While the technical and professional aspects of public relations may have to be assigned to specialists, the board sets policies and determines what should go into the program. As one training manual for board members put it, "Public relations seeks the active support of those individuals and groups in the community whose support the council needs in order to live and grow. It is more than publicizing, more than making council contacts. Public relations is the winning and keeping of consent. Consent takes many forms, but all are active and positive. Approval is voiced, cooperation is given or offered, the individual joins or encourages others to join, money or other tangible support is given, a job is taken and done. Public relations is not content to build a general climate of passive good will in which these things might happen. It is planned and conducted so that these things will happen. Consent must be systematically won. The 'public' is many publics. Different groups are moved to action by different things. Effective publicity must be planned, focused, appealing, repetitive. What the council does is as important as what it says it does. How the members feel about it has a very great bearing on the idea the public has of it. In sum, good public relations is concerned with: The policy decisions a board of directors makes; the morale, attitude, and action of its members; a very wide range of activities designed to inform, promote, and persuade action. Public relations uses a wide range of methods and many media. In addition to press, radio, and TV there are: house organs, magazines, brochures, flyers, reports, public appearances, letters, movies, exhibits, demonstrations, posters, personal contacts with key individuals, speeches, visits, official representation, services rendered, satisfied customers, the voice on the telephone. Excellence and effectiveness are not judged by how many inches of type, how much time on the air, or even how many of these means are used. Effectiveness is measured by how much greater consent the council enjoys—how ready the community cooperation, how great the demand for the program, how willing the volunteers, how generous the support. The board is the trustee of a vital community resource. It must manage the affairs of Girl Scouting as if it were a public trust—as indeed it is. To act in this spirit helps to create consent. Every official action taken, if it impinges in any way on the public, adds to or diminishes the consent the council enjoys. . . . Members of boards of directors have key roles to play in fostering permanent relationships with the leadership of other institutions and organizations. This is a crucial part of a total public relations program, and of the individual board member's job." [7]

In accepting board membership, the individual should be prepared to give active, enthusiastic support to the agency. He must spread information about the agency in his day-to-day business and social contacts. The board member acts as a two-way line of communication between the agency and the public. He should be prepared to answer criticisms and should strive always to clear up inevitable misconceptions about the work of the agency. If he does not have the answer to questions raised he should refer the questions to someone who does or should seek out the correct answers himself. Good public relations starts with the board itself. Board members can help by assisting the nominating committee to build a strong board. The public relations abilities of prospective board members should be considered by the nominating committee as they review qualifications. Board members can help the agency by seeing that in public contacts people are asked to do specific things and things that are within their power and means. Board members can interpret the importance of good standards for program and services and can help people understand that a good program costs money.

The Public Relations Committee

The public relations committee of the board is the place where recommendations in regard to public relations policies and program should be formulated for board action. In his complete manual of public relations for churches, Stuber discusses the role of the committee chairman and tells how the committee should be organized. [8] In their classic volume on the interpretation of social welfare, Baker and Routzahn identify eight "publics" which must be considered in formulating the public relations program. They are: 1) The agency family consisting of board, committees, and staff. 2) Volunteers. 3) Clients. 4) Cooperators. 5) Supporters. 6) Key persons. 7) Special publics. 8) General public. They indicate that these various "publics" require special treatment and urge an individualized public relations program.[9] Golden and Hanson offer detailed directions for how to plan, produce and publicize special events.[10] Quite frequently the public relations committee of the board is asked to develop a plan for the publicity of these events. Depending upon the nature and size of the event, it may be necessary to employ outside specialists to develop the actual material needed.

Public agency boards have a real responsibility to educate the taxpayers and legislatures because almost always program improvements require capital or operating budget appropriations. In one eastern community, the school board produced a brochure to inform the public about the importance of a school bond issue. As reported in the press, "On Tuesday, parents and residents of the Nyack school district will go to the polls to decide on a $2,004,144 bond issue—and if the electorate is not informed on the matter at hand, it is through no fault of the Nyack Board of Education. The five member board has presented its case to the public in a detailed brochure that might well stand as a model for all metropolitan school districts. It has presented the problem in the schools, explained the proposed solution, explored the pros and cons, and answered questions that might not have occurred even to voters. From the presentation emerges, perhaps a picture typical of suburban communities. 'Today there are twenty-six percent more boys and girls in our schools than in 1950. . . . Today, we are using all our available classrooms for the education of these young people. . . . Next year we will be short twelve classrooms with an expected pupil increase of another three hundred boys and girls. In the next four years, our best estimates show that thirty-eight percent more pupils will be enrolled in the Nyack schools.' To deal with the problem the board consulted with an advisory committee of thirty-three laymen, and their answer, which the board agreed is 'the only answer, other than excessive and costly crowding or a more expensive attempt to rent [space]' is now going before the voters." [11]

In addition to the brochure which is often used, boards can reach a nationwide audience through the use of closed-circuit television.[12] Another device being used is the news conference or press conference. In one such conference held at the headquarters of a "beleaguered antipoverty agency" the board chairman "laid some of the blame for the agency's troubles on the board of directors" and said, "There is no question our board has not assumed as much responsibility as it should. We have to take on greater responsibility for this program and we have to do a better job." [13] Candor such as this is good public relations, provided the board does respond to the challenge of the chairman.

Bright provides the public relations committee and the board with basic points to remember about public relations programs and how to plan them. First, public relations planning must be based on facts, services, and needs. Second, the public relations program must have goals. Third, the public relations program must have a long-range plan. Fourth, in good public relations the agency keeps its community relations strong but also works with the family of agencies to which it belongs. Fifth, the public relations program must focus upon whom you want to reach and why, and for what purpose. Sixth, know the group you are trying to reach. Seventh, personal contacts and direct methods are the most valuable. Eighth, the board, the regular staff, and special public relations staff when utilized must coordinate their efforts. Ninth, the various groups and individuals must have specific assignments. Tenth, public relations requires good timing of the efforts. Eleventh, the public relations program costs money and must have a budget.[14]

All agencies are well advised to put their policies into writing and to make them public. Seeing to it that this gets done is a shared responsibility between the board, the public relations committee and the staff. Policy changes as they occur should also be widely publicized.

Often it is good public relations as well as good planning to set up committees of citizens to help formulate the answer to a pressing problem. One southern city reported: "A study of the 'acute' problem of finding a place to put all of Alachua County's school children next year will be continued by a principals' and citizens' committee structured by the school board Tuesday. . . . The new committee will be composed of principals and two parents from each of seven schools most affected plus a representative each of the Chamber of Commerce, League of Women Voters and Citizens Committee for Public Schools." [15]

The Board and the Constituency

In spite of the fact that all of the efforts of the board are directed to seeing to it that the needs of its constituency are met, few boards have given much attention to creating regular and formal channels of communication with the persons served. Very often the board is a group quite apart from the service clientele. Perhaps they do not want it to be this way but a study reveals that many board members have little insight about the way their decisions affect the people served.[16] Undoubtedly, much of the unrest that prevails today is because many people do feel shut out from the "establishment" or group that controls the agencies they need to utilize. This seems to be changing and many efforts are underway to decentralize large central agencies so that smaller community units may have direct representation on the board. Youth-serving agencies are making deliberate efforts to bring more young people on boards. In the hospital field, efforts are made to solicit patient opinion about services rendered. In the welfare field, clients are being brought into direct communication with boards and in one state it was recommended by one of the party platforms that clients have two seats on the citizen's advisory board.[17]

Clearly, the board has some kind of relationship with the constituency. The question is what kind of relationship? If the board operates on the assumption that its job is to develop services *for* a group of people this will imply one kind of relationship. If, on the other hand, it sees the need to develop services *with* people this puts a different light on the matter. Under the latter philosophy the board will want representation of the constituency either through formal or informal channels. Certainly a minimum to be sought after would be regular and continuous communication with those served to get fresh data on the way services are being rendered and the way they can be improved. The traditional gap between the board and the constituency can be narrowed by encouraging client representation on the board and its committees. The utilization of advisory committees as discussed in an earlier chapter [18] is another way of bringing to bear client experiences and viewpoints. The same holds for the policy of open board meetings and public hearings on vital agency matters. The development of an overall agency representative council including board, staff, clients is another way of approaching the matter of getting broader representation and, of course, better public relations.

As the author stated in an earlier book, "If we believe that . . . constituency has a function within the agency beyond that of merely accepting services, we must think through the possible place of such a group in the total administration process of the agency. Among the many things constituency can do are these: First, constituencies can be very active in helping the agency understand basic human needs which must be met; Second, constituency can give expression regarding the kinds of programs or services that are most likely to aid in the meeting of these needs; Third, constituency can function at the vital point of policy determination;

Fourth, constituency can be a potent resource for agency interpretation and support; Fifth, constituency can assist the agency in evaluating the quality of its work and can suggest modifications and improvements." [19]

Kahn speaks of the importance of a "community presence" and indicates that increasingly board and staff are also service recipients in modern social welfare. He says, "Both direct-service volunteer and board-level participant in policy and planning represent, at any given moment, a *community presence* in relation to a social welfare service. Such a presence dramatizes the public's interest and concern and symbolizes its full participation in a network of service and institutional provision. In a modern democratic society, client, staff and board may become the same people at different times and in different relationships. The offering and taking of service becomes increasingly the extension and acceptance of a right. The development of new social provisions reflects community decisions in which all segments of society begin to have a part. The issue then is not whether the citizen should have a policy role in social welfare but rather how the role may best be supported and implemented." [20] Following along in this vein the commissioner of welfare in the nation's largest city established "client or welfare advisory groups . . . designed to provide a new channel of communication between clients as a group and the department." At the same time, he announced the decentralization of the department so that district offices would have more decision-making powers.[21]

Student participation in the government of colleges and universities was discussed in a recent statement prepared by three national bodies in higher education. These groups said, "When students in American colleges and universities desire to participate responsibly in the government of the institution they attend, *their wish should be recognized* as a claim to opportunity both for educational experience and for involvement in the affairs of their college or university. Ways should be found to permit significant participation within the limits of attainable effectiveness. The obstacles to such participation are large and should not be minimized: inexperience, untested capacity, a transitory status which means that present action does not carry with it subsequent responsibility, and the inescapable fact that the other components of the institution are in a position of judgment over the students. It is important to recognize that student needs are strongly related to educational experience, both formal and informal. Students have a right to expect that the educational process will be structured, that they will be stimulated by it to become independ-

ent adults, and that they will have effectively transmitted to them the
cultural heritage of the larger society. If institutional support is to have
its fullest possible meaning it should incorporate the strength, freshness
of view and idealism of the student body." [22]

It is reasonable to assume that boards will accelerate their efforts to
bring more constituents into their work and that in so doing they will
bring into being better and stronger services.

The Board and Interagency Relationships

With interagency cooperation an imperative today, it is necessary that
each board determine what its relationship should be with other boards
in the family of agencies. As stated by one national group, "The community relations function, as an aspect of the public relations function,
involves understanding the objectives and programs of other groups and
organizations within the community; keeping these groups and organizations informed of the activities, purposes and accomplishments of the
Girl Scouts; and working toward common goals for a better community
with organizations whose philosophy and objectives are compatible with
those of the Girl Scouts." [23]

No agency can do its work with maximum effectiveness unless it is
clear about the work being done by other agencies and unless it works
cooperatively in overall community programs. While the program and
service-rendering tasks are obviously delegated to the professional staff,
the board has a major role to play in community planning and in for-
malizing policy relations between agencies. Boards will work with other
agencies on formal and informal studies of community needs and problems. They may establish joint committees to explore a need and determine the proper auspices for a new service. There may be joint meetings
of boards in the same field of service, in the same geographic area, or in
complementing fields of service. New agency programs should be approved by the board only after full discussion with allied agencies who
may have related or even similar offerings. Representatives from other
agencies frequently serve on boards so that the point of view and experience of sister institutions can be utilized in policy decisions. In many
instances agencies agree to work together on a joint sponsorship basis for
a particular type of service needed by the agencies and of import to the
community. In the area of board member education and training, a

common pattern is for agencies to get together often under the leadership of the community council.

As a matter of board policy it is very important that there be spelled out in detail the way that the agency works with other agencies. Such written statements should be widely distributed.

In a brilliant summary of his many years of experience with inter-agency joint planning and collaborative practice, Buell comes to several conclusions which have serious implications for boards. "1) . . . Progress toward effective planning and coordination will not come simply by talking about it. Nor will it come by waiting for all the obstacles now confronting us to clear up—lack of money, personnel, competitiveness and the like. The resources now at our disposal in money, personnel and skill are simply enormous compared with the time I began my professional life. What we must do is grasp the nettle and determine to develop experimentally better ways and means of using whatever is at hand. 2) . . . The local community must be the focus for joint planning and coordination. This is true despite the extraordinary increase in both federal and state money now supporting these services and the element of control emanating from them. Yet the *community* is where people live and have their problems. In the main, this is where direct service is provided. . . . Planning and coordination at this level must set the pattern. 3) . . . If the community is to be the focus for planning, specialized agencies should act accordingly. That is, they must be clear about their role in meeting the totality of the community problem of their specialized concern. . . . 4) . . . Generally speaking, most people are of good intent. Again, within reasonable limits, they usually want to do the right thing, provided they know what it is. 5) . . . Basically, what has been lacking is the acceptance of a common community program goal and the development of effective methods necessary to plan and coordinate it. Disparate goals have been, and still are, the rule. The one attribute which all agencies have in common is their separate desire to provide more and more service to meet a human need as they see it. But the provision of service is not a goal in itself. Service is simply a means of solving a problem—in this instance community problems in the fields of health and welfare. Here then is the underlying difficulty. Generally speaking, our complex structure of health and welfare services has lacked any common, clearly conceived community problem goal. Lacking clear problem objectives to which to relate our separate services, efforts to develop coordinated programming and operations were in the last analysis doomed to frustration. 6)

. . . Structure is of secondary importance to clear goals and effective implementing methods . . . one should not confuse the purpose of securing widespread participation of a more or less educational nature with the purpose of securing community action at strategic points. Different structures, different representation and leadership, are required for these two purposes." [24]

While one may not be willing to go the full way with Buell, it is certain that agencies are giving way in the "agency-mindedness" and separatism and are seeing the necessity to work together on the solution of hard-core community problems. This can well lead to a reduction in the number of agencies and the increase, through merger, in the multipurpose agency which organizes and offers a manifold attack on a stubborn problem. While it is unrealistic to assume that any board will willingly preside at the liquidation of its "empire," sound community policy making is pushing agencies to justify their existence and to harness their energies more effectively with their cohorts. Critical evaluation of what the agency is doing and with whom it is doing it will be a major task for many boards in the years ahead.

The Board and Community Planning

In almost every community today and certainly in all of the urban areas of the nation the community planning movement is gaining ground. The seriousness of the urban problem and the failures of existing agency structures have accelerated the pace to develop new delivery systems for needed services. In a report prepared for the International Conference of Social Work, Northwood says, "In short, many of the traditional 'solutions' and strategies of work have come under critical scrutiny because they do not seem to be solving the problems of the city or preparing for tomorrow's society of abundance. Probably the main impetus for the developmental approach arises from the flood of local agency and citizen activities in response to the worsening of urban conditions. With the encouragement and enablements of the federal government, undoubtedly the volume of activity will increase. Thus, there is a growing backlog of experience, theory, and research that is necessary to a comprehensive developmental approach. However, at the present time there is little planning, articulation, and regulation of the myriad local efforts. The net result is that there is much wasted effort, useful information is not exchanged, fruitful approaches are not tested adequately to determine their boundaries, and so forth. Although there is a marked growth of planning centers at all levels of government, these are not given a place in a plan. All this activity indicates the imperative for planned development." [25]

If community planning is to emerge as a viable force in controlling the deterioration of community life and in enhancing the human environment, board members must take the lead. Although they may represent but one agency or service, in an operating sense, they must enlarge their concerns to take in the whole community.

MacRae underlines the critical challenges facing community welfare planning: "Rapid urbanization has exacerbated the strains and tensions which are always present in city life. Our economy shows an increasing inability to use the unskilled and the under-educated. Armies of children and youth swarm in our communities, demanding enormous increases in educational, welfare and leisure time services. Millions of these children present far more than the usual problems of growth and development. They come to our cities as refugees from areas of grinding poverty and deadening segregation. Sharp increases in the proportion of the aged in our population present communities with a range and severity of problems for which they are ill equipped. Medical care facilities and personnel are proving inadequate to demands, and rising costs make equitable distribution of medical care a growing problem. The steady erosion of natural resources and the alarming disappearance of open spaces is creating a crisis in recreational facilities. The existence of persistent pockets of shattering poverty has affronted the conscience of America. All of these facts supply sufficient yeast to cause ferment in the most stable society. An additional ingredient has been added which has shaken even the most complacent. We are living in a time when our Negro fellow citizens have decided they have waited long enough for America to redeem its promise of opportunity for 'life, liberty and the pursuit of happiness.' This long pent up cry for social justice and equal opportunity will not be denied. Nor should it be. In fact, the vigor of the protest is a cause for rejoicing rather than dismay." [26]

Certainly agency business "as usual" is neither possible nor desirable in the face of the staggering problems that beset us. Fortunately, many boards are reaffirming their commitment to community planning and lending strong support to those enterprises which seek to create new ways of meeting community needs. This reaffirmation grows out of a long and great tradition of citizen participation in this country. Stumpf examines the three-fold nature of citizen participation: "A look at citizen participation in the United States reveals that the personal responsibility of each individual in his roles of private citizen, member of a voluntary group association, and voter-taxpayer is one of the benchmarks of this nation and of our organized community life. The American ways of community growth and development and of problem-solving involve three inter-related systems: 1) The individual has personal responsibility as a private citizen either to help himself through his own efforts or to pay for what he wants done to satisfy his needs and wants, with his payment made on a profit-making or non-profit-making basis. This is the private enterprise system of meeting one's needs and wants. 2) If independent action through private enterprise is not satisfactory to solve one's problems, then the usual alternative has been to find other people with the same unmet needs and to set up a voluntary group. Thus, there is a second national tradition of citizen committees and voluntary associations, frequently starting as self-interest groups but usually rather quickly becoming interested in both self and others, but frequently employing technical or professional persons to help them. This is the voluntary group enterprise system of meeting human needs and wants. But this system is much greater and more influential than the sum of its parts. It has become a virtual unofficial government which not only holds sway over the destiny of many areas of American life, but also provides the country with the widest and deepest experience in decision-making and problem-solving short of the government itself. Indeed, it may be the chief training ground for citizens and citizen leaders who are to participate in government. 3) If voluntary group associations on local or national levels do not meet human needs, then government is used. And in some aspects of life, such as general police and health protection, governmental organization was set up immediately upon recognizing that individual responsibility or private enterprise would not suffice, without trying a voluntary association way. A characteristic of good modern government is the employment of some technical or professional persons to work *with* citizens, not just *for* them, in solving problems. With or without technical assistance, government is a third system for problem solving, in addition to its general function of providing society with a framework of law and order. It seems important, as we consider community development in the United States and who participates in it, to recognize that these three systems and their variations are the American ways of meeting needs and solving problems." [27]

The three systems referred to by Stumpf are brought into a working relationship in over two thousand communities by some kind of health and welfare council. These councils have been generally regarded as the community's means of planning for services to meet health, welfare and recreation needs. Four types of activities have been conducted by these councils. They are: community policy planning, problem-solving planning, interagency program development and coordination, and agency administrative planning. As has been stated by the parent body for this movement, "representative Councils have developed the following distinctive features: an overall community point of view, detached from the administration of any particular service program; broadly representative citizen leadership and involvement; the merging of professional and lay interests in common concern for action; community sanction, stemming from a wide cross-section of membership and continuity of community financial support; accumulated community organization knowledge and skill; and, utilization of the fact-finding and research evaluation function in influencing community budgeting of health and welfare programs. A unique characteristic of Community Health and Welfare Councils is their ability to view and carry out planning in a broader way than can any single agency or group of agencies. They are able to bring objectivity into the assessment of individual agency programs. They can determine community priorities and help achieve a balanced pattern of services." [28]

There can be no question but that the board of a local agency should be active within the framework of the community council. In fact, it is impossible for any agency to do a good job unless it coordinates its work with that of other agencies and plans jointly with them. Board representatives selected to serve on the community council have a tremendous responsibility and should be chosen with great care. They must be able to represent their agency and at the same time have the larger picture of the community and its needs in mind. To a certain extent the dual role of representing the agency and at the same time planning for the total community may cause strains and even conflict but in the final analysis, what is best for the community is certainly the goal of all.

NOTES

1. *A Blueprint for Board Members* (Omaha: United Community Services, 1958), pp. 21-23.
2. Harleigh B. Trecker, *Social Agency Boards as Viewed by Board Members* (School of Social Work, University of Connecticut, 1959), pp. 35-45.

3. Gene Harlow and Alan Scott, *Contemporary Public Relations: Principles and Cases,* pp. 3-4. © 1955 Prentice-Hall, Inc., Englewood Cliffs, N.J.
4. Scott M. Cutlip and Allen H. Center, *Effective Public Relations,* p. 6. © 1958 Prentice-Hall, Inc., Englewood Cliffs, N.J.
5. Reprinted with permission of The Macmillan Company from *Public Relations for Educators* by Gloria Dapper, p. 5. © 1964 by Gloria Dapper.
6. *Ibid.,* pp. 7-27.
7. "Public Relations Point of View" (New York: Girl Scouts of the U.S.A.). For use by National Training Corps in Nationwide Training Council Boards, 1964–1966.
8. Stanley I. Stuber, *Public Relations Manual for Churches* (New York: Doubleday, 1951), Chapter 25.
9. Helen Cody Baker and Mary Swain Routzahn, *How to Interpret Social Welfare* (New York: Russell Sage Foundation, 1947), pp. 10-25.
10. Hal Golden and Kitty Hanson, *How to Plan, Produce and Publicize Special Events* (New York: Oceana Publications, 1960).
11. Judith Crist, "Nyack Tries Educating the Voters, Too," *New York Herald Tribune,* September 30, 1956.
12. "Columbia Trustees Prepare TV Report for 170,000 Alumni," *New York Times,* September 19, 1968.
13. Douglas E. Kneeland, "Haryou-Act Faces Broad Overhaul," *New York Times,* June 16, 1966. © 1966 by the New York Times Company. Reprinted by permission.
14. Sallie E. Bright, *Public Relations Programs—How to Plan Them* (New York: National Publicity Council, 1950).
15. "Alachua Board Provides Group to Continue Study of Schools," *Jacksonville Times-Union,* January 12, 1968.
16. Trecker, *op. cit.,* pp. 37-39.
17. Recommendation of Democratic Party Platform, Connecticut, June 1968.
18. See Chapter Two, *infra.*
19. Harleigh B. Trecker, *Group Process in Administration,* revised and enlarged (New York: Woman's Press, 1950), pp. 125-126.
20. Alfred J. Kahn, "The Citizen's Role in Social Welfare Policy," *Children,* September-October, 1963, p. 188.
21. *The Welfarer* (Published for Employees of the New York City Department of Welfare), March 1966, p. 1.
22. *Statement on Government of Colleges and Universities,* American Association of University Professors *Bulletin,* Winter 1966, statement adopted by A.A.U.P., American Council on Education, Association of Governing Boards of Universities and Colleges.
23. "Definition of Community Relations as Used in Girl Scouting," adopted by the National Board of Directors, October 1959.
24. Bradley Buell, "Structure and Substance in Interagency Joint Planning and Collaborative Practice," a paper presented at the National Institute on Service for Handicapped Children and Youth, March 12, 1963, Chi-

cago, Illinois (New York: Community Research Associates, Inc.), pp. 3-6.

25. Lawrence K. Northwood, "Imperatives for a Developmental Approach," in *Social Welfare and Urban Development* (New York: National Association of Social Workers, 1966), p. 15. Reprinted with permission of the National Association of Social Workers.

26. Robert H. MacRae, "Inventory and Challenge: New Directions for Community Welfare Planning," paper presented before the National Social Welfare Assembly, November 30, 1965.

27. Jack Stumpf, "Roles and Relationships of Participants," in Roland L. Warren (editor), *Community Development and Social Work Practice* (New York: National Association of Social Workers, 1962), pp. 22-23. Reprinted with permission of the National Association of Social Workers.

28. *The Role of Community Health and Welfare Council* (New York: United Community Funds and Councils of America, January, 1965), p. 10.

10 *The Board and Social Action on the State and National Scene*

Most services in the areas of health, welfare, and education are organized and delivered to people in the local community. The majority of governing boards are essentially local in character. Yet increasingly these boards must establish relationships with state, regional, and national bodies. It is the rare board that can carry on its work without doing so.

As was pointed out in the previous chapter, boards are active in community councils which function primarily on the community level. They should also be active in the newly emerging regional planning bodies and in the state associations. Because of the larger role of the federal government in financing local services and in standard setting for these services, the board must also think through its relationship with the federal government.

Naturally, all agencies must operate within the framework of state and federal laws, and some local agencies, such as school boards, are clearly agents of the state. In the voluntary field many agencies are members or affiliates of national agencies and in so affiliating they must relate appropriately. In addition to following national standards for accreditation of services, they have a role in forwarding the national goals. Since health, welfare, and educational needs cannot be separated from the physical environment, increasingly these services are being brought into overall regional planning.

189

Apart from the structural relationships, it is strikingly evident that the problems and needs of the local community are often national in character and there is a close interweaving of local, state and national interests involved in their solution. Carter points this out when he observes, "We have moved rapidly from an atomistic society of small communities and slow communications to a molecular Nation of large cities and instant communications. Where once National and international events came to us almost as history and seemed little related to our reality, we are assaulted now by a seemingly endless flow of occurrences and crises in which we had no role and of which we were not aware until they burst upon us; we are asked daily to assume new responsibilities by persons we do not know with respect to problems we had not thought to be ours and without understanding how they came to be ours. This is not to underrate the complexity and difficulty of our present problems, but to stress our changing perception of them. In the past, as sports or machinery became more complex and demanding, we have tended to hand them over to experts; we have sought in the same way to hand over our social problems to experts, but are less happy about it because we haven't seen more results." [1]

Since it is clear that the local community cannot be healthy in an unhealthy nation and that the local agency, no matter how successful, cannot achieve its full potential without widening its concern and increasing its involvement, boards are called upon to review their policies of social action. In doing so they must come to some agreement as to what are the most critical social problems facing the nation.

National Social Problems and Issues

In a recent study of national social problems and issues the causative factors were delineated as follows: "There are many factors contributing to serious social problems, poverty and deprivation in the midst of our growing national affluence, with consequent increases in the number of persons requiring financial aid and a wide variety of specialized health, education, social and related services. These factors, many of which are interrelated, include: the population explosion of the past twenty years, with its concomitant increase in those in our population who are the most vulnerable—the very old, the very young, and the mentally and physically disabled; the increasing industrialization which is creating at the same time technological unemployment and, in certain skilled categories, labor market shortages; the revolution in agriculture which is producing surplus rural families, Negro and white, who migrate to the big cities in search of a livelihood, but find themselves beset with problems of education, training, housing, acculturation—and unemployment; problems associated with industrialization, such as the evolution of a national labor market replacing local ones, resulting in unprecedented population mobility. Ours has become a rootless and restless nation with more than thirty million Americans moving each year—at least five million from one state to another; the growing number of chronically ill, and the lag in wide application of a great body of knowledge regarding prevention and treatment of disease. Despite popular impressions, the poorest in our population receive the least amount of medical care, and the lowest quality; the newly discovered one-fifth of our nation's families who are unable to secure work or to earn enough to meet minimum levels of subsistence for health and decency; the large numbers of our adult population who are too illiterate, undereducated or unskilled to obtain work in today's labor market or to qualify for technological training; the increasing strains on family life resulting in more family disorganization, divorce, desertion, separation, illegitimacy and juvenile delinquency; the persistence of racial discrimination in jobs, education and housing, despite the various statutory provisions against it." The same study listed the "substantive problems of national significance" as: "racial discrimination and civil rights, and services related to improved race relations and equal opportunities; poverty, and services related to income maintenance, job opportunities and specialized services for low-income families; ill-health, and services related to the financing of medical care, improvement in availability and quality of health services, health manpower, and basic medical research; mental illness, and services related to the development of community-based mental health services, preventive mental health programs, manpower and research; crime and delinquency, and services related to protective, preventive and correctional programs and rehabilitation of criminal offenders; slums and crowded inadequate housing, and services related to slum clearance, rehabilitation, urban renewal and public housing to improve living conditions of low-income families; aging, including a wide variety of problems of older people, and specialized services to help the elderly; unemployment and problems created by automation, and services related to the development of new job opportunities, training and manpower development; deficits in education at all levels, and specialized programs for deprived populations, ranging from preschool education through adult basic education and training; leisure time, and services directed toward constructive recreational activities, particularly programs which will improve physical fitness, mental health and social relations; broken families, and services aimed at the stabilization and improvement of healthy family life; abused, neglected and unwanted children, and child welfare programs to serve them and their parents; the population explosion and services related to family planning and population control; central city decay, and programs related to the social aspects of the revitalization and reconstruction of the cities; migration, and specialized services for populations on the move." The same study lists "a number of major areas of national concern regarding the capability of existing systems to deal with these and related social problems. These concerns are in three principal areas: financing, availability and utilization of manpower, and the effectiveness of program. Included are national issues such as: the amount and distribution of governmental and voluntary funds to be made available for social purposes; the utilization of professional, quasi-professional and non-professional manpower in the light of manpower shortages in such fields as social welfare, health, education and training, mental health, urban renewal, etc.; the need for definite information regarding the relative effectiveness and cost of various program strategies for dealing with these social problems; the need for more effective coordination and integration of programs at the Federal, state and local levels; the need to develop new and innovative systems to deal with social problems that have persisted in spite of past and present efforts; the need to bring all segments of the American public into full and appropriate participation in the formulation and development of policies and programs; the need to eliminate all existing administrative structural barriers to the full availability and accessibility to established programs and to protect the rights of all citizens; the need to recognize the international nature of the responsibilities of the United States for social progress and development throughout the world." [2]

Some of the above problems are approached in a systematic way in a recent report prepared by the National Association of Social Workers.[3] While no one agency, or any one profession for that matter, can hope to solve all of these problems, the problems are interrelated and call for action on a wide front. Boards must take such action.

Former Secretary of the Department of Health, Education and Welfare Wilbur J. Cohen lists some of the major domestic problems facing our society as: "1) The most pressing domestic problem calling for national solution is racial inequality and discrimination—an intolerable condition in a democratic society. . . . 2) A second national problem is poverty, the stimulation of continued economic growth, and the provision of jobs for the disadvantaged. One of the most significant developments of recent years has been the growing consensus that productive and satisfying jobs and income security should be assured all members of the labor force; and that an adequate income should be provided under dignified conditions for workers and non-workers alike. There is widespread agreement that poverty can and must be eliminated. . . . 3) A third problem is the future of our educational system. Today, too many of our schools are in trouble financially, socially, and culturally. They are inadequately financed, inefficiently organized and unable to meet the demands of an increasingly complex society in the decade ahead. 4) A fourth problem is the inadequacy of our health care system. There are very serious deficiencies in the way health care is organized, financed, and delivered in the United States. . . . 5) A fifth problem is the quality of our environment. The air we breathe is polluted, our cities are becoming jungles of broken down tenements, concrete and macadam are rapidly replacing the green grass; we drive miles to parks that may be overcrowded when we get there. We must find ways to improve the quality of the environment around us. . . . 6) A sixth problem is the communications gap—not only among the races but between the young and the old, the poor and well-to-do. We must begin talking with each other rather than at each other. . . . 7) A corollary to the communications problem is that today many of our essential institutions are not able or willing to respond effectively to society's needs. They must be strengthened perhaps reconstituted to that end. We need to start with our basic institution—the family. All of our efforts in health, education, and welfare are designed to promote a wholesome and stable family life. This is the basis for efforts to assure every family access to family planning information and services. . . . 8) Finally, there is the problem of maintaining the commitment of the American people to social progress and to the supremacy of human values. . . . I can't provide a blueprint for the future. But I would like to identify certain elements that will determine our response. Perhaps the most important factor is the general and widespread recognition that these are national problems, requiring a national solution. I believe there is no longer any serious debate—as there was as little as five years ago—that, for example, many people in this Nation are not getting adequate medical care or satisfactory nutrition or that job opportunities are closed to whole segments of our population. Many of the searing ideological issues have been largely resolved. The question now is not *should* these problems be solved but how best *can* they be solved. What kind of a mix of Federal, State, local, and private initiative can best do the job effectively while conserving the values that are important to the American people?" [4]

The Importance of Agency Action

Most agencies in their constitution and bylaws state broad purposes and goals in the realm of human betterment. For example, the national voluntary agency in the field of family service listed as one membership requirement that "the agency must direct efforts toward the improvement of social conditions that have a negative effect on family life." [5] Earlier, the same agency said, "The family service agency has a particular responsibility to take leadership in working for the improvement of social conditions and the establishment of adequate community welfare and treatment services." [6] Currently they say, "The primary purpose of the Family Service Society is to preserve and strengthen the family as the basic unit of society. As a part of this, and in accordance with our bylaws, it is appropriate for the Family Service Society to engage in social welfare action to prevent social conditions which would have a harmful effect on families and their members." [7]

Other agencies and organizations have similar and related aims insofar as the achievement of social welfare goals and programs are concerned. While it is necessary that agencies avoid partisan politics in the sense of endorsing specific candidates for office, it is important that they contribute their experience and knowledge in the development and formulation of legislation which will result in meaningful programs for people. Consequently, the legislative committee of the board which screens bills and makes recommendations to the board regarding pending legislation is a most important committee. Also, it is important for the agency to participate in legislative conferences and to present testimony at public hearings. Recently, the national Advisory Council on Public Welfare, operating under Congressional mandate, conducted regional hearings throughout the country. Participants in the regional hearings reflected the views of 43 national voluntary organizations, 54 state voluntary organizations, 60 state public agencies, 75 local voluntary groups, 51 local public agencies, 20 schools of social work, and 39 assistance recipients or former recipients. Three hundred forty-nine persons thus had an opportunity to present their views. The importance of the regional hearing approach is evident in the quality of the findings of the Council as reproduced in their monumental report.[8] In this instance, not only did the Congress benefit but there were benefits to everyone who took part because their understanding of the problem was undoubtedly deepened as a result of this experience.

In addition to taking an active part in hearings, the agency board should be well versed in the state and federal legislative process. Ordinarily, procedural documents can be secured for use by the board's legislative committee and in orientation of new board members.[9] Frequently there are community or statewide training conferences conducted by such organizations as the League of Women Voters which will provide excellent background information. When the agency is genuinely interested in legislative matters, formal board action will be taken and views of the board conveyed to the legislators and to the community.

It should be pointed out that some organizations operate under very restricted charters and must choose carefully the legislation with which they can be concerned. For example, the Girl Scouts are chartered by Congress. The charter reads, "Girl Scouts of the United States of America, local councils, other units holding a credential, and members of the Girl Scout movement shall not involve any part of the Girl Scout organization in any issues of a political or legislative character except those of a legislative character directly affecting the corporate rights of Girl Scouts of the United States of America or local units." [10] Under these circumstances it is indeed clear that the organization as an organization is sharply restricted in what it can do. Furthermore, to determine what legislative matters directly affect the corporate rights of the organization will require legal counsel in many instances. When agencies are in doubt as to what their legal limitations are they should check carefully their articles of incorporation including their constitution and bylaws. If these seem to be too restricting it may be the decision of the board to seek a revision and updating.

In any event, each board should issue a clear policy paper on legislative and social action matters so that everyone will be in agreement as to what steps are legal as well as desirable. It is evident that there is a marked trend toward much wider involvement of agencies in considering the great national problems which exist today. Some take a vigorous position on general matters of the common welfare. Other boards work explicitly to bring into law programs which they deem to be important for all people.

When an agency board becomes aware of its wider tasks and when it seeks to commit its energies to the bringing about of social change, it can secure much help from other agencies and from state and national bodies. In addition, it must develop a plan for selecting those problems and issues with which it will be concerned and a plan for developing the best ways of going about getting action. Lourie observes that the development of a plan is difficult. He says, "Present leadership is divided among many units of professional and community concern. There are many points of leadership but nowhere, particularly at the local community level, is there consistent lay or professional leadership that has become the focal point of effective community planning. We are still uncertain about the competence needed to handle different degrees of maladjustment. I know of no community plan that clearly defines organizational responsibility, that coordinates and engineers the flow of problems among the several systems of service. No one force can stand alone. Each, while making its contribution, must also face certain realities . . . some principles that need consideration [are]: First, any successful program should be based on long-range social goals and within a system of priorities. Constant re-evaluation of these goals is needed to prevent incrustation. Second, new situations demand new approaches and devices in community planning. We should not resist them. Without new approaches, problems can become overwhelming. Third, no helping agency can stand alone. None is all-encompassing. Collaboration in an atmosphere of trust is essential for successful programming. Agencies sometimes will have to accept assignments of responsibilities of a community rather than choose their own. Fourth, cultural patterns must be considered in any planning effort. Unassimilated cultural groups need full consideration. Fifth, in any American community we cannot consider our job successful if any group is denied equal rights and equal opportunities. Ultimately a democracy cannot uphold a single standard while practicing a double one. Sixth, all changes come hard. Resistances are present in the face of any change. These need to be analyzed, understood and dealt with intelligently. Seventh, change is produced by the cooperation of social forces. If the avenues of cooperation are not adequate in a community, they need to be realigned. . . . In all these senses, public and voluntary efforts share a true and deep partnership." [11]

Understanding Social Action

The board which commits itself to the taking of action in behalf of needed social programs must spend time defining the concept. Wickenden says, "Social action is the term commonly applied to that aspect of organized social welfare activity directed toward shaping, modifying, or maintaining the social institutions and policies that collectively constitute the social environment. This can properly be regarded as one of the two interrelated aspects of the social service function which a United Nations expert group in 1959 defined as 'organized activity that aims at helping towards a mutual adjustment of individuals and their social environment.' Social action is concerned with the better adjustment of the social environment in order to meet the recognized needs of individuals and to facilitate those social relationships and adjustments necessary to its own best functioning. . . . Efforts to effect or prevent a change in social policy must be directed in the long run to the social instrumentality vested with the power of decision. This may be a legislative body with the power to enact or modify law; an executive agency with power to propose such changes and carry them out when enacted; a court in which public policy may be tested; or a non-governmental body whose practices, with respect to employment, housing, discrimination, or other factors of social relationships, have the effect of social policy. In this context 'policy' may be defined as a settled course of action, typically incorporated in an institutional mechanism, such as a law or program through which such a policy is put into effect. . . . The specific areas of social action activity on the part of social welfare organizations are as diversified and inclusive as the goals of social welfare itself. In recent years, however, the following have taken a high priority in the nationwide efforts of social welfare organizations: strengthening the public welfare programs; extending the social insurance system with special emphasis on adding health benefits for the aged; federal and other measures to prevent and mitigate juvenile delinquency; civil rights legislation; better provisions for community programs to aid the mentally ill, mentally retarded, and chronically ill; housing and urban development; provisions for youth employment, manpower training and the stimulation of voluntary services; and better provision for groups with special needs including the aged." [12]

Gardner, in his critical essay on leadership, says, "If social action is to occur, certain functions must be performed. The problems facing the group or organization must be clarified, and ideas necessary to their solution formulated. Objectives must be defined. There must be widespread awareness of those objectives, and the will to achieve them. Often those on whom action depends must develop new attitudes and habits. Social machinery must be set in motion. The consequences of social effort must be evaluated and criticized, and new goals set." [13] But Gardner observes also that "very few of our most prominent people take a really large view of the leadership assignment. Most of them are simply tending the machinery of that part of society to which they belong. The machinery may be a great corporation or a great government agency or a great law practice or a great university. These people may tend it very well indeed, but they are not pursuing a vision of what the total society needs. They have not developed a strategy as to how it can be achieved, and they are not moving to accomplish it." [14]

Not everyone ignores his responsibility to take "the large view." An executive of a national community planning group presented a paper on "Assigning Priorities in Public Policy." In his discussion of the needs of older persons he said, "For public policy to have meaning, it must be directed to public purposes—to public goals. And it must be rooted in a commitment to that purpose and to those goals. Our purpose is . . . the decency, dignity and self-respect of every individual. Our goal, too, is a society which itself has the decency and dignity to assure that for every individual. Our purpose is to make possible the independence, the self-reliance, and the self-determination of all of the aged who can attain it and continue it, and the most enlightened, civilized, and humane services for all who need them." He then went on to list as priorities: financial independence, social security and public assistance, living arrangements, health services, personnel, comprehensive planning and community organization, public education, and top quality in all services. He closed his remarks by noting: "In a democratic society, public policy is shaped by those who care most, who know what they want, and who work hardest to get it most skillfully, and most persistently. If I were to select one imperative ingredient for success in achieving public policy, it is persistence—the ability to outlast others, to stay with an issue and press for a purpose longer and more energetically than others." [15]

It is a responsibility of the executive to take leadership with his board in the realm of public policy. He is obligated to share his views based upon his experience and his competence. The board is not obligated to follow his advice and frequently does not. Nevertheless, a first step in the process of social action is for someone to take leadership.

One such leader is Youngdahl, who defines social action "to mean those activities and processes that have for their purpose the end result in social policy, legal or extralegal, of new social services or the modification or elimination of existing ones. It includes such things as fact-finding, research, the dissemination and interpretation of information, analysis of community needs, organization, and other efforts to mobilize public understanding and support in behalf of some community service or legislative or other proposal. Social action can be geared to a problem in a local community, to one that is statewide, or to one that is national in scope. Does a social agency have a role in social action? I answer in the affirmative and in so doing I include all agencies, public and private, secular and religious, local, state, and national. No agency can abdicate this responsibility if it has an interest in the people it serves. Agencies exist to serve their own clients, actual or potential, but regardless of their constitutional or other limitations they can hardly be classified as a social agency if they are not effectively interested in people in general, and particularly in the areas or aspects of human relationships in which the agency participates and has special skill. It is not expected that all agencies will carry the same role in social action, but all agencies have some role to play. In some instances it will be direct and major, and in others minor and supporting." [16]

The Voluntary Agency Board and Social Action

One of the striking changes of the last decade is the increasing frequency with which voluntary agency boards take a stand on social issues. For example, in the case of one national agency, its board of directors underscored the urgency of the Report of the National Advisory Commission on Civil Disorders. In a formal statement unanimously adopted, the board stressed that there exists an "unparalleled opportunity" not only to avoid violence, but to "make possible a far too long delayed reconstruction of our decaying central cities . . . because of the Report's specific programs in education, welfare, employment and housing." The board called on all communities to "respond constructively to the Report—because our tradition of social justice demands it, because the integrity and well-being of Jewish communal life requires a just American society, and because we must continue to be fully involved with others in strengthening democratic rights." The board asked federations to study the report as a basis for "grappling actively with the problem of poverty, to promote specific projects using the expertise of Federations and their agencies, and to work in close cooperation with other Jewish and non-sectarian organizations and with Urban Coalitions. It asked that communities bring to responsible officials of government the depth of support for the needed measures." [17]

In another instance, a board committee of a youth agency "told the Board of Elections . . . of alleged 'severe irregularities and harassments by local inspectors that had prevented the registration of many of New York's eligible citizens, and had delayed and inconvenienced other citizens who had managed to register.' A delegation from the board and the community met with the Elections officials and brought with them affidavits testifying to abuses." [18]

Stein highlights the fact that board members of voluntary agencies have a special role to play in social action on important issues. "Board members of voluntary agencies . . . are assumed to have a special right to speak because they are social agency board members and therefore are both knowledgeable and public-spirited; their names carry weight in the community. Legislatures which hear no opposition to punitive welfare measures from agency board members would have every reason to feel that no responsible or at any rate significant opposition exists. Moreover, voluntary agencies can carry on their special functions—innovation and experimentation, for example—only by the grace of the existence of government-supported social welfare. Board members may take whatever position they wish on any given issue—whatever the position, it is better than apathy. . . ." [19]

A voluntary family service agency took vigorous action in behalf of dependent children in their state who were being subjected to restrictive eligibility policies by the state welfare agency. Their outstanding leadership in this cause resulted in receiving an award from their national agency, "For Outstanding Achievement by a Member Agency in Promoting Significant Community Action to Benefit Family Life." [20]

The Board of Directors of the National Federation of Settlements and Neighborhood Centers took formal action in relation to the national problem of poverty. A portion of their statement reads, "NFS is concerned with the continuing crisis in American life, as evidenced in the neighborhoods served by our member centers. Deep chasms divide racial, ethnic and income groups. We continue to be plagued by poverty in the midst of affluence. Acting out of a deep sense of national urgency, the NFS calls upon the President, the Congress and the American people to reassess their commitments and re-order priorities in dealing with problems which beset us. The solution of these problems requires federal leadership, effective legislation and adequate funding. The federal government, we believe, has not yet measured up to its responsibility in such fields as Civil Rights, Housing, Education, Health and Welfare, and Income Assurance. . . . NFS believes the effective war on poverty must be waged by every level of government, federal, state, and local, and in coalition with all of the private sector, including commerce and industry, citizen groups and voluntary agencies such as NFS and its members. . . . NFS pledges that its members will play an increasingly active role in the organization of their neighbors for self help. Its members will work, alone and in coalition with others, to help their neighbors broaden their opportunities for citizen action and direct access to the highest sources of federal, state and local authority." [21]

In one of the most challenging presidential addresses ever delivered to the National Conference on Social Welfare, Solender identified seven tasks of social welfare's lay leaders: "First, the nation's major social problems, social welfare's role in meeting them, and the way this role is discharged must be reexamined thoroughly. This study must be fresh and nondefensive, probing the depths of issues and revealing their complexity and their relation to other social concerns and fields. . . . Second, courageous, comprehensive, long-term social planning to fill unmet needs must be the order of the day. Such planning must focus on the needs of people and communities rather than of institutions. It should not shrink from radical institutional changes which may be required and must emphasize rehabilitation and prevention. . . . New dimensions of public understanding of social needs, their impact on people, and the requirements for social services which they evoke are an urgent necessity. We must achieve—especially on the national level—a concerted, total-field approach to this problem with its nationwide implications. . . . Third, the third action area consists of creative participation by all connected with social welfare in articulating and implementing the evolving role of government in meeting social needs. Forces in American life which minimize this function of government must be resisted. Major social concerns are national in scope and are so complex that public initiative is indispensable to their solution. This is the case for public welfare as well as for housing, health, services for the aged, education, and other areas. To those who claim that liberty is eroded by greater governmental action in these fields there must be an emphatic response that the persistence of social deprivation is the greatest deterrent to realization of the rights of all people. The general welfare responsibility of government, sanctioned in the Constitution, warrants effective public action in these areas. . . . Fourth, a confident, forward-looking redefinition of the role of voluntary social welfare in light of the maturing of public services is imperative. Voluntary agencies have a unique position in a democratic community. They reflect the impulses of a free people acting autonomously to establish community services to meet their requirements. . . . Fifth, social welfare must meet the demands of change in the preparation of professional social workers equipped for leadership. . . . Sixth, a sixth direction must be that of increasing the representativeness and deepening the quality of lay leadership. This applies to public as well as voluntary services, inasmuch as a greatly expanded role for laymen should be sought in public agencies through citizens' advisory groups and the like. Social welfare agencies must overcome the charge of lack of inclusiveness in the composition of their governing boards by including unrepresented groups, especially those which are less developed socially. . . . There must be greater fluidity in board memberships and active programs to recruit and develop new leaders. Rotation systems can assure a constant flow of fresh leadership, encourage potential leaders, and bring new minds and faces to policy-making groups. . . . Seventh, there must be broad-gauged research in social welfare. Unresolved social problems must be probed for new insights that can be used in solving them; the needs of individuals, groups, and communities must be intensively examined; new social science knowledge must be tested and verified; and programs, methods, practices, and structures must be critically evaluated." [22]

Principles of Procedure in Social Action

Out of his long experience as a leader in social action, Youngdahl has "set forth in outline form some basic principles of procedure relating to an agency's role in social action. 1) All social action stems out of individual conviction. If the administrator, the staff members, the board members, and other participants of a social agency have convictions on some unsolved problems relating to the people they serve, some kind of participation in social action will be inevitable. 2) Sound convictions are built upon information and facts. Therefore, research and fact-finding are a necessary base to any social action effort. . . . 3) All agencies have a responsibility of initiating social action on any problem that concerns its clients. . . . 4) In order to initiate action, an agency must first identify a problem. The reason an operating agency has such a unique role to play in social action is because it is in such a good position to recognize need. It is a recurring problem among its clients—a problem that cannot be solved by casework or group work per se, but only by some larger action, such as a new law, a new preventive service, or provision of something that is lacking. . . . 5) After identifying the problem, the next step is to define the scope of the problem and the breadth and degree of understanding necessary to mobilize the forces for an effective solution. In some instances the scope will be as narrow as the geographic limitations of an agency which serves a small segment of a city. . . . In other cases, the problem cannot be solved without mobilizing the forces of an entire metropolitan area. . . . In still other cases . . . state action may be required. Finally, in some instances national action is necessary. The agency, then, will assume basic responsibility for the action movement and it will vary from an individual operating agency to a council of social agencies, to a state community organization body, and on the national front to some such agency as the National Social Welfare Assembly, the National Association of Social Workers, or some similar body which is willing and able to assume the task. . . . 6) When the operating agency has turned over the problem to someone else, it has accomplished a major responsibility but it does not end there. All social agencies have a responsibility for giving a supporting role in matters of social action in which health and welfare aspects of the people of the community are involved. . . . 7) An administrator of a social agency has a responsibility to give continuous interpretation not limited to the agency's own problems, but to the broad welfare problems of the community. In a city like St. Louis, for example, there are at least three thousand board members of social agencies. Generally speaking, they represent significantly important segments of the community. Perhaps it is not an exaggeration to say that almost any worthwhile project could be established if only large-scale support of social agency board members could be had. There is a resource here which has hardly been tapped, and the responsibility of social agency administrators and staffs seems clear. Moreover, the greater the spread of interest and understanding to nonsocial work groups, the greater the effectiveness of the action movement. 8) A council of social agencies or a Health and Welfare Council has a responsibility of a definite nature to initiate action movement as well as to stimulate operating agencies to make suggestions and to participate. . . . 9) To be successful, all participants in an agency, all agencies in a community, all communities within a state should have some part to play in an action effort. . . . 10) The sound approach, whether to a board or to the citizenry in general, is not the slap-dash overnight type but rather the gradual, sober, evolving one, which can get understanding and, from that, action. . . . 11) Frequently a community's strategy is involved in a social action effort. There are so many things that different agencies and groups want to have done at a given time and any effort to get them all is usually doomed to failure. Therefore, a system of short-term and long-term priorities should be established. . . . For any important success, the whole must be considered. . . . 12) The real test or yardstick in social action is the democratic process. This frequently requires bowing to defeat when "the voice of the people" says no. There are times, however, when a numerical minority can act in behalf of the majority, but such a procedure requires high integrity. Even in such cases the majority acts by acquiescence and, of course, they always have the power of the veto. Participation in social action is a responsibility of all social agencies. It is a function that should not be considered peripheral or extracurricular but as an integral part of an agency's job. To be carried out professionally, this function requires high integrity, and the utmost skill, patience, and devotion to the needs of people." [23]

NOTES

1. Lisle E. Carter, Jr., "National Purpose and the Need for Community," in *The H.E.W. Forum Papers 1967–68* (Washington: Department of Health, Education, and Welfare), p. 97.
2. *A Study of the Future Role and Programs of the National Social Welfare Assembly and the Report of the National Social Welfare Assembly Study Committee* (New York: 1966), pp. 13-16.
3. Nathan E. Cohen, *Social Work and Social Problems* (New York: National Association of Social Workers, 1964).
4. Wilbur J. Cohen, "Where Do We Go From Here?" in *The H.E.W. Forum Papers 1967–68* (Washington: Department of Health, Education, and Welfare), pp. 144-149.
5. *Membership Requirements for Agencies* (New York: Family Service Association of America, 1964).
6. *Scope and Methods of the Family Service Agency* (New York: Family Service Association of America, 1953).

7. From a letter by Mrs. Raymond H. Kierr, President of the Family Service Society of New Orleans, to members of the Louisiana Legislature, June 29, 1960.
8. *Having the Power We Have the Duty,* The Advisory Council on Public Welfare, Report to the Secretary of Health, Education, and Welfare, Washington, D.C., June 29, 1966. 148 pages.
9. *Law Making in Connecticut.* Prepared by the Institute of Public Service, The University of Connecticut, January 1963. *Social Action Guide* (New York: National Association of Social Workers, 1965).
10. Blue Book 1967, p. 22. © Girl Scouts of the U.S.A. Used by permission.
11. Norman V. Lourie, "Our Common Cause: Viewing Social Trends in Welfare," *Viewpoint,* No. 11, Spring 1964. New York Charities Aid Association, New York, N.Y.
12. Elizabeth Wickenden, "Social Action," in Harry L. Lurie (editor), *Encyclopedia of Social Work* (New York: National Association of Social Workers, 1965), pp. 697-703. Reprinted with permission of the National Association of Social Workers.
13. John W. Gardner, "The Antileadership Vaccine," *Annual Report of the Carnegie Corporation of New York,* 1965, pp. 5, 7.
14. *Ibid.,* p. 7.
15. Philip Bernstein, "Assigning Priorities in Public Policy," *Council Reports* (New York: Council of Jewish Federations and Welfare Funds, Inc., April 1967).
16. Benjamin E. Youngdahl, *Social Action and Social Work* (New York: Association Press, 1966), pp. 105-106.
17. *The Jewish Community Newsletter* (New York: Council of Jewish Federations and Welfare Funds), April 1968.
18. *Mobilization for Youth.* New York, N.Y.: Office of Public Relations and Information, October 20, 1965.
19. Herman D. Stein, "Board, Executive, and Staff," in *The Social Welfare Forum, 1962.* Official Proceedings, 84th Annual Forum, National Conference on Social Welfare, New York, N.Y., May 27-June 1, 1962. Published by Columbia University Press. P. 227.
20. *Margaret Elden Rich Memorial Award* (New York: Family Service Association of America, 1961).
21. *News and Roundtable* (New York: National Federation of Settlements and Neighborhood Centers), July 1968, p. 5.
22. Sanford Solender, "The Challenge to Social Welfare in America," in *The Social Welfare Forum, 1963.* Official Proceedings, 90th Annual Forum, National Conference on Social Welfare, Cleveland, Ohio, May 19-24, 1963. Published by Columbia University Press. Pp. 13-22.
23. Youngdahl, *op. cit.,* pp. 106-109.

11 *The Board Faces Pressure, Conflict, and Confrontation*

Most books about the board fail to pay much attention to the kinds of pressures, conflicts, and confrontations that have to be faced and dealt with at one time or another. Perhaps this area has been neglected because in an earlier time pressures were less prevalent and problems of conflict appeared less frequently. Perhaps the whole matter of trouble and conflict was ignored because to admit that such things happened in the sacred halls of the board was unseemly and inappropriate. Perhaps society itself was more settled, even tranquil compared to today. Perhaps the sharp divisions so prevalent now were beneath the surface and not ready to come up. It is interesting to observe that an authority on higher education wrote in 1965, "Thus far in the history of higher education in America, pressures for modifying the layman structure of boards of trustees either to include members of the faculty or the president of the institution have not prevailed." [1] Undoubtedly true in 1965, but scarcely the case in the decade's turbulent latter half when higher education faced incessant demands for restructuring.[2]

Boards today are deep in action on a number of fronts. As put by one school board member, "Challenge is the name of the contest in which we compete. Youngsters dare us to find a way to educate them successfully; parents demand that we do it; teachers test the scope of our authority; finance boards fault our fiscal responsibility; and some pressure

207

groups cry: 'Throw the bums out and let us do it right!' The honor of wearing the armband of leadership in public education will be ours only so long as we channel the steam of our contenders into controlled, constructive, and creative force for change. This requires serenity born of confidence in ourselves and knowledge that such an uproar is 'much ado' about something so important that everyone has an opinion to express. Such serenity reduces the sting of criticism without blunting its prod. By listening carefully, discussing openly, thinking imaginatively, and acting with integrity, we can meet the challenge. School board members still hold the greatest single unit of power in the local decision-making process, but everyone has such a stake in public education that no one can claim a monopoly. Confrontation is the climate in which we act during the negotiation process, or when parents push for sidewalks, special education or less crowded classes, or when fiscal authorities screen budget requests or proposals for new schools. In such cases, school boards are usually on the defensive, but now they must collectively take the offense in a crucial political confrontation. They must confront Connecticut voters, contenders for General Assembly seats, and gubernatorial candidates with the facts which make certain changes necessary to assure viable public education in the foreseeable future." [3]

It is most important that boards understand that there will be many times when they must cope with stress, pressure, conflict, and even confrontation. They must understand the nature of conflict and learn how to deal with it. In addition, they must be ready to recognize that at times they will be confronted by "raw power as it is exercised by pressure groups in the metropolitan areas." [4] The superintendent of schools of a large city "vividly described the pressures from teachers especially those identified with unions; he showed how the dynamic forces for and against segregation have functioned; and he depicted the sporadic emotional outbursts from frustrated groups ever present in an urban complex where there are millions of people huddled together in a space where it is a chore to breathe let alone live in comfort. He noted that members of boards of education, lay citizens, students, and teachers are not the tractable, easily maneuvered pawns that educational writers and non-practitioners might encourage one to believe. He said that the wide hiatus between what we think should be done and what can be achieved is a disturbing prospect at best and often a distressful one as well." [5]

The Increase in Conflicts

Even the casual observer can see that there is a marked increase in the number of conflicts and in the sharpness of confrontations. Why is this so? Probably no one can be sure but it is evident that society is in a turmoil and some would say that revolutionary changes are underway in this country and abroad. Obviously, it is a time of dissent and challenge to existing authority and the board is a body with legal authority so it can expect to receive some of the brunt of the movement for change. It is also a time of rising expectations with a marked increase in activism, even militancy, on the part of client groups and some staff groups. In many situations the term conflict is too mild and confrontation seems to be more descriptive of what is taking place. The dictionary refers to "conflict" as "to come in collision or disagreement; to be contradictory, at variance, or in operation." [6] "Confront," on the other hand, is "to face in hostility or defiance; oppose." [7]

As pointed out in the previous chapter, the nation has many unsolved problems and patience has been running out on the part of many people. The large agency which is a prototype of society's bigness and impersonal nature seems to be remote to many people. In addition, they may feel quite unable to be a real part of the agency and quite lacking in power. Because communications tend to take a considerable amount of time and changes take even more time, some persons are weary of waiting and are seeking involvement on their own terms. Frequently, conflicts and confrontations signify a deep discontent with the agency, often of long duration, and the eruption of feelings which have been kept in check is an outcome of old grievances.

Recent trends toward collective bargaining with regard to salaries and working conditions for staff have been noted in both public and private agencies.[8] In most of the community services economic rewards have been slow to come for professional and nonprofessional workers as well. While salaries are better than they have been there is reason to believe that boards will find themselves in negotiation with employee groups regarding salaries for the foreseeable future. There may be some prolonged conflicts as staff members use pressure to have their demands for better salaries met. Boards will be seeking additional resources from the public in order to improve salaries.

The failure of the community service system to deliver what the people want is another factor to consider. Even in the best of communities there are huge gaps in service, duplication of service, overlapping, and absence of real coordination. Consequently the people are quite rightly asking for changes often of a very basic nature. Boards are being asked to look at the way their agencies are operating and are being urged to create more efficient programs and services.

Pressures and Conflicts Within the Agency

During the course of a program year there is more than a fair chance that the board will have to deal with pressures and conflicts that occur within the agency itself. One potential source of conflicts is with the staff. Increasingly, staff members are interested in securing better salaries and working conditions and are turning to labor legislation which affords them the right to collective bargaining. In addition to adequate salaries, fringe benefits, and working conditions, staff members often call for a larger voice in policy decisions and urge higher standards of professional service. In those agencies where there is a long tradition of board and staff working together such problems are less likely to arise.

Frequently the constituencies or clientele of the agency organize to bring pressure on the board for a modification of services or even for a restructuring of the agency. They too may ask for opportunities to participate directly in policy making. Often there is resistance to changes in agency policies, programs, and services and the board is strongly challenged by the people they serve.

Another area of possible conflict is within the board itself. Factions or cliques may seek to take control of the board and the agency itself. Efforts may be made to remove an officer or key committee chairman, or the chairman of the board for that matter. Disagreements can become so pronounced that resignations result. Power struggles can erupt, as happened in a large city school board where, it was reported, "the Board of Education, unable to resolve a split that came out in the open at a turbulent meeting Wednesday night, is expected to make no further attempt for the time being, to elect new officers." [9]

An important area of disagreement within many agencies is the extent to which the board should have central powers and the extent to which their powers should be decentralized or allocated to community or regional units. As reported in the press, "The mental health program . . . is divided into two camps. On one side is the Mental Health Department and its policy-making Board of Mental Health. They want to retain strong central control. On the other side are the community-oriented citizens groups. One of the most powerful and effective lobbies in the state, these associations want a decentralized department and strong regional mental health authorities. The battle has been going on for a decade. It broke out into the open during the drafting of the 1965 statewide mental health plan. It surfaced again last week when leaders of the Association for Mental Health, representing the local groups, presented their views at a meeting of the Board of Mental Health. . . . The whole issue may spring up again at the next session of the Legislature. AMH is considering introducing a bill to reorganize the department. The AMH wants mental health services to be organized along the lines of local school systems. . . ." [10] In large cities the issue of decentralized control of the public schools is a major issue and often a source of heated conflict.[11]

Increasingly, professional workers take issue with decisions affecting their clients. An extreme example was reported in a large eastern city. "Thirty-four social workers and social work students were arrested in front of the City Department of Social Services yesterday after they had sat on the sidewalk to protest the new system of simplified welfare payments. The protest was the first composed largely of professional social workers . . . who had found the new payment system completely inadequate for their clients . . . [they] contended the system had been introduced for 'political expediency' to hold down welfare costs." [12]

Still another area of possible conflict is that of local agency and national agency relationships. When the local agency is a member of or an affiliate of a national, there are times when one group or the other may feel differently about a major matter of policy. Also, there may be differing interpretations as to whether or not the local agency is adhering to national policies and standards. In extreme situations nationals have been known to drop local affiliates and demand that the local cease using the national name. These cases are rare and for the most part the working relations between nationals and locals go along smoothly. This is especially true when locals take an active part in the affairs of the national body and representatives of local affiliates are elected to the national board and serve on national committees.

Conflicts between the board and the executive happen every now and then. When working relationships are poor and when roles have not been clarified these conflicts can result in the resignation or even dismissal of the executive. This seems to happen without regard for the type of agency whether it be educational, health, social service, or cultural.

In the case of the resignations of two county health commissioners in the midwest, a newspaper commented editorially, "When the County Board of Health loses Commissioners at this rate, it is pretty obvious that something is wrong. . . . [The resigning doctor] described in bitter terms the conditions which impelled him to ask to be released from his contract. '. . . since my training has been based on honesty, ethics, and high moral standards free from political pressures, prejudices and favoritism, I feel that I can no longer do justice to the practice of my profession as a public health physician and administrator under the existing conditions . . . these conditions, in my opinion are malignant and entirely detrimental to the practice of good preventive medicine and the basic principles of public health practice, the specialty for which I have been trained. . . .' " [13]

After a long and bitter struggle between a board of education and a superintendent of schools, the superintendent agreed to resign. The resignation resulted in a special study of the situation made by a committee appointed by the State Commissioner of Education. The report reveals the depth of the conflict when the board's reasons for requesting the resignation of the superintendent were contrasted with the superintendent's appraisal of the situation. The board said, "1) The Superintendent did not properly interpret the Board's views to the community or to the staff. 2) The Superintendent was not the kind of chief administrator the Board felt it needed; namely, one who would effectively recognize the Board's intent and more rapidly execute its formal policies. 3) The Superintendent did not take sufficient initiative in curriculum matters. Instead, proposals for curriculum changes usually arose from Board members or principals. 4) The Superintendent, as executive agent of the Board, did not carry out the Board's policies to its satisfaction." On the other hand, the superintendent gave the following reasons why the board had requested him to resign: "1) The Board's method of operation was faulty in that the Board moved into areas and activities which were more properly the province of the Superintendent and the staff. 2) The Board's lack of feeling for effective human relationships was the prime reason for a lack of effective working relationships between the Board and the staff. 3) The Board does not understand the principle that democratic leadership is essential in school administration to effectuate change but would prefer a Superintendent who would rule by fiat. 4)

The Board often acted without professional advice and in this way limited the Superintendent's opportunity to display dynamic vitality." [14] Apart from the validity of either set of claims is the fact that the conflict was allowed to reach such proportions that it could not be worked out without serious hurt to all involved and without serious implications for the educational program of the city.

Examples such as the foregoing are indicative of a serious problem which prevails when expectations are not clear and when roles go unspecified. Although the conflict may seem to be limited to the executive and the board, it is reasonable to presume that it "spills over" and affects the entire staff to some extent.

Pressures and Conflicts from Outside the Agency

It should not be surprising that most agencies designed to render services to the community are subject to pressure from the community from time to time. Also, these pressures have been known to result in serious conflicts and even confrontations. If the board has thought through and developed a satisfactory policy statement on community relationships [15] these pressures can be channeled into positive support for needed changes in agency services and programs. If the board's relationship with the community is vague and unclear the actions taken by local groups can be a trial. Increasingly the activists in the community are submitting requests for new, modified, or expanded services. Usually the board does not have the ready funds to meet these requests at once. Often the community seeks a change in policies as enunciated by the board and on occasion the community may disagree with the board about program and service decisions. Complaints about the professional staff are sometimes delivered. These complaints may have to do with the way service is being rendered or with the personal qualities or political views of the staff. Criticisms are quite common, particularly in those cases where little attention has been given to developing community understanding of what the agency does and how it tries to do it.

Public as well as private agencies may get pressures from governmental units with reference to standards of service, the overall quality of the program and fiscal responsibility of the agency. On some occasions serious conflicts arise over the fundamental control of the agency. This is especially true in the case of some of the recent federally supported antipoverty efforts. [16]

Legislative committees have offered criticism of agencies, as is illustrated by this example: "A pamphlet offering 'confidential help for the unmarried mother' sent sparks flying yesterday at a legislative committee hearing. The pamphlet, printed by the Department of Welfare, was dramatically produced . . . at a finance committee hearing on the department's budget. . . . 'What about this?' the . . . Senator demanded. . . . He held the piece of literature aloft to show a front page bearing a picture of a young woman embracing an infant over the words, 'confidential help for the unmarried mother.' If you are a pregnant girl or mother, not married to the father of the child, and do not know where to turn with your problem, says the pamphlet, qualified agencies . . . stand ready to help you. . . . I think a pamphlet like this, declared [the Senator], tends for moral degeneracy." [17]

Boards may receive strong suggestions from federated financing groups or from community planning bodies asking them to add or drop a service. Now and then there are heavy pressures to bring about the merger or amalgamation of agencies and often this leads to conflict. On occasion agencies are invited to participate with other agencies in special projects and such participation may result in disagreements as to purposes, methods, and procedures.

In his discussion of pressure on school boards, Tuttle observes, "We have the multitude of organizations of lay citizens in every conceivable area of life (business and industrial organizations, farm groups, labor groups, professional groups, and a host of others) whose interest is indirect but nevertheless real when their attention is focused on the schools and public education. . . . Whenever one special organization or element in a community attempts to influence action by the school board without consulting others who should be equally concerned, or when movements for control are made secretly and without revealing all the factors involved, the result is almost certain to be dissatisfaction and strife within the community unless the board keeps a firm guiding hand on the situation." [18]

One of the criticisms leveled against government employees, usually quite unfairly, is that they "shirk on the job." In one eastern state the Finance Commissioner sent a letter to all state commissioners requesting them to review the work habits of their employees in order to correct instances of "shirking on the job." "Instances of apparent inattention to duty on the part of a small number of state employees have given rise to several recent taxpayer complaints," the letter states. "The cited instances include groups loitering over coffee in corridors of state buildings; excessive time spent on coffee breaks in state cafeterias; prolonged newspaper reading at desks; loud social conversation conducted in large offices open to public view interfering with the work of other employees; and other examples of shirking on the job." The letter calls for a personal review of working habits by each commissioner to insure that the job performances of all state employees "measure up to the high standards the taxpayers have a right to expect. The effective and conscientious work of the great majority of our state employees has thus been brought under criticism because of the careless behavior of a few. It is essential that this situation be corrected," [19] the letter states. One cannot help but wonder if such an approach is fair to the "great majority" and whether it would not have been better to counsel directly with the "few" careless ones.

Until the 1960's it was unusual for the agency to be faced with a "sit-in." Now it occurs quite frequently. How often does one read stories about sit-ins at colleges, welfare agencies, Selective Service boards, etc. Such pressures, conflicts, and confrontations within the agency or from outside of the agency make it necessary for the board to develop an understanding of the nature of conflict and to develop ways of dealing with it.

Understanding the Nature of Conflict

Lest it be thought that conflict is without positive implications, an excerpt from an employee magazine reveals that when differences are dealt with creatively, genuine power can be released. "The American system . . . recognizes that people seldom achieve complete agreement on anything, and it wisely foresees that by airing all views, we will arrive at a synthesis which represents the best to be found in each. In organizations, too, this principle can bring strength which could never exist in a wholly autocratic unit. Conflict is as inevitable as the changing of the seasons. The important element is how the natural differences of thinking people are resolved. In recent times, we have seen considerable emphasis focused on the kind of organization in which the power of decision is highly restricted. A single individual or a single clique having the reins of authority simply passes the word, and that settles that. This kind of decision making, while seldom popular, often gets a grudging nod of approval from those impressed by speed and impatient of debate.

We see also the kind of organization which seeks always to compromise. A willingness to give and take is regarded as a desirable trait in individuals and many an organization has come to admire itself extravagantly in following a similar pattern. The fact is, however, that neither authority nor compromise uses conflict creatively, in the way that it can be molded into an effective force. Dictatorial disregard of all opinion may move swiftly, but so the more rapidly will it arrive at disaster. Compromise leaves scars on both sides of a controversy; in attempting to please everyone, we usually reach the point of pleasing no one at all. The organization which recognizes the necessity and the power of conflict deals with it quite differently. In any clash of two viewpoints, the ideal solution is very often neither one nor the other, but a third course which draws from each. By close attention to such methods, the organization uses its human resources in the most effective way, it encourages original thought, and it proves often that the whole can be greater than the sum of its parts. And what is the organization? It is simply the aggregate of all its people, each of whom in his daily associations has the opportunity for creative solutions which advance the interest of all. Conflict among individuals is like any form of energy. Locked in, it builds up pressure for the eventual blow-off. Permitted to escape bit-by-bit and dissipate itself in hasty expedients, it becomes useless. Handled with respect and employed to purpose, it is a force which can move the earth." [20]

In a review of current behavorial science knowledge concerning leadership, it was pointed out that "as people think together in the planning and performance of work, it is almost certain there will be different points of view, and feelings and emotions will arise. Conflict, then, is almost certain to appear. The direction the manager provides, when faced with conflict, will in large measure determine whether or not people will gain increased understanding and acceptance of the resulting course of action. Thus, the manager should take the opportunity to relieve or 'work through' conflict, rather than suppress, smother, deny, or avoid it. The key to gaining high creativity and involvement is the proper handling of conflict. As conflict is tolerated, and even encouraged relative to the situation at hand, creative ideas are likely to be stimulated. A further consequence is that the ideas probably will open up alternative courses of action. Experimentation with these alternatives allows the manager to help people improve their performance in an atmosphere of acceptance of change. The manager creates the atmosphere in which the amount the person talks is consistent with his contribution, and coordinated with what others are talking about. Listening is coordinated to what is being said so that people are hearing one another. The problem solution is being moved forward by people building on one another's ideas." [21]

Boulding remarks that "conflict is a phenomenon so omnipresent in social life that we tend too easily to take it for granted, almost like speaking prose. When we examine it, however, we see that it is a phenomenon which is susceptible to analysis, and it is our hope that this analysis will have the very practical objective of the better management of real conflict. The very term 'conflict management' expresses our objectives perhaps better than 'conflict resolution.' 'Resolution' has an air of finality which we do not particularly mean to convey. We are not 'against' conflict. It is indeed an essential, and for the most part, useful element of social life. There is, however, a constant tendency for unmanaged conflict to get out of hand and to become bad for all parties. The objective of conflict management is to see that conflicts remain on the creative and useful side of an invisible but critically important barrier that divides the 'good' conflict from the 'bad.' . . . Peacemakers are seldom popular with the contending parties, even though they are praised in the Beatitudes. Without peacemakers, however, both organizations and societies have a tendency to fly apart into meaningless conflict. We might almost define the objective of a peacemaker as seeing that conflict makes sense." [22]

In a brilliant exposition of how to diagnose an issue and its cause and how to decide on the best course of action, Schmidt and Tannenbaum say that the person's "ability to deal effectively with differences depends on: his ability to diagnose and to understand differences; his awareness of, and ability to select appropriately from a variety of behaviors; and his awareness of, and ability to deal with, his own feelings —particularly those which might reduce his social sensitivity (diagnostic insight) and his action flexibility (ability to act appropriately)." They go on to point out that "differences among people should not be regarded as inherently 'good' or 'bad' . . . and there is no one 'right' way to deal with differences." [23]

Every work situation has some stress and strain in it and to understand differences and conflict it is necessary to look at how the individual is adapting to and functioning within the group situation. Tannenbaum observes that "an individual at work—whether he is a rank-and-filer or manager, and whether his job is in industry, government, education or any other formal organization—he is engaged in a task which he is called upon to perform, and he is typically imbedded in a small group of individuals with whom he collaborates in getting a larger job done. His work group is then interrelated with other work groups in a larger complex, which is called an organization. This organization is itself imbedded in a cultural context which in many ways affects the organization's functioning. In trying to understand this individual, we need to see him not only as a product of the task, the work group, the social organization, and the culture of which he is a part, but also as a product of his past and present experiences off the job." [24]

In his penetrating analysis of bureaucracy, Hook makes the observation that "the democratic view to which we North Americans are all committed in theory, although our practice does not always reflect it . . . asserts that, by and large, adult human beings who have access to relevant sources of information are better judges of their own interests than any group of administrators, bureaucrats or experts. The most relevant source of information for most people is their own experience and their reflection upon that experience. In the basic affairs of life, this is obvious and can be denied only by paternalists who believe that the human estate is one of perennial childhood. After all, those who wear the shoes know best where they pinch. The expert may know best how to correct shoes that pinch, but the criterion of proper correction is set by the consumer." [25]

Etzioni supports this view and carries it further in his evaluation of confrontations which have taken place at universities. He says, "Personally, I favor maximum feasible participation of all groups in all private governments through a sharing in the decision-making process. It is the most effective way to communicate needs, to counter oligarchization and to educate the membership to responsibility. A university is, in part, a political being; actually, I do not know of a corporate body which has no political facets. Differences of needs among its member groupings are inevitable. The grouping that is least organized and which generates least power is the one whose needs are most likely to be neglected. Students in a multiversity, for instance. True, where the purpose of the institution is service to a client (welfare, health, justice and educational institutions) those in power will heed to a degree the client's needs without any pressure exerted on them by the clients, because of their moral commitments or the fear of public outcry or legislative intervention. But they will heed them earlier and better if the clients ('cases on relief'; students) generate some pressure of their own. . . . From the beginning of political philosophy, writers favoring rule by elites have suggested that the needs of those lower in rank can be upwardly communicated without actually cutting these individuals in on the power. But experience shows that when students (or welfare clients, or the poor) are unable to back up their communications with some pressure, their communication is often, too often ignored. It is easy for the beleaguered administrator (or elite) to respond to all other demands first." [26]

Since criticism, differences, conflicts, pressures and confrontations are so prevalent in the life of every board, it is imperative that ways be planned to deal constructively with them.

Dealing with Differences and Conflicts

The advice offered by a school board association for handling of complaints and criticisms would seem to apply to other agencies as well: "An acceptable and uniform system for handling complaints and criticisms should be adopted as official board policy. The following outline of procedure would seem to be a satisfactory guide. 1) The channel for complaints and criticisms on which action is requested should always be through the superintendent to (if necessary) the board. An individual member has no legal right to promise action or correction, and he has a moral obligation to refrain from doing so. Rather than conducting his own investigation of a complaint, a board member should refer the matter to the superintendent for staff investigation, study and a report to the board. 2) A serious complaint or criticism should be presented to the board as a written, signed statement, or alternatively the individual should be invited to appear before the board and the matter should be a part of the agenda. 3) Individual board members should inform the superintendent of complaints and criticisms even though no action is requested. In turn, the board should be kept informed by the superintendent so that no pressure of which he is aware should erupt in community gossip before board members have knowledge of the facts in the case." [27]

When controversy and conflict arise it is important that the board think through the steps that are involved in turning the conflict into constructive action. Follett [28] and others have discussed the steps involved. First, the board officers and the executive must accept the fact that a problem exists and must be willing to bring the matter out in the open.

Differences cannot be worked out unless people know what they are and what may be their bases. Second, there must be a genuine desire to end the conflict. This requires that the parties search for areas of common ground upon which they can begin discussions. In the strictly disruptive confrontation it has been markedly evident in recent months that the disrupters do not wish to find any common ground and do not wish to work toward anything constructive. Their goal is continued conflict rather than to arrive at integration or reconciliation. Third, assuming that there is a genuine desire to work together, it is necessary for persons to focus on the issues rather than the conflict itself. Usually conflicts have dramatic features which are not necessarily the most significant ones to understand. When people agree to work together to define the issues it is easier to locate the specific points of difference and at the same time personality factors can be lessened or even completely defused. Fourth, in involved and complicated issues it is advisable to break them into constituent parts so that the separate facets of multiple problems can be examined. In this way progress toward ultimate solutions can be realized as partial agreements emerge. Fifth, check always for agreement on basic assumptions and premises. Many conflicts arise because there is a marked discrepancy in what each party believes to be the legitimate purpose of the agency and the capability it has for meeting needs. Furthermore, it is always helpful to refer to standards of desirable practice and the ideal situation even though such an ideal may not be achieved. Sixth, assess regularly to see what progress is being made and what areas of agreement have been reached. As areas of agreement emerge accent should be placed on them because they represent positive and constructive accomplishment. Seventh, utilize the listing of alternative solutions as possibilities even though none of them may seem to have unanimous backing at the start. Eighth, work always with the evolving situation emphasizing the search for reconciliation rather than the prolongation of the disagreement.

As Schmidt and Tannenbaum point out, the management of differences calls for skill in creative problem solving. Frequently the board chairman and the agency executive demonstrate some of the things they see happening when the leader "wishes to transform . . . conflict into a problem solving situation: he can welcome the existence of differences within the organization; he can listen with understanding rather than evaluation; he can clarify the nature of the conflict; he can recognize and accept the feelings of the individuals involved; he can indicate who will make the decision being discussed; he can suggest procedures and ground rules for resolving the differences; he can give primary attention to maintaining relationships between the disputing parties; he can create appropriate vehicles for communication among the disputing parties; he can suggest procedures which facilitate problem solving." [29]

Among the several approaches to dealing with differences and managing conflict are such things as special committees, open hearings, outside studies by consultants, arbitration proceedings, policy statements, statements of clear codes and policies, and so on. In a number of colleges and universities the entire student body and faculty have conducted symposia and workshops designed to further understanding of the problems of higher education and society.[30] This kind of a planned symposium where differences can be brought out in the open should do much to facilitate a meeting of the minds. Also in the university setting it was reported that alumni, faculty and students would participate in the selection of a new president.[31] The Association of Governing Boards of Universities and Colleges in annual conference were urged to develop a university-wide approach to the handling of student demonstrations.[32]

In one situation the Board of Regents of a state university issued a policy statement on student demonstrations.[33] Clear policy statements can be helpful in creating understanding of the conditions under which the agency will do its work. Ordinarily such statements are more meaningful if an effort is made to involve various parties in creative discussion prior to the issuance of the statement. While the board must accept the responsibility for determining what the policy shall be, one can assume that there will be greater acceptance of it if many persons are involved in the work leading up to the statement. This procedure was followed by a west coast university in the development of a new code of student conduct.[34] It is extremely important that all groups be brought into consideration lest concessions to one group bring about protests from other groups.[35]

While it may take longer to develop understanding and consensus if all conflicting parties are brought into conversations and discussions, there really is no substitute for face-to-face deliberations where the differences can be brought out into the open and considered. Hurry-up efforts to effect conflict solution will only lead to further difficulty at a later time.

In summary, it seems clear that pressures, conflicts, and even confrontations are on the rise and that boards will no doubt be faced with more of them. Many of today's conflicts seem to be related to the changes that are sweeping the nation if not the world. They are societal in nature and are symptomatic of the revolutionary struggles that are going on in many of our basic institutions. Unfortunately, the forces of repression are also at work and there are worrisome signs that peaceful change based upon rational methods is under attack. There are grave dangers in the philosophy of repression and suppression of conflict. Conflict must be looked upon as a symptom that all is not well. It must be seen as a force which can be handled properly and can lead to creative changes making for a stronger society.

As the board deals with the many pressures and conflicts of today it must understand that there are differing bases and causes which must be studied, analyzed, and understood. In addition, each example must be looked at in the social context within which the agency finds itself.

Most minor incidents of complaint, criticism, and pressure can be handled by the executive and the staff without great board concern. However, major issues do have to be faced by the board because board policy is very often at the root of the difficulty. Certainly the alert board will think through what is involved in handling pressures, conflicts, and confrontations and will be seeking constantly to clarify its principles and procedures for use in these situations. It is clear that two conditions make for prevention of some conflicts and for resolution of those that do occur. First, policies and roles must be clearly stated, and second, wide involvement of board, staff, constituency, and community is essential in working through any major conflict situation.

NOTES

1. S. V. Martona, *College Boards of Trustees* (New York: The Center for Applied Research in Education, Inc., 1965), p. 99.
2. *Crisis at Columbia.* Report of the Fact-Finding Commission Appointed to Investigate the Disturbances at Columbia University (New York: Vintage Books, 1968).
3. Laura M. Pope, "Crisis and Challenge Are School Board's Daily Fare," *Connecticut Education*, May 1968, p. 2.
4. "Dilemma of the Idealist," *The Community School and Its Administration*, April 1965, p. 1.
5. *Ibid.*, p. 2.
6. *The Random House Dictionary of the English Language* (New York: Random House, 1967), p. 308.
7. *Ibid.*, p. 9.
8. Archie Kleingartner, "Nurses, Collective Bargaining and Labor Legislation," *Labor Law Journal*, April 1967.

9. Leonard Buder, "Officers Stay on at School Board," *New York Times,* August 23, 1968. © 1968 by the New York Times Company. Reprinted by permission.
10. David H. Rhinelander, "Mental Health Group Split on Centralization," *Hartford Courant,* March 24, 1968.
11. Fred M. Hechinger, "Local Control of Schools a Growing National Issue," *New York Times,* October 13, 1968.
12. Francis X. Clines, "34 Local Workers and Students Seized in Protest at Welfare Headquarters," *New York Times,* October 10, 1968.
13. "The County Health Mess," *Akron Beacon Journal,* April 14, 1961.
14. "Board-Thorne Conflict Is Fundamental, Authorities Overlap, Study Group Says," *West Hartford News,* June 6, 1963.
15. See Chapter Nine.
16. Peter Gall, "Poverty and Politics—Bickering in City Halls Brings Early Defeats for Antipoverty Effort," *Wall Street Journal,* October 6, 1965.
17. "Pamphlet Detailing Assistance to Unwed Mothers Irks Senator," *Journal-Every Evening,* Wilmington, Delaware, February 19, 1958.
18. Reproduced from *School Board Leadership in America,* 1963, pp. 61-62, by special permission of the author and copyright owner, Edward Mowbray Tuttle.
19. "Shirking Reports Spur Check on State Workers," *Hartford Courant,* March 16, 1960.
20. "The Power of Conflict," *Better Living—Employee Magazine of E.I. Dupont De Nemours & Co.,* March-April, 1959.
21. Leroy G. Malouf, Jane S. Mouton, Robert R. Blake, "A New Look at the Functions of Managing People," *Personnel Administration,* March-April 1965, p. 31.
22. Kenneth E. Boulding, "Two Principles of Conflict," in Robert L. Kahn and Elise Boulding (editors), *Power and Conflict in Organizations* (New York: Basic Books, Inc., 1964), pp. 75-76.
23. Warren H. Schmidt and Robert Tannenbaum, "Management of Differences," *Harvard Business Review,* November-December 1960, pp. 107-108.
24. Robert Tannenbaum, "New Approaches to Stress on the Job," in *Recent Research on Creative Approaches to Environmental Stress.* Proceedings of the Fourth Institute on Preventive Psychiatry Held at the State University of Iowa, Iowa City, April 26, 27, 1963.
25. Sidney Hook, "Bureaucrats are Human," *Saturday Review,* May 17, 1958, p. 13.
26. Amitai Etzioni, "Confessions of a Professor Caught in a Revolution," *The New York Times Magazine,* September 15, 1968, p. 97.
27. *Boardsmanship—A Guide for the School Board Member,* Fourth Edition, 1969, pp. 18-19. Revised by the staff of the California School Boards Association, Sacramento, California. Used by permission.
28. Mary Parker Follett, "Constructive Conflict," in Henry C. Metcalf and L. Urwick (editors), *Dynamic Administration—The Collected Papers of Mary Parker Follett* (New York: Harper, 1942), pp. 35-49.

29. Schmidt and Tannenbaum, *op. cit.*, pp. 112-114.
30. Aeis Salupkas, "Stony Brook to Study Campus Unrest," *New York Times*, October 10, 1968.
31. James R. Sikes, "Bigger Role Seen for L.I.U. Students," *New York Times*, October 10, 1968, p. 33.
32. Israel Shenker, "Educators Assess Their Own Faults," *New York Times*, October 10, 1968, p. 29.
33. "Georgia Colleges Quietly Take in Stride Regents' Ban on Disruptive Protests," *New York Times*, October 13, 1968, p. 49.
34. Gladwin Hill, "Coast Regents Set Up Students' Code," *New York Times*, May 30, 1965.
35. Fred M. Hechinger, "Ragged School Truce," *New York Times*, September 21, 1966.

PART FIVE

THE CONTINUING DEVELOPMENT

OF BOARDS

12 *Evaluation of Board Performance*

There is growing evidence that boards must look at their work more carefully and must devote more time to systematic evaluation of their efforts. Their responsibilities to society are so awesome that they must guarantee to themselves, as well as the people they serve, that they are doing the best job possible.

It is well known that the quality of board performance has a great bearing on the quality of services and programs provided by the agency. When there is an effective board there is a far better chance that the program and services of the agency will be good. Board members need to know how well they are doing their job and should not be permitted to go on year after year without a thoughtful, complete, and accurate appraisal of their inevitable strengths and limitations.

Evaluation means the making of a systematic effort to ascertain the extent to which the board is achieving its goals. Since it can be assumed that in any human enterprise there will be both successes and failures, evaluations can be expected to reveal that some aspects of the work are being done quite well and other aspects less so.

A careful search of the literature reveals that little has been done by boards in terms of either self-evaluation or evaluation by an outside group. There are some studies [1] but the number is not large. Perhaps some of the conflicts referred to in the previous chapter could have been avoided if more time had been spent by the board in critical self-appraisal. Evaluation which grows out of crisis and confrontation is never

227

as productive as evaluation which is a continuous part of the work of the board.

The Importance of Planned Evaluation

To a certain extent the good board is continuously evaluating its work as it goes along. Also, other people are making evaluations of them even though they may not be expressed as such. The most useful kind of evaluation is the one that is deliberately planned and conducted by the board itself. There are many reasons why planned evaluation is of great importance. First, the changing nature of the community and the mounting demand for community services make evaluation more crucial than ever. Also, the trend toward wider participation on the part of the community makes it essential that the board take a look at itself to see if it really is composed of the right people in terms of representativeness. Second, evaluation is needed to help the board determine the extent to which it is achieving its objectives and fulfilling its role in agency administration. While it is difficult to separate board appraisal from total agency appraisal, the board does have specific tasks and these tasks can and must be looked at. Third, planned evaluation will help board members to see their strengths and their weaknesses and will point up areas within which work can be improved. Fourth, as a result of systematic study, officers and board members can learn how well they have been doing their individual jobs and can get both satisfaction and guidance for the future. Fifth, such findings can lead to growth and development on the part of the board members and an increase in their own fulfillment as servants of the community. Sixth, a board which shows regard for evaluation of its own work sets a kind of tone for the entire agency and makes others in the agency not only respect them but may stimulate them to evaluative efforts of their own. When an evaluative point of view permeates the agency, great strength can result for all units. Seventh, the continuous assessment of strengths and weaknesses on the part of the board has value for the organization as a whole and highlights the points at which change is needed. Creative flexibility emerges out of systematic appraisal. Rigidity can be avoided and organizational change can be fostered. Eighth, when a board engages itself in serious evaluation it is demonstrating to the community that it takes its responsibility seriously and expects to render an accounting of its stewardship to the community. The more open the evaluation the greater the likelihood that understanding will emerge. Ninth, the evaluation process itself can be one of considerable impact on the board member who is earnestly seeking to provide better leadership for the agency in the community. Tenth, boards that have engaged in evaluative studies of their work report that such studies lend perspective to their jobs and help them to see the large tasks ahead.

In spite of the fact that evaluation is important, there seem to be obstacles to it and difficulties in getting it underway in many agencies.

Obstacles to Board Evaluation

One of the major obstacles is the fact that board members give their time voluntarily and there is some feeling that it is unfair to subject their efforts to critical appraisal. This same feeling is less likely to exist with reference to paid workers but it is a factor in the hesitancy with which some boards approach evaluation of their own efforts.

Another problem is that boards become very busy and express the feeling that they do not have the time to engage in evaluation. While this argument does not really hold up, it is an easy way of avoiding self-appraisal and everyone can claim it.

Unfortunately, critical inquiry and evaluation hold a negative connotation to many people. Thus, they look upon board evaluation as being only a search for "something wrong" and fail to see the positive contribution that careful study makes.

Another block is the charge that there is an absence of precise instruments of evaluation. This is undoubtedly true; however, it need not be a deterrent to action. In every situation subjective judgments have to be made, even in those fields where the most precise tools are available. Perhaps those who object to and resist evaluation are actually fearful that the results will be disconcerting or even embarrassing to them. If this is the case one can wonder if they should be in board service, anyway.

Leadership in Evaluation

Who is responsible for board evaluation? Certainly the chairman of the board and the executive must take leadership in this matter. They must motivate the board and stimulate a desire for evaluation by them. They may recommend the assignment of the responsibility to the officers, or to the executive committee, or to a special committee. Under some circumstances they may wish to recommend the calling in of consultants either from the agency or from outside. They should urge each committee [2] to conduct at least an annual evaluation of its work and should provide assistance and instruments for the committees.

One of the most important aspects of board evaluation is the establishment of a climate or mood within which appraisal can be carried forward. Here the total board must play a prominent role. What are some of the characteristics of an effective climate for self-evaluation? First, self-evaluation should be thought of as a positive, stimulating, exciting adventure. It should be considered as an opportunity for progress and a challenge for improvement. Second, an effective climate is a climate within which constructive criticism, the search for facts, and emphasis on strengths as well as weaknesses are put forward. Third, an effective climate calls for a searching *together;* the development of a creative partnership where board, staff, and community are working together in harmony. Fourth, an effective climate for self-evaluation must be free, frank, open, and based upon clear channels of communication between board members, staff members, persons served, and community representatives. Fifth, an effective climate must stress those aspects of the board's work where needed changes and improvements are most evident. Sixth, an effective climate provides sufficient time to do the self-evaluation without feelings of frantic hurrying or pressure.

Board members and staff members must join together in developing and carrying forward a sound and complete process of self-evaluation. They must understand the stimulation and values of such efforts and must be strong advocates of the process. A first step is to determine the focus of the evaluation. Ordinarily the focus must be related to the basic purposes or objectives of the board and what it sees as its primary task. In fact, some would say that three-fourths of the evaluation process hinges around the spelling out of clear objectives. Otherwise, there is no framework for the evaluation effort. One way to go about it is for the chairman to appoint an evaluation committee made up of board members assisted by staff members. This special committee may draft the self-evaluating plan stating the goals or objectives of the appraisal, the methods to be used, and the time schedule to be followed. Then comes the gathering of information from minutes of board meetings, interviews, hearings, observations, questionnaires, and special studies. It is then necessary to correlate these facts with the purposes of the board and ascertain the extent to which these purposes are being achieved. Usually, it then becomes necessary to outline the changes that are proposed for board methods and procedures. These changes may relate to the way members are selected, the way the board is organized, the way meetings are conducted, relations with the staff or community, and many other areas of board performance.

There are some special questions that always arise in self-evaluation efforts. One such question is how far can the board go with a "do it yourself" approach? When does the board need outside consultation? Another question is, how far can you study the work of the board without studying the work of the agency as a whole? A third question is, should the board wait until the completion of the self-study before making changes in its work? Still another question is, must the board have complete agreement about recommendations or is there room for alternate approaches?

Fortunately today boards do have available the assistance of outside consultants either from their national agency or from government or professional management consultant firms if they wish to have help. Outsiders can provide significant data with reference to national standards, national trends, and comparative experiences. Often it proves to be a wise investment for the board to engage an outside consultant, especially when there are major problems to be considered. The outside consultant can bring a fresh, more objective look at the work and can bring wider experience and at least a different point of view. When the board has gone as far as possible with self-study the assistance of the outside consultant is often valuable.

Criteria—Essential for Evaluation

Criteria are standards or measures by which the board can assess the extent to which it is performing its tasks in a satisfactory manner. They are of essential importance to the evaluation process. The formulation of criteria and the construction of an evaluation instrument which arranges these criteria in logical order is a vital step in the evaluation process. The thirty-six suggested criteria which are offered below were prepared by the author [3] and have been used successfully in a number of studies of agency boards.

A Yardstick for Measuring the Board

THIRTY-SIX SUGGESTED CRITERIA FOR BOARDS TO USE IN SELF-EVALUATION

	Rating		
Criteria or Measures of:	Yes	No	Need To Work on This
A. *Selection and Composition*			
1. The agency has a written statement of qualifications for board members.			
2. The Nominating Committee works on a year-around basis and solicits staff, board, clientele, and organization suggestions for nominations to the board.			
3. The agency is always thinking ahead and has a pool or reservoir of potential board members for the future.			
4. The board is composed of persons vitally interested in the work of the agency.			
5. The board is widely representative of the community.			
6. There is a satisfactory combination of experienced and new board members to guarantee both continuity and new thinking.			
7. The agency has a formal plan for limiting the tenure of board members which specifies rotation so as to assure a steady supply of new board members.			
B. *Orientation and Training*			
1. The agency has a clearly written statement outlining the duties and responsibilities of the new board member.			
2. The agency has a written plan which it follows in its program of orientation for its new board members.			
3. The agency has a board member manual which it supplies to all board members. The manual is revised periodically.			
4. The agency has a plan for and program			

Rating

Criteria or Measures of:	Yes	No	Need To Work on This
of board member training carried on throughout the year.			
5. Board members participate in community, state, regional, and national training opportunities.			

C. *Organization of the Board*

1. The board has a simple, concise set of bylaws which provide clear duties for the officers of the board and spell out the procedures by which the board transacts its business.

2. The board has an elected executive committee to handle matters which may come up between meetings.

3. The board has working committees such as program, personnel, legislation, public relations, etc., through which work is channeled.

4. Committee assignments and responsibilities are in writing and copies are supplied to committee members.

5. Committee assignments are reviewed and evaluated periodically.

6. Working relations between the executive and the board are clearly defined and understood.

7. Board and staff members are clear about their specific duties and responsibilities.

D. *The Board at Work*

1. There are regularly scheduled board meetings at least ten times per year.

2. Meetings begin on time and end on time as per agreed-upon schedule.

Rating

Criteria or Measures of:	No	Yes	Need To Work on This
3. There is adequate preparation of material including agendas, study documents, etc. in advance of board meetings.			
4. Board meetings are characterized by free discussion, general participation, active thinking together.			
5. Board meetings deal primarily with policy formulation, review of plans, making board authorizations, evaluating the work of the agency.			
6. Routine matters, that is, items requiring official action but little discussion are handled with dispatch.			
7. Minutes of board and committee meetings are written and circulated to the members.			
8. Regular reports of committee work are made to the board.			
9. The board spends some time on matters of community, state, and nationwide concern within the field of service of the agency.			
10. Individual members of the board accept and carry assignments within the area of their special talents and competencies.			
11. Board and staff members work together on specific programs and projects from time to time.			
12. Executive functions and direct services are left to the staff.			

E. *Evaluation of the Board*

1. Board members give sufficient time to the work of the agency and have a good record of attendance at regularly scheduled board and committee meetings.

	Rating		
Criteria or Measures of:	Yes	No	Need To Work on This
2. The board conducts an annual review of its own organization and work.			
3. The board has an agenda of future plans for the agency scheduled in terms of program priorities.			
4. New leadership is emerging constantly from the board and its committees.			
5. The board participates actively in community-wide social welfare planning programs.			

The Principles of Evaluation

When the board decides to conduct a self-evaluation it is important that it be clear about the principles which underlie such an effort. Eight principles seem to be evident. First, the *Principle of Purpose*—The first principle to observe is that of careful and thoughtful formulation of purposes. The specific purposes of the self-evaluation should be developed and stated in advance so that those persons working on the study will know what the goals are. Second, the *Principle of Participation*—Board members, staff members, and community representatives should be involved in planning, conducting, and analyzing the self-evaluation effort. The more people involved the better the opportunity to bring about real change in attitudes and understanding. Third, *the Principle of Planning and Preparation*—Careful advance planning and preparation is essential to the success of all self-evaluation efforts. Planning committees should be widely representative and should be well staffed. Work must be done enough ahead to allow for steady progress in the evaluation itself. Fourth, the *Principle of Progressive Development*—Self-evaluation should move from the simple to the more complicated forms of study. Self-evaluation should be planned over a period of time and should block out steps which can be taken in an orderly manner. Fifth, the *Principle of Pace and Timing*—It is important to begin with people where they are ready to begin and to move along with them as they are ready to move. Evaluation efforts which overwhelm the participants are of little use. Sixth, the *Prin-*

ciple of Continuity—The self-evaluation committee should make an effort to provide a continuous flow of material which can be put together in periodic summaries of what has been covered and what lies ahead. Seventh, the *Principle of Wholeness*—Self-evaluation is better when an effort is made to concentrate on the board in relation to the total agency in the community. This procedure introduces timeliness and relevance and results in greater learnings. Eighth, the *Principle of Follow-up*—The board must seek a constant feedback of material and recommendations for change should be put into effect as they emerge. Recommendations should include what are seen to be the steps necessary for their implementation.

One of the great benefits to come from evaluation is the improvement of the board and its members. In the next chapter, ways of improving board service will be outlined.

NOTES

1. Harleigh B. Trecker, *Social Agency Boards as Viewed by Board Members* (School of Social Work, University of Connecticut, June 1959).
   School Boards and School Board Membership—Recommendations and Report of a Survey, New York State Regents Advisory Committee on Educational *Leadership,* December 1965.
2. Alvin Schwartz, *Evaluating Your Public Relations* (New York: National Public Relations Council of Health and Welfare Services, Inc., 1965).
3. *The Board of Directors of a Neighborhood Center* (New York: The National Federation of Settlements and Neighborhood Centers, 1960), Appendix.

13 *Ways of Improving Boards*

When one evaluates the work of any board it usually shows that there is room for improvement. This is true for almost any kind of organization and especially true for the community service field where challenges have been so marked in recent years. Yet, it is still unusual for an agency to have a comprehensive and well-operated program of board education and development.

Community policy in health, education, welfare, recreation, and other fields is frequently determined by the board member group. The kinds of services available in the community are influenced to a substantial degree by the actions taken by board members. Even though they carry heavy responsibilities and make decisions which impinge upon the entire community, there is little in a way of systematic, ongoing, community-wide programs of selection, placement, and education of board members. This important group of community policy makers has been largely ignored in terms of research, study, and the provision of training opportunities. As a result, there are a number of stern problems coming to the fore. There is always real difficulty in securing enough qualified key leaders for major posts on community agency boards. There seems to be considerable feeling on the part of board members that they are not having a good experience on boards and frequently the community feels that the board does not represent them all. Fundamentally, board members report that they lack the substantive content of their fields of service and do not know what basis to use in making vital decisions. This has resulted in confusion, lack of focus, and sometimes in serious community errors.

The Need for and Importance of Board Education

Almost all of the board members interviewed in our study [1] placed great value on board member education. They observed that there was so much for them to learn that a program of continuous education was indispensable. As pointed out by Sprafkin at a university-sponsored institute for board members, "In this scientific and technological age, all of us are called upon to devote countless hours to preparing ourselves for whatever work we propose to do in society. We must be trained if we are to function productively in the world as it is today and as it will be tomorrow. This is as true for board members as for members of our staff. If education is needed for social workers, why not for those who determine programs and direct agencies? Board members increasingly feel the need for planned programs and studies designed to help them develop their skill as board members. No longer do people become board members merely to sit and to listen. They expect to work, they expect to assume responsibilities. Board membership is not only an honor; it is also a profound community trust. Effective participation on the board is something which can and may be learned. Board member education must be continuous, first, because the modern social agency is becoming increasingly complex and tends to become more so. Secondly, rapidly changing social conditions make it imperative for board members to keep themselves informed about the most important new developments. Thirdly, the job or function of the board member has become more clearly defined than it was in the past. Fourthly, new knowledge concerning group leadership and group participation is forthcoming all of the time, and new knowledge about social and health services is emerging. Thus, to function at his maximum, the board member must be kept informed and up-to-date. He needs to know about the agency and its purpose, its historical growth, development and programs; about the community of which the agency is a part; and about the board itself—its responsibilities, its way of working, its composition." [2]

The chairman of a school board asked his board members to take courses of study to become more efficient. [3] He wanted them to study school law, government finance, educational philosophy and community-wide education.

In discussing trustee education in the library field Young observes, "Trustee education is a continuing responsibility of state trustee groups which is complicated by the constant turnover of trustees. Associations provide basic publications (trustee manuals, newsletters, bulletins) and plan for programs which help the library trustee serve his local library effectively but also see it as a unit in a larger plan for statewide library development. Information on the directions of library service, the problems of manpower, plans for interlibrary cooperation, financing and taxation, policy setting, etc., are subjects which trustee associations consider with their memberships on a regular and repetitive basis." [4]

What Board Members Say About Training

A number of years ago, the author interviewed a sample of board members to find out what kind of training they were getting and how effective they thought it was. Some agencies had been giving more attention to education and the developing of the skills of the board members. These agencies had prepared handbooks, manuals, and other written materials. Conferences had been arranged and workshops had been offered. More thought was being given to orientation as the start of board member education. One experienced board member saw great value in what her agency was providing. She said, "The agency has developed and made remarkable progress in the past ten years, because the board, through better training, has learned how to increase their skills and competence. Improvement of the agency has come with the increased knowledge of board members." The same study found that a frequent method of training was the wide use of written material, but many board members did not feel that it was helpful because they did not take the time to read it or because they did not understand it. One board member with many years of experience said, "The staff should be more careful in their presentation of written material by putting it in language that the board members who are lay persons can understand. The staff may use their technical language unconsciously and it is clear to them but may not necessarily be meaningful to the board members. The whole matter of written communication is a difficult one." Conferences and workshops were thought to be of much more value than the printed word. In evaluating an interagency conference, a board member observed that "these events are beneficial as they help us to get a better understanding of our agency by comparing our work with the work being done by similar agencies. The conference was a broadening experience for me." Board member institutes were also thought to be valuable. As reported by one board member, "It would be helpful to new board members and stimulating to seasoned board members if institutes were available to them fairly regularly during their board service." Many of the board members interviewed felt that in order to evaluate the work of their agency, and then to go beyond this and learn the overall social needs and problems of the community, they should have broader and better educational programs. This raises the question of time available for such training. As one board member put it, "The problem in providing training for board members is always the time limitation." Some suggest that training events should be integrated with committee work and the board meeting itself and that training should be continuous as well as through special events.

Approaches to Board Improvement

If it can be established that boards are seriously interested in improvement, and evidence points that they are, then it is important that an overall approach be developed. It would seem that the officers and the executive, or the executive committee and the paid worker would take responsibility for lodging the task with the appropriate group. Perhaps a committee on board education would be the best approach.

Actually, the board has several sources for educational programs. First, within the local agency it is possible for them to put on orientation programs, workshops, conferences, institutes, and other special events. They can prepare written material such as manuals, newsletters, and substantive articles. Second, the local agency can cooperate with other agencies in its field of service through state, regional and even national efforts. The same kinds of educational efforts can be made but they will be on a broader basis and less focused on the single agency. Third, the agency can work in cooperation with allied agencies on the local, state, regional, or national level and high-level training efforts can be produced. State education associations,[5] welfare conferences, library associations, and health associations usually devote some time to board training. Fourth, the agency can develop training programs with the public adult education system of the community or with the higher education system. Both of these avenues are becoming more and more utilized as avenues for the continuing education of board members. It is likely that the education committee of the board will explore all approaches and utilize those that are most pertinent to the needs of their group.

Perhaps the starting point for many agencies is to assess the motivation of their members to learn to serve better. Blair's observations about American legislatures would seem to apply to boards also. He said, "It is generally agreed that the starting point for improving legislatures is the legislator himself, for if a community—whether local, a state, or the nation—is to have a great legislative body, some of the best of its interested citizens must be willing to serve as members." [6] In his research on developing responsible public leaders, Nelson claims that "man must accept the responsibility, first, for his own life, secondly, for the lives of others around him, and thirdly, for his own society so that his public responsibilities ought to be the final crown of his life, the climax of his education. Public service should thus be, first of all, an ideal carried in the citizen's mind. . . . If an optimum level of leadership performance is to be achieved, a number of different operations must harmonize. Ways must exist to identify leadership potential throughout society. The opportunity for the training and expression of this potential must exist to translate it into a capability. There must be a general recognition that society has a claim on the exercise of this potential in public leadership roles. Persons with this potential must be motivated to respond to society's claim. The process of selection must match the specific requirements of a given position with the person who meets these requirements. The tasks, in order, are to identify, develop, recruit, assign, and retain." [7]

In his discussion of organizational renewal, Gardner stresses selection when he says, "The first rule is that the organization must have an effective program for the recruitment and development of talent. People are the ultimate source of renewal. The shortage of able, highly trained, highly motivated men will be a permanent feature of our kind of society; and every organization that wants its share of the short supply is going to have to get out and fight for it. The organization must have the kind of recruitment policy that will bring in a steady flow of able and highly motivated individuals. And it cannot afford to let those men go to seed, or get sidetracked or boxed in. There must be positive constructive programs of career development." [8]

In addition to selecting the right people and giving them a good start on their work through orientation, the agency education committee must determine *with them* what their educational needs are. Bell and his colleagues have pointed out the differences among persons in public leadership positions and have suggested that adult education efforts have to be planned in terms of these differences.[9] Reeves tends to support this thought in his writings about school boards.[10] In her valuable discussion of adult volunteers as learners, Naylor urges collaboration and cooperation between the learners and the teachers.[11] Sprafkin says that "to do an effective job board members need to know what is expected of them; what kinds of deliberation they will have to make, what decisions to take; what the purpose, function, and structure of the agency are; what services the agency offers; what jobs the staff members carry; what is the calibre and quality of the work done; and how the agency is related to other agencies in the community." [12] Probably most board members would agree with these categories but would put specific emphases on certain ones depending upon their situations.

After determination of what is needed the education committee has to think about curriculum content and methods of presentation. Here the rich literature of adult education is enormously helpful.[13]

The Board Member's Manual

In her classic presentation, Demorest pointed out that the board member's manual is a basic tool in board education. She observed that "agencies have put their manuals to work by: distributing them to new members as they are elected to membership; discussing the manual at a general orientation meeting of new members; holding separate meetings with each new member, giving and discussing the manual in advance of a general board meeting and asking members to come prepared to discuss; holding series of discussion groups on separate chapters, with the manual as resource material; using the manual in connection with board members institutes specifically for orientation of new members; scheduling regularly a separate item in the manual on the agenda for each board meeting, either for a short report or for discussion." [14]

The author has collected and examined a substantial number of board member manuals. They range from the highly detailed national agency manual [15] to the relatively concise manuals of small agencies. The introduction to one such manual reads: "You are welcomed to the Board of Directors of the . . . Clinic. As a new member there is certain information which you will want to know and perhaps refer to in the future. With this in mind, the following material has been prepared. It is a very brief statement of the operations of the Clinic and the means by which services are carried out. During your association with the Clinic, it is hoped that you will be active on Board committees, participate in regular Board meetings, learn to know the staff and gain first-hand knowledge of the Clinic. We are looking forward to a happy and meaningful association." [16] The manual lists the names, addresses, telephone numbers and terms of office of all the board members. The reader is then given "A Quick View of the Clinic and Its Departments and Operations." Here, in short paragraphs, the history, finances, and services of the clinic are described. The administrative setup is outlined and the work of the several departments is discussed. An organization chart of the agency follows. Next, the bylaws are presented and after this, the policies of the clinic are given in detail. The manual closes with highlights from annual reports. This twenty-eight-page document is well written and should be of great value in the education of new board members and should be a constant source of reference for experienced board members.

The board member manual of a neighborhood service organization [17] is set up in kit style so that a number of exhibits can be included. The manual begins with an historical statement about the agency, office locations are outlined and the articles of incorporation are given. The bylaws, a chart of agency structure, the committee organization, the agency program and areas of service follow in this order. The manual closes with a statement of personnel policies and practices.

Increasingly, manuals are being designed and produced in a flexible style so that new material can be inserted. This is very important because every manual has to be revised at periodic intervals and, in addition, new material is coming out all of the time. The loose-leaf, numbered section approach makes for a format that will allow for modification of material or insertion of new material without redoing the entire manual.

It is interesting to note that few of the manuals say much about board member education or the opportunities and expectations in this regard.

Board Member Institutes

One of the major methods used in board education is the special institute. The author has participated in many such institutes and has collected reports from a substantial number of them.[18] Without question the well-planned and well-conducted board member institute can make a considerable contribution to the growth of board members. The same holds for the periodic conferences and workshops that are offered by agencies and by groups of agencies. By concentrating attention on the role and responsibility of the board member it is possible to develop new insights and stimulate new awareness of important skills.

Usually the board member institute is planned by a staff and board committee. Any planning committee making decisions about the program of the institute must secure answers to the following questions: 1) *Who* are the board members who will be participating in the institute? 2) *What* do they want and need from the program? 3) *How* can we find out what their needs are? 4) *What* experience do they bring to their job as board members? 5) *What* training have they had in the past? 6) *How much* time can be devoted to the institute? 7) *What* do the board members need most of all now? 8) *What* is the best way to present material so that learning will take place? 9) *What* leadership do we have available in our community to help put on the program? 10) *How* can we stimulate board members to participate? 11) *What* is our basic purpose for this institute; *what* do we want to accomplish?

Content seems to emerge around a number of headings. The community, the agency, the board itself, board-staff relationships, and agency-community relationships are frequently included in the program. Purposes may range from the giving of information to the development of leadership skills.

Increasingly, agencies are setting up committees to be responsible for planning the board member institute either for their agency or in cooperation with other agencies. As one watches these committees at work it is possible to summarize some of the principles which must guide them. First, there must be a careful formulation of the purposes to be served by the institute. Not everything can be accomplished in one event, so realistic objectives should be set in relation to the time available. Second, board members, new and experienced, should be involved in deciding upon purposes, planning the program and conducting the institute. The more people involved the more likelihood that there will be good participation and a maximum amount of learning. Third, the principle of individualization is important. By this we mean that efforts will be made to study and understand the board members as individuals with unique needs which differ from the needs of others. Questionnaires, interviews, and other devices can be used to find out what the members need and to plan accordingly. Fourth, the institute should be seen as *one part* of the total program of board education of the agency. This of course assumes that the agency has a total training plan for its board members as is recommended by Naylor [19] who also outlines a very complete course for board members.[20] Fifth, it is urged that the institute provide opportunities for more than just listening to presentations. While lectures to introduce subject matter and stimulate thought are valuable, the real learning comes when board members are given the chance to discuss the material and relate it to their own situations. Sixth, each board member institute should be evaluated at the conclusion by those who have participated and their suggestions should be incorporated into the planning of the next event.

Board Education for Community Leadership

To an ever-increasing extent board education is being focused upon community understanding and community leadership. As Solender puts it, "The responsibility of the board member is to know his community, to understand his community. A board member who is invited for the first time to take a seat on a board should say, 'I want to have an orientation to a series of things. I want to know the community and especially the community which this agency is designed to serve. Don't tell me first about the work which the agency does. Tell me first about the people it serves and what their life needs and problems are, because the whole purpose of the organization is to minister to the needs of people. I want to know who the people are, what their needs are, their problems, their hopes, their frustrations, their aspirations. Tell me first about these things. Let me know and understand the community and tell me what changes are happening in this community which we are serving. What are the new and emerging problems? What are the conflicts over changes which are occurring and which are altering the way of life, the setting in which these people are living? Help me to know these people as individuals, help me to understand the community, the community forces which are at work, the dynamics, the conflicts, the issues. Let me understand that that's where I must start. I want to know this broadly about the community and I want to know this about the agency's clientele in particular; and I want to know it no matter what the clientele is. If the clientele is a poor community, a lower socio-economic group, a group that is faced with poverty, I want to understand them; if the clientele of my agency are middle class people, I need to know as much about them because I know that middle class people are afflicted with serious social problems which sometimes are overlooked in our very appropriate preoccuption with the tragedy of poverty in American life. I want to understand the needs of these people no matter what their socio-economic class is, and I want to try to gain insight into these needs.' " [21]

In response to a growing awareness of the complexity of community problems a university developed a community leadership seminar [22] to which board members were invited. The program, which was planned in cooperation with the board members, took into account the changing urban situation and crucial problems of urban life. Outside speakers were brought in from agencies and from universities. Among the presentations were, "The Community Development Revolution," "Law and Order in the Ghetto," "The Failure of the Push Toward Integration," "The Changing Urban Community," "The Black Leader: Powerful or Powerless?" and "The Urban Crisis." Board members who took part in the seminar had an opportunity to listen to the presentations and then to ask questions and formulate their own conclusions in small discussion groups. Universally, they reported that the experience was a meaningful one for them and helped them to rethink the bases upon which they would attempt to make community policy decisions. Everyone agreed that this high-level program could best be offered by a university because of its traditional role as an agent of knowledge search and as an objective appraiser of the community situation.

Certainly there is a great need for a concerted effort on the part of community policy makers to deepen their understanding of the forces at work in these revolutionary times. Board members are faced each day with critical decisions growing out of the new demands for service. They must understand the community and social change.

NOTES

1. Harleigh B. Trecker, *Social Agency Boards as Viewed by Board Members* (School of Social Work, University of Connecticut, 1959), Chapter 6, pp. 45-61.
2. Benjamin Sprafkin, "How to Become a More Effective Board Member," in *Institutes for Board Members*, a Publication in the Social Life Series of the Richmond School of Social Work, Virginia Commonwealth University, March-April, 1968, p. 25.
3. John W. Slocum, "School Trustees Asked to Study," *New York Times,* February 24, 1959, p. 31.
4. Virginia G. Young (editor), *The Library Trustee—A Practical Guidebook* (New York: R. R. Bowker Co., 1969), p. 167.

5. See Edwin M. Tuttle, *School Board Leadership in America* (Danville, Illinois: The Interstate Printers and Publishers, 1963), Chapter 26, "State Association Work-Type Meetings," p. 203.

6. George S. Blair, *American Legislature—Structure and Process* (New York: Harper and Row, 1967), p. 419.

7. Charles A. Nelson, *Developing Responsible Public Leaders* (Dobbs Ferry, N.Y.: Oceana Publications, 1963), pp. 31-37.

8. John W. Gardner, "How to Prevent Organizational Dry Rot," *Harpers* magazine, October 1965, p. 20.

9. Wendell Bell, Richard J. Hill and Charles R. Wright, *Public Leadership* (San Francisco: Chandler Publishing Company, 1961).

10. Charles E. Reeves, *School Boards—Their Status, Functions and Activities* (New York: Prentice-Hall, 1954), Chapter 16, "The Development of School Board Efficiency."

11. Harriet H. Naylor, *Volunteers Today—Finding, Training and Working with Them* (New York: Association Press, 1967), Chapter 9, "Adult Volunteers as Learners."

12. Sprafkin, *op. cit.*, p. 21.

13. See Malcolm S. Knowles (editor), *Handbook of Adult Education in the United States* (Chicago: Adult Education Association of the U.S.A., 1960); J. R. Kidd, *How Adults Learn* (New York: Association Press, 1959); Cyril O. Houle, *Continuing Your Education* (New York: McGraw-Hill, 1964); Harold J. Alford, *Continuing Education in Action* (New York: John Wiley and Sons, 1968).

14. Charlotte K. Demorest, *The Board Members' Manual—How to Produce and Use It in Board Education* (New York: National Publicity Council for Health and Welfare Services, Inc., 1951).

15. *The Council Manual* (New York: Girl Scouts of the U.S.A., 1969).

16. *Board Member Manual,* The Hartley-Salmon Child Guidance Clinic, Hartford, Connecticut, 1967.

17. *Board Member Manual,* Neighborhood Services Organization, Detroit, Michigan, 1960.

18. Harleigh B. Trecker, *Social Agency Board Member Institutes—An Analysis of the Experiences of Eighteen Cities* (New York: Community Chests and Councils of American and the National Social Welfare Assembly, Bulletin No. 161, May 1952); *Board Member Institutes,* The Council for Spartanburg County, Spartanburg, South Carolina, January 1958; *So You're on a Board—Digest of Board Members Institute,* Community Council of Waterbury, Connecticut, April 1959; *Summary Board Member Institute,* Junior League of Dayton, Ohio, and the Volunteer Service Bureau, February 1960; *1960 Board Members Institute,* Greater Hartford Community Council, April 1960; *More Power to You,* Institute for Board Members, United Community Council, Akron, Ohio, March 1961; *Summary—Board Members Institute,* Greater New Britain Connecticut Community Council, December 1962; *Summary of Talks on Developing an Effective Agency,* Rhode Island Council of Community

Services, Providence, 1962; *Proceedings Board Members' Workshop,* Council of Social Agencies of Flint, Michigan, March 1963.

19. Naylor, *op. cit.,* Chapter 10, p. 116 ff.
20. *Ibid.,* pp. 169-171.
21. Sanford Solender, "Understanding Responsibilities," in *Institutes for Board Members,* a Publication in the Social Life Series of the Richmond School of Social Work, Virginia Commonwealth University, March-April 1968, pp. 6-7.
22. *Community Leadership Seminar,* School of Social Work, University of Connecticut, 1967–1968.

14 *Boards Must Meet Continuing and New Challenges*

In this closing chapter an attempt will be made to look at some of the continuing and new challenges that boards will face in the period ahead. Some of the major policy issues that boards will have to deal with in the community service field will be stated. New responsibilities of boards or new emphases on continuing responsibilities will be suggested. True, the challenges will be seen as immense, but by no means insurmountable. While the tasks of boards can be expected to become more difficult, the contributions that they make will be even more significant than they have been in the past *if* they choose to respond vigorously and positively to the opportunities that are now present.

To a certain extent, the material in this chapter is predictive and perhaps questionable in its certainty. The margin for error is possibly high because no one really knows what the future holds for them. Yet it is essential for boards to try to look ahead and make some calculations about the future. In their monumental work, *The Year 2000—A Framework for Speculation on the Next Thirty-Three Years,* Kahn and Weiner say, "There are very good reasons for trying to imagine what the world may be like over the next thirty-three years. The most important, of course, is to try to predict conditions in reasonable detail and to evaluate how outcomes depend on current policy choices. If only this were feasible, we could expect with reasonable reliability to change the future

249

through appropriate policy changes today. Unfortunately, the uncertainties in any study looking more than five or ten years ahead are usually so great that the simple chance of prediction, policy change, and new prediction is very tenuous indeed." [1] In spite of this difficulty the authors urge policy research, for "in policy research we are not only concerned with anticipating future events and attempting to make the desirable more likely and the undesirable less likely. We are also trying to put policy-makers in a position to deal with whatever future actually arises, to be able to alleviate the bad and exploit the good. In doing this, one clearly cannot be satisfied with linear or simple projections: a range of futures must be considered. One may try to affect the likelihood of various futures by decisions made today, but in addition one attempts to design programs able to cope more or less with possibilities that are less likely but that would present important problems, dangers, or opportunities if they materialize." [2]

Fortunately for board members, in the various fields of community service a substantial number of future oriented studies are being made. For example, board members of institutions of higher education now have *Campus 1980—The Shape of the Future in American Higher Education.* In this landmark book the editor observes: "Nineteen eighty is imminent if one thinks in terms of the lead-time which large social organisms like universities need to adapt themselves to changes in the environment. One might think that the future shape of higher education would be quite clear by now. And indeed some things are clear—there are curves that can be projected to yield quite reliable ideas of the future. But the challenges facing the colleges and universities are so formidable that the next decade may well demand radical changes. So while some prospects for American higher education in the year 1980 are almost inevitable, others are shrouded in uncertainty." [3]

One place for boards to begin is with an assessment of their own strengths and weaknesses as instruments of social policy making.

Boards Today—Strengths and Weaknesses

As boards prepare to meet the continuing and new challenges of this time in history, it is encouraging to note that they have many strengths upon which to build. The fact is that the boards responsible for community services in health, education, welfare and other fields have a proud history and a rich record of accomplishment. In spite of inadequate support, and often overwhelming demands, these boards have demonstrated the worth of and the need for the services they represent. This does not mean that the boards or the agencies they represent are perfect. Perfection is always in short supply in the realm of human affairs. And throughout this book mention has been made of many shortcomings. Yet, over the years, the adequacy of the efforts of these agencies has far outweighed the inadequacies that exist.

Perhaps the greatest strength of the board system is the vast amount of highly motivated citizen energy which it releases and brings to bear on society's problems. The men and women who give of themselves to community policy making are a rich resource, in fact, an indispensable resource. Mumford says, "In discussing the role of planning, we all too easily get lost, however, in details of political organization, economic support, population movements, transportation facilities, metropolitan or regional government; and we neglect the factor that is central to all of these things: the dimensions of human personality. The answer to the problems of human organization and human control will not come from computers; the answers will come from men. And it will not come from the sort of men whom we have indoctrinated with the myth of the machine—the disoriented experts and specialists whose uncoordinated and lopsided efforts, uncorrected by the more humane wisdom of their peers, and untutored by historic experience, have produced the overmechanized, standardized, homogenized, bureaucratized life that now surrounds us increasingly on every side." [4] The answers to the problems of the day will come from men. Boards are made up of millions of men and women who will be in the best position to work toward the solution of the critical ills that beset us.

But just as there is strength in the legions of board members who serve, there is also weakness and that weakness is the system that tends to limit and even hamper the attempts at innovation so greatly needed. Because the board system is long-established, and because the services under board control are likewise old, innovation comes hard. While our community service system is not static, it is admitted by many board members that changes are needed. And it is further admitted that change is difficult, often made more so by the rigidities of board members who serve too long and are unwilling to step aside for new persons to have an opportunity to serve and to bring new ideas.

Concern and conviction that communities shall be better places for everyone is an essential strength of the dedicated board member. Today's board member must begin with this fundamental regard for his community. He must make an effort to be intelligently informed. He must always be interested in new ideas, in experimentation, and in planned change. He must believe in freedom, a variety of approaches, and in critical evaluation. He nurtures his respect for the competence of professional workers and believes in the system through which professionals and citizen leaders work together. In fact, this working together of the trained person and the community representative is one of the great strengths of the system. Every community problem today is complicated and solution requires that professional knowledge and skill be blended with citizen insight and participation. Professionals and board members are both needed and it is to the credit of them that the system of joint leadership works remarkably well. Yet there is a weakness here also. It is that the pathways to board responsibility are sometimes needlessly restricted to a small segment of society and the means available to persons who would get professional education are often inadequate. There must be a widening of the channels for involvement for both groups.

Board members tend to know more about the community than any other group of people. This knowledge is a great strength. But often the board member becomes narrowly specialized, as does his cooperating professional colleague, and vision vanishes in the partializing of problems and the fragmentation of services. Even today it is difficult for many people to see the whole community and more difficult to speak for it. Narrowness must give way to breadth of concern for interrelated problems.

In spite of the realities of overspecialization and fragmentation in the community welfare system, vast changes are taking place. Striking among these major changes is the way the modern community is reorganizing its efforts to meet human needs. These changes are making a difference to boards and to agencies. The emergence of a creative partnership between government, voluntary agencies, and the business community is heartening. All share in the task of protecting and nourishing the nation's most important resource, namely, *its people*. Thus, there is being created a network of interrelated and cooperating forces which are striving to produce a new social welfare system. Today the community social welfare system is complicated and it is to be doubted that it will ever be simple again. The product of the system is the provision made in any community at any time for the prevention and relief of individual and group stress and the enhancement of the individual's social functioning through the enlargement of social opportunities. It is recognized that there must be a clear division of responsibility between governmental and voluntary agencies and that the functions and tasks of the various agencies must be understood by all. Also, there is increasing emphasis on the continuous coordination of services and programs and this is a strength upon which to build. In addition, there is more in the way of ongoing evaluations of services leading to change, modification, and improvement. While evaluation efforts are not yet sufficient, there is a trend toward more systematic study of results of programs.

An agreement seems to have been reached to the effect that services provided by either governmental or voluntary agencies must measure up to four essential criteria. First, there must be a sufficient number of adequately trained personnel fairly compensated for their efforts to render effective services with equality for all people. Second, there must be adequate standards of services for all people on a nationwide basis. Third, there must be sufficient administration and organization services. Fourth, there must be continuous research and study as to the effectiveness of services. While progress in meeting these four ideals is uneven, the fact of their acceptance as goals is a strength.

Perhaps the greatest problem faced by boards is their inability to unlock a sufficient number of new sources of vitality in their agencies and in their communities. It is the job of the board to awaken the community to its potential for continuous growth through change and challenge. The challenge is a commitment to a better future for mankind. As Harrison puts it, "The grandeur of human destiny becomes really manifest only when man is released to some extent from the battle for physical existence, and learns that on a constantly rising scale he can become a small creator. . . . Let us make our approach to science then the human one. Our great interest is in man, and we can see man best in all his humanness and incipient godliness against the background of progressing nature. Perhaps by this means we may reach some realization of what man has been, why we are here, and most important—what man may be. . . . We must grow with our universe. It is turning out to be much more marvelous than man has ever dreamed, more beautiful while more complex, fuller of that which is considered good than philosophers of earlier years could dare to expect. Man's new directions of thought are filled with meaning for the coming races of mankind, and would lead him to new fields of awareness, new challenges of attainment, and new realizations of human destiny." [5] Boards must become instruments for the creation of new awareness and new conviction on the part of many people.

An eminent social scientist put the issue this way: "Now and during an indefinite span of years ahead, there is urgent need for the confident exercise of social intelligence. As a nation, we will be called upon to make choices that call for a full appreciation of consequences. As a society, we function under a system of decentralized decision making. In all walks of life, we endeavor to preserve the individual's right to decide for himself. This is probably what freedom means to most of us. It is certainly the nature of our pluralistic society. As self-governing individuals, we must live in the same world with a totalitarian state that denies in its organization and ideology all that we cherish. If we are not to embrace, in self-defense, the very attributes of our competitor for survival, we must learn to excel in terms of our own attributes. Freedom must show its greater strength: *the capacity of citizens to make wise choices.* To this end, we must be self-aware; aware of our psychological strengths and weaknesses as individuals, aware of our social roles as citizens or as parents or in our work or play, aware of the interrelation of churches, and labor unions, and business, and professions, and other groups, aware of the forces that make for productivity or self-development or moral virtue, aware of the nature of American culture and of other cultures we must understand in order to remain free." [6] Boards of community service enterprises must be leaders in "the confident exercise of social intelligence." This is one of their strong points.

In one of his greatest speeches President John F. Kennedy said, "We can have a new confidence today in the direction in which history is moving. Nothing is more stirring than the recognition of public purpose. Every great age is marked by innovation and daring—by the ability to meet unprecedented problems with intelligent solutions. In time of turbulence and change, it is more true than ever that knowledge is power; for only by true understanding and steadfast judgment are we able to master the challenge of history." [7] Board members as recognizers of and spokesmen for public purposes have made a great contribution and will continue to do so. But they will face enormous challenges and problems in this era of revolutionary change, and the way boards respond will have much to do with how society survives the racking tortures of these troubled times.

Challenges and Problems in an Era
of Revolutionary Change

In what kind of an atmosphere or social environment will boards be carrying on their work in the period ahead? This is hard to predict, yet some things seem to be quite clear and they will influence the work of boards and to a large extent determine *what* boards will work on. The listing which follows is by no means exhaustive. Nor are the problems and conditions mutually exclusive. In fact, they tend to interlock and overlap. Society is a fabric of closely woven strands of experience, feelings, and needs. Today it is an unhappy society in many respects and the problems seem both harsh and overwhelming. Yet, the problems and challenges must be faced. And boards as instruments and architects of public policy must be both forthright and fearless in facing them.

Rapid revolutionary changes will continue. If one can be sure of anything it is that rapid revolutionary changes will continue and the pace of change will be even more swift. The country is in the latter third of a century of turmoil and transition. Toynbee puts it this way: "The entire planet is now going to become a single home for the whole of mankind —all races, people, classes and individuals are demanding a share in the power and the wealth, that till now has been a monopoly of the few. . . . Our technological production has made welfare for all seem at least possible, and poverty for the majority, therefore, seems no longer tolerable —the world revolution is sweeping away the old barriers between the peoples of the world and is sweeping away the privilege enjoyed by a small minority." [8]

Fifty years ago most Americans did not have telephones, automobiles, or even electricity. Air travel, worldwide radio and television, reaching out to the moon and Mars, are commonplace today but were unknown to most people prior to 1920. The use of atomic energy is less than twenty-five years old. The nuclear submarine, missile, jet plane, and man-made satellite are all products of the past fifteen years. There is a vast revolutionizing change in human living as a result of these technological accomplishments. The impact of these changes on the individual has been tremendous. As Leavis put it, "The advance of science means a future of change so momentous that mankind will need to be in possession of full humanity to cope with it." [9] A foundation report said, "In a time of breathtaking technological and social change, there is a need for people who understand the process of and the nature of change and who are able to cope with it." [10]

In appraising the changing world Mumford observes: "The human prospect today is both brighter and darker than it has ever been in the historic ages. For the first time, mankind exists as a self-conscious collective entity, bound together by communication at the speed of light, and by transportation at the speed of sound; we command physical powers that were once locked in the depths of nature, and knowledge enough in every department of thought, if we had the good will and the social imagination to use it, not merely to free the race from the old threats of starvation and destitution, but to give to every human being on the planet the cultural resources for personal development and enjoyment that only a minority ever participated in on any scale in the past. But, at present these happy prospects are heavily overcast by well-justified fear and dismay. The method of thinking that has made these advances possible, and the very technology that has brought them to the point of realization, are at the same time working in precisely the opposite direction. As our machines become more automatic, more intelligent, more self-governing, the life that they make possible in our communities becomes humanly less interesting, partly because we have transferred too many of our activities, even thought itself, to these mechanical agents. What is just as bad, the whole apparatus of power on which we necessarily depend has gotten out of control and is running away with us. As a result we have only replaced the old slavery of production with the new servitudes and compulsions of consumption; and in comparison with the power and resources now at our disposal the net human gain has been dismally small." [11]

Koontz observes that the challenges facing corporation boards today are related to the many changes that have come about during the past fifty years. He lists the need for flexibility in changing times and says boards should "not only be able to move with it, but, in order to have time to plan, be able to forecast it." He urges the provision of a "balanced environment for creativity" and stresses the fact that "a business enterprise exists as an economic instrument of society. Those who manage it fulfill their social obligations only if they obtain results (in terms of products or services) which society wants, at the least cost in terms of material and human resources." [12] Gardner reflects that the major changes in our history were converted into challenges that "demanded everything of us that we could give. . . . The challenges pulled us on to greatness. . . . Don't be fooled by appearances. A nation doesn't run on dollars or wheels or skills or natural resources. Those are all enormously useful ingredients or instruments or by-products or end products. But a nation runs on motivation, on aspiration, on a vision of what it might become. A nation needs challenge. A people has to want something . . . it is not enough to reassert values. Hell is paved with reasserted values. Action is needed. Such values cannot be said to be alive unless they live in the acts of men. We must build them into our laws and institutions and our ways of dealing with one another. That is slow, arduous, painful work. But it is the great work of our generation. Each preceding generation had its great work to perform—founding the nation, conquering the wilderness, settling the land. Ours is to make this a livable society for every American, a society in which no children's growth will be stunted or fulfillment impaired by circumstances that can be prevented, a society in which ignorance and disease and want will tyrannize no longer, a society that does not assault the senses with ugliness nor the mind with mediocrity nor the spirit with bleakness." [13]

Boards must meet the challenge of change with an awareness of the fact that they, as community policy makers, have a special responsibility to see to it that human needs are met to the fullest extent possible.

The urban crisis will continue and may even become more serious. The urban crisis, which has been building up for a century, will continue and may become more serious before solutions are found. Boards, for the most part, will do their work in the midst of this crisis. Sherrard claims, "There is no escape from the city; it surrounds us. The city has given way to the metropolis and the metropolis to the megalopolis. There is no room for transportation that can move fast enough or far enough to escape it. Nor is there any escape internationally. The same pattern of growing urbanization and metropolitanization is found around the world. By the end of the century, half of the world's population will be living in cities of more than 100,000 population, and by the middle of the next century, barring cataclysmic occurrences, the entire world will consist of one large urban culture with more than eighty percent of the population living in or around such cities. . . . This is a world-wide revolution fully as important as the industrial revolution itself, the agricultural revolution, or the earlier shift from a hunting to a settled agricultural economy. But the most frightening aspect of this current economic and social revolution is its speed. These drastic changes in population and patterns of settlement are taking place over a much shorter period than the earlier revolutions, and we have very little time to contemplate the problem before we take action to avoid world-wide chaos. Furthermore, judging from recent events in this country, we have very little time to avoid national chaos." [14]

Barr warns that "the problems of our cities have unquestionably grown to almost intolerable proportions—pollution, transportation, adequate housing—and the whole gamut of problems associated with the ghettos. The costs associated with these projects are staggering. In one area alone—housing—to move from the current level of about 1,400,000 starts a year to a 2,600,000 rate which is widely advocated at the moment, would place at least an additional $20 billion strain on our credit markets annually, and unquestionably an additional strain on our Federal budgetary resources. The other issues which I have mentioned—pollution, urban transportation, and the problems of the ghetto—fall roughly into the same category as housing. Financing these programs will be a great additional burden on our capital markets and on state and local government tax revenues. In addition, unless I am sadly mistaken, they are going to produce a sizable claim on our Federal tax revenues." [15]

In a nationwide report on how to make our cities and suburbs livable, Abrams' foreword calls attention to the fact that "public policy is now the most important force in determining whether our suburbs grow well or badly, whether our journeys to work will be comfortable or tedious, whether we breathe good air or bad air, whether our slum neighborhoods will continue to seethe with tension and violence." [16]

Increasingly boards are acting on the urban crisis. As one national agency reported under the caption *Federations Act on Urban Crisis,* "Ninety-five leaders from forty cities in an all day session June 14th exchanged experiences in dealing with America's critical urban problems. . . . Stressed were: leadership in community-wide efforts such as the Urban Coalitions; active support for massive governmental action, especially adequate appropriations by the Congress, as imperatives for effective action; demonstration projects and services. . . ." [17] It can be expected, in fact demanded, that agency boards will be involved more and more in working on solutions to the problems of the cities.

The struggle for racial justice and equality of opportunity will continue. The long struggle for racial justice and equality of opportunity for everyone is certain to continue. The survival of the nation depends upon the resolution of this struggle. It will be resolved. In spite of presently polarized hostilities and the seeming increase in support of black separatism, an integrated society will be achieved. In recent years the conscience of the nation has been touched and awakened. In spite of the many violent confrontations, especially in the large cities, progress is being made. All levels of government—federal, state and local—are engaged in human rights programs. The stern problems of employment, housing, education, and civil rights are being tackled with more energy than heretofore. While it is evident that much more must be expended in the way of both money resources and human energy, it seems apparent that there will never be a turning away from this problem. Fortunately, the problem is now being defined as national rather than regional. All sections of the nation have a great stake in its solution. An enormous body of literature in all fields is emerging and a considerable wealth of experimental material is being made available.[18] Although solutions will not be easy and it will take many years to create a truly just society, there is a genuine motivation for change. Future generations will look upon this period in history as a major turning point. Community service agencies and their boards have given and taken leadership in the field of human rights. They will be called upon to invest more of their time upon this matter in the years ahead.

The human services of education, welfare, health, and recreation will continue to have high priority. Boards are finding and will find even more interest in the human services. The need for programs of education, social welfare, health services, recreation, and the like for all people is firmly established. It can be expected that there will be tremendous growth in all of these fields. However, the growth will be uneven and some fields will be difficult to master. Poverty and the kinds of programs needed to help people out of the depths of economic deprivation are the number one concern of many people. A small start has been made but much remains to be done. The nation has not yet mobilized its resources to combat the problem of poverty although more has been accomplished during the past five years than at any time in history. Much progress has been made in dispelling the notion that poverty is solely the fault of the individual. As Frankel pointed out, the poverty problem is essentially a result of past depressions, recurring recessions, wars, and the fear of war. Welfare programs of both governmental and voluntary agencies are the creations of necessity, the product of "the chronic emergency that has been with us since the moment that Western society cast its fate irreversibly with machinery, cities, productivity, and economic growth." [19] The doctrine of personal blame or fault is no longer reasonable or rational when it is revealed that millions of Americans live in poverty. According to the Conference on Economic Progress: "In 1960, more than seventy-seven million Americans, or more than two-fifths of a nation, lived in poverty or deprivation. . . . In poverty were almost ten and one-half million multiple-person families with annual incomes under $4,000 and almost four million unattached individuals with annual incomes under $2,000—approximately thirty-eight million Americans or more than one-fifth of a nation. . . . In deprivation, above poverty but short of minimum requirements for a modestly comfortable level of living, there were almost ten and one-third million families with incomes from $4,000 to just under $6,000 and more than two million unattached individuals with incomes from $2,000 to just under $3,000—more than thirty-nine million Americans, or almost more than one-fifth of a nation. . . . With less than half the income required to place them above poverty, there were almost three and one-third million families under $2,000 and about one and three-fourths million unattached individuals under $1,000—more than twelve and one-half million Americans." [20]

It is not surprising that a nation which permits millions of its citizens to remain illiterate has a poverty problem. A study of the Cook County (Illinois) Department of Public Aid concluded that more than half of the 282,000 recipients were actually functionally illiterate.[21] And this problem will grow worse unless it is faced and solved. Automation is already seeing to it that without education the individual cannot secure employment. In his discussion of automation Bush says, "We shall encounter serious problems as mechanization proceeds. . . . The lot of the poorly educated or insufficiently skilled, always hard, will become harder. The man-in-the-rut, who loses his rut, will need retraining at society's expense and, as we have already come to know the training will not always take. The old, like the young, will need more care, shelter, and protection. All these groups and some others will need greater help from society than they are at present getting. This is a price of progress: it need not be too high for what is thereby achieved." [22]

Conant in his challenging and disturbing volume on *Slums and Suburbs* [23] sounds a clarion call for the nation to face up to the inadequacies in education in the central city areas. In discussing family problems, Frankel claims: "Some of the major factors behind family problems are already well known. They include inadequate schools; crowded living conditions; ill health, physical and mental; the steady pressures, humiliations and hostilities under which racial and ethnic minorities live, the influence of culture which makes much of technique and little of ideas and purposes. . . ." [24] It is impossible to solve family problems or the problem of poverty without taking into account the total context within which these problems occur. Better schools, better health services, modernized welfare programs, strengthened social insurance programs, better housing, and equal opportunities are all involved.[25] Insofar as the income maintenance programs are concerned, they are already undergoing much review and changes are bound to be forthcoming. Certainly the nation will continue to broaden and strengthen the social security system and this act in itself will remove many people from the public assistance programs. Family allowances, already being made in many countries, will be provided in this country. Some form of a guaranteed income will emerge; in fact, controlled experimentation in this regard is now underway.[26] The poverty problem will not simply disappear. The "welfare problem" will not disappear. New ways will be found to meet the basic needs of the many millions of young and old who are victims of an economic system that has no use for either.[27] That government on all levels will play an even larger role is self-evident. With almost one million people in need of public assistance in New York City alone, it is obvious that increased government support is required and since the problem is national in scope there must be national standards.

Hand in hand with efforts to eliminate poverty, in fact basic to such efforts, is the strengthening of the educational system particularly in the inner portions of the large city where the poor live. Also, the provision of decent housing [28] and the availability of health services are essential. In spite of the many problems now prevailing and the enormous price that must be paid for neglect of these problems over the years, many gains will be made. While human services may never catch up with the technological changes of the last century, attention is finally being focused on them.[29]

Priority setting and resource allocation will be major decision areas. Every level of government and every social institution will face a major challenge at the point of setting priorities and determining how resources are to be allocated. Domestic goals and requirements will have to be balanced against diplomatic and military demands.[30] National purposes will have to be reviewed and restated and decisions will not only have to be made, they will have to have the support of the people. Governmental and voluntary agencies will be called upon to develop much better systems through which responsibilities will be allocated and accepted. To a considerable extent this exercise in purposing, setting priorities, and allocating resources will be a new experience for many people. Frankly, because resources have been so plentiful and because pressures for change so minimal until recent years, many agencies and programs have simply gone along without much planned change. In his fascinating speculation about America in the twenty-third century Gardner says, "If society is going to release aspirations for institutional change—which is precisely what many twentieth century societies deliberately did—then it had better be sure its institutions are capable of such change. In this respect the twentieth century [is] sadly deficient. Because of failure to design institutions capable of continuous renewal, twentieth century societies showed astonishing sclerotic streaks. Even in the United States, which was then the most adaptable of all societies, the departments of the Federal Government were in grave need of renewal; State government was in most places an old attic full of outworn relics; in most cities, municipal government was a waxwork of stiffly preserved anachronisms; the system of taxation was a tangle of dysfunctional measures; the courts were crippled by archaic organizational arrangements; the unions, the professions, the universities, the corporations, each had spun its own impenetrable web of vested interests. Such a society could not respond to challenge and it did not. . . . Twentieth century institutions were caught in a savage crossfire between uncritical lovers and unloving critics. On the one side, those who loved their institutions tended to smother them in the embrace of death, loving their rigidities more than their promise, shielding them from life-giving criticism. On the other side, there arose a breed of critics without love, skilled in demolition but untutored in the arts by which human institutions are nurtured and strengthened and made to flourish." [31]

Challenges to the system will continue. The community welfare enterprise is under challenge and the challenges will continue. Although some would view these challenges with dismay, and even alarm, it is evident that in the long run positive change comes about when enough people get interested in working for it. Although the methods being used by some groups to force changes in the system are certainly to be questioned, there is reason to believe that a tide of change is getting underway partly as a result of the challenges put to the agencies of education, welfare, government, and the like. Major groups challenging the system include the "consumers" or clientele being served, the staff workers, and the community at large. In addition, many agencies are challenging their own methods and are working for new structures and new ways of involving more people in the decision-making process. The way that the board meets the challenge of various groups is most important. Boards and administrators must listen to the ones who are challenging them and must invite these challengers to play a vital role in the services they are advocating and seeking.[32] Every community service agency of today came about because someone or some group challenged the status quo and worked for change. It will continue to be the task of the board to respond to all voices that challenge them.

Consumers of services will play a wider role. One of the striking changes in the past few years has been the fact that consumers of community services are being invited to play a larger role in determining what those services are to be and in making the policies that guide them. This trend will continue and will be accelerated in the years ahead. In the fields of education, welfare, housing and urban redevelopment, health care, highways, physical and social planning, and elsewhere, vigorous efforts are being made to get the advice, counsel, and support of the persons most affected by the programs. In the case of federal programs particularly, legislation requires that people be given a much greater voice in determining what the program shall be. For example, the historic Economic Opportunity Act of 1964 in Section 202(a)(3), dealing with community action programs, states that the program must be "developed, conducted, and administered with the maximum feasible participation of residents of the areas and members of the groups served." [33] This legal mandate has had a profound influence on the program [34] and has been subject to much review and some criticism.[35] The fact remains, however, that the Congress made "maximum feasible participation" a basic requirement and this same requirement has been written into the laws authorizing other federally supported programs. Any move as major as this one is bound to run into difficulties in implementation. However, in almost every sector of the human services enterprise efforts are being made to involve the people who are no longer willing to be mere recipients of programs and policies determined only by boards or administrators. While the evidence is most conspicuous in the fields of education,[36] antipoverty, and welfare today, there is reason to suspect that the "closed shop" board or administrative body is being opened up in many, many fields. This is a reality of this decade and it will continue.

Government responsibility for the human services will increase. Although there will be much discussion and some resistance, government on all levels will be called upon to spend more money upon and give more leadership to the human services. This is not a new trend but, as emphasized by a recent national foundation report, "human needs are today served by government to an extent never imagined at the dawn of the American Republic. Regardless of varying political philosophies, there is nearly universal agreement on the new role of government in certain functions of human welfare. This unanimity stems not from a preference for public over private efforts but from the nature of modern society. Only government can marshal the resources needed to cope with certain complex and costly functions of society. Far from implying a forfeit of private responsibility, government expansion poses special challenges to individual initiative and ingenuity. While not entirely precluded from boldness and imagination, responsible government in the democratic society cannot habitually experiment and venture beyond public sentiment; thus, the private organization must be the innovator, the risk-taker and the pioneer." [37] Striking evidence of the immensity of the problem is the fact that in New York City alone it is anticipated that public assistance costs for the year 1969 will exceed one billion dollars and will be the largest of all budget items percentage-wise.[38] Health, education, and welfare costs consume the largest part of the budgets of state governments also. With an increasing population and ever-widening concepts of needs to be met, government will have an ever-increasing responsibility.

Professionalization of services will continue. In every field of community service activity there will be an increase in the need for and number of professionally qualified workers. The kinds of problems that are being dealt with require the most sophisticated of professional preparation. Fortunately, the American system of lay and professional cooperation is well established. There should not be any serious strains in relationships between lay boards and professional workers except in the basic economic area. The central problem for boards will be to get enough qualified staff and to provide conditions whereby present staff can keep up with the changes that are occurring in their fields.

New coalitions of business, labor, government, and civic organizations are being formed. Only dimly perceived at this time is the formation of new coalitions of business, labor, government, and civic organizations dedicated to a united attack on social problems of the community.[39] Business has taken special leadership in recent years and it can be expected that this leadership will continue.[40] The private sector is seemingly less in opposition to the public sector of community life and there are hopeful signs that a new design for community planning is emerging.

The movement toward coalition has profound implications for agencies and boards. Their knowledge, experience, and insight should be put to work in cooperative ways with these new overall organizations.

The ten challenges of change sketched above are by no means the only ones to consider. They are, however, major factors to take into account as the board plans its work for the decade ahead. It is now possible to predict some of the major policy issues that citizen boards will have to face more directly in carrying forward their work. Some of these issues will be presented below.

Policy Issues Boards Must Face

More and more, boards will be confronted with major issues of policy. Their time will be devoted to a considerable degree in working on these matters.

As Kahn and Weiner point out, "New and rapidly innovating technologies; vast political, social, and economic upheavals accompanying the worldwide mushrooming of population, the continued development of mass communication; and the less spectacular but equally consequential processes of urbanization, industrialization, and modernization are obvious facets of the second half of the century. It is a truism that the pace with which such changes are taking place has reduced the reliability of practical experience as a guide to public policy and has diminished the usefulness of conventional judgment in dealing with social problems. On the other hand, traditional or unalterable factors in man, societies, and culture continue to play important, even decisive roles. Policy-makers, in many fields, given so much new information to assimilate, so many new variables to assess, and so little experience directly relevant to the new problems, can no longer be as confident of the applicability of traditional wisdom and can no longer rely so much on the intuitively derived judgment that once seemed adequate to resolve issues and to achieve fairly well-understood goals." [41]

Some of the issues that boards must face more forthrightly in their policy-making role can be identified because boards are already grappling with them. Other issues are only dimly foreseen at this time but signs are on the horizon. It can be predicted with some confidence that most boards of directors will be faced by the six issues outlined and discussed below.

1) *The issue of agency control.* To a great extent boards have tended

to be the controlling administrative body insofar as the agency is concerned. But now others are asking for a share in the creation of policies and in the decision-making process. In large cities and in large bureaucratic agencies the issue is being stated as centralization versus decentralization of control and authority with a strong tide running in favor of decentralization.[42] On the whole this is a healthy trend if it means that more people want to participate responsibly in the affairs of community agencies. A willingness to assume responsibility is far to be preferred over apathy and every effort should be made to involve more people in the affairs of every community agency. This does not mean a giving up of legally conferred responsibilities on the part of the board. It means, rather, a wider sharing of responsibilities with a larger universe of people who assume legal roles through due process. Decentralization of control to where people live is not in itself a process which does away with central control. Every service-giving agency, public or private, which serves large areas of the community needs both central authority and decentralized responsibilities which are clearly understood.[43]

While public education systems have been the chief target of decentralization advocates, there is reason to believe that other service fields will likewise feel the pressure to restructure their agencies to bring the people in the neighborhoods into closer collaboration.

The issues of control and involvement are not limited to centralization versus decentralization. A big drive is underway on the part of professional workers and agency clients to have a much more active part in decision making. As one teacher puts it, "Many believe that the demands of . . . teachers to have a greater say in the formulation of school policy are indicative of our desire to take over and run the school system or merely to participate in national teacher militancy. This is erroneous, and I deem it most unfortunate that our thoughts on the subject have been so misconstrued. Instead, it seems to make sense that they who daily spend full time with students should best know the youngsters' needs, as well as what programs are or are not successfully meeting those needs. It is also true that classroom teachers have firsthand knowledge of many budgetary needs, such as books, teaching materials and additional teaching staff, in the various buildings. Teachers know better when they are fully prepared to commence a new program because they are the ones who have to teach it. . . . It is not our aim to infringe on the state-granted prerogatives of the Board of Education, but we do insist on having a strong say in what is recommended to it in every area which pertains to us and the teaching of children entrusted to our care." [44] Feelings such as these are often expressed by other groups of professionals in other fields. It need not be implied that these persons wish to usurp the board's responsibility to govern but they do want a voice which is listened to and responded to. Another group seeking a much greater voice is the welfare client population.[45] The welfare rights movement is relatively new, but it augurs a considerable amount of rethinking of welfare policies and in at least one state a welfare commissioner is recommending that representatives of the poor be placed on the citizens advisory board.[46]

That there is a struggle for power and control cannot be denied. It will loom large as an issue which boards must continue to face. Solution will not come from ignoring the issue or from frightened capitulation to unreasonable demands from persons who seek to tear down rather than build. Every board, however, would be well advised to look critically at itself and assess honestly the extent to which it actually is broadly representative of all strata of society.

2) *The issue of responsible participation.* If it can be assumed that boards are seriously seeking the broader involvement of people and seriously interested in allocating some of their powers and responsibilities not only to staff but also to clients and the community, then the issue of how to bring about wider and more responsible participation must be looked at. This will call for a basic rethinking of the agency and the board point of view and philosophy and it will require soul-searching of the highest order.

The essential issue is the creation of better channels of communication between the board, the staff, and the people being served. In addition to the wider use of committees, advisory and administrative, which has been discussed earlier,[47] there is a trend toward broadening the base of the nominating committee, and in many cases board members, instead of being appointed and ratified, are elected by the constituency.[48] While these efforts have not always been successful there is reason to believe that progress is being made. A major counterargument to the electing of client members to boards is that they become swallowed up by the board and lose their "action" power.[49] Others stress the fact that electing community representatives does not necessarily mean that they will be permitted to work on real policy issues.[50] Apart from all of the arguments, pro and con, it is certain that boards will have to look at their own selection procedures and find ways to broaden the base from which members are chosen.

3) *The issue of service organization, availability, and delivery.* At issue in every field of service and in every community is the fact that services are not properly organized, are not generally available to all people, and are not "delivered" efficiently. Furthermore, there is a minimum amount of solid research of an evaluative character and no one really knows much about the effectiveness of alternative approaches. In his discussion of the needs and problems of the inner city, Sherrard says, "Traditional methods of doing things are not good enough. A good deal more imagination, ingenuity, boldness, and experimentation must be demonstrated if we are to have any substantial effect on the desperate situation in the inner city. I have myself reached certain rather pessimistic conclusions. If for no other reason, the sheer size of the problem precludes placing major reliance and expanding our principal resources on individualized services. While in the last analysis much human communication must take place on a one-to-one basis, if we are truly contemplating social change our efforts must be placed in a broader methodological context. . . . No major field of human activity in this country operates with less theoretical and scientific guidance than the field of social welfare. In a time of unprecedented social change most social agencies which should be most sensitive to the need of innovation, flexibility, and experimentation appear quite content to continue along lines laid down during the first half of this century, if not in the last. Considering the amount of money spent on social welfare in this country, the situation is an outright scandal. No major corporation could hope to stay alive more than a few years without an active research and development department. Some models readily adaptable to the social welfare field exist in certain industries which have organized research and development programs industry-wide, and in some cases world-wide, funded on an equitable assessment basis. There is no comparable activity worthy of the name in our field." [51]

Burch and Newman are especially critical in their indictment of the existing service delivery system in the human needs area. They list three problems: "First, fragmentation—Services tend to operate in isolation from each other, treating the individual consumer as a series of compartments rather than as a whole, living organism. Sometimes as many as ten different agencies may be related to a family without any coordination among them. In other cases, the lack of comprehensive overview has permitted serious gaps in service to exist between the fragments. The individual must deal with arbitrary and sometimes irrational differences among agencies in eligibility determination and must submit again and again to the same questions in intake interviews each time he encounters a new agency. Second, unresponsiveness—Human service agencies are presumably well-meaning. However, due to such varied factors as professional tunnel vision, ignorance of reality, tradition, statutory limitations, overwork, indifference, and class or status differentials between producer and consumer of service, many, perhaps most, health, education, and manpower services currently being provided by large public and voluntary agencies are off target in one way or another as they touch the lives of people. Third, inaccessibility—Human services are often difficult of access to the people who need them most and who may have the least skill in navigating the channels necessary to obtain service. The most obvious kind of inaccessibility is location. It is not uncommon for a clinic or an employment office to be two bus rides and an hour and half from where the potential consumer lives. Other accessibility factors may include such things as the hours a service is open, the attractiveness of the office, the courtesy of the receptionist and staff, the necessity for an appointment, waiting lists, long sojourns in the waiting room, and most basically, awareness that the service exists." [52] In their discussion of neighborhood service programs, now in only a beginning stage, Burch and Newman hold out much hope as does March [53] in his exciting presentation of "The Neighborhood Center Concept." Geismar [54] and others [55] have developed pioneering material on understanding and serving the multiproblem family.

Grosser calls attention to the fact that there has been a great expansion in the number of persons served by human service agencies and to a great extent a "public policy objective is to provide service to a full spectrum of the nation's population"; [however,] "agency programs have generally been offered in a style very different from that of the target population, and have been staffed by professionals who tend to differ from the clients in ethnicity, education, and other indices of social class. Agency programs and policies have usually been created by central decision-making bodies far removed from the service neighborhood. These factors have produced a gap between the service institution and the target population. The non-professional worker, indigenous to the population served, is seen as a bridge between the institution and the lower class community. The expansion of staff to include some members of this class as dispensers of service does not require the service agency to alter its program, replace its present staff, or revise the legislative or corporate mandate under which it operates. The use of local persons is perhaps the least threatening way of developing rapport with the new client." [56]

There can be no doubt that there will be major reorganization of services in the period ahead. The form that the reorganization will take is not entirely clear but some features are evident. Boards will need to consider policies which step up the coordination of services, and decentralize services. They may be considering the matter of mergers of several agencies. They certainly must be very cautious in instituting new services without careful study. Further proliferation of services on any level of government and by any agency, without intensive efforts to coordinate existing services, will only contribute to the confusion that now exists.

4) *The issue of manpower, recruitment, utilization, and salaries.* It can be predicted with certainty that most boards in all fields of service will have to work hard on the matter of manpower recruitment, utilization of manpower, and salaries for both professional and nonprofessional workers. The personnel committee of the board, already busy, will be even busier.

New patterns of manpower utilization are evident today in the human services. While professionalization continues at a rapid pace there is substantial interest in and use being made of the nonprofessional worker in auxiliary jobs.[57] In every field of health, education, and welfare there is a shortage of trained workers. This shortage has been reported in numerous studies.[58] In some instances community-wide manpower programs are underway with attention focused on better methods of recruitment, better utilization of existing personnel, and better scales of remuneration.[59] Volunteers are also being used with a new awareness of the contribution that they have to make. Plans of staff development are coming to fruition and it is evident that retraining in the human services will occupy the attention of many agencies.[60] The board will face many issues in the realm of personnel and will have to take continuing responsibility for developing and implementing personnel policies and practices consonant with the needs of the era.

5) *The issue of finance and budget.* Already at issue, and certain to continue so, is the matter of how to finance the human services and how to budget the available money. Every board has characteristically struggled with these problems and has devoted much time to them. There is reason to believe that even more time will have to be given to the money problem. Despite the great increase in the gross national product and the growth in government responsibility, the percentage expended on the

human services has lagged behind expenditures in other areas, notably national defense. Firmly established is the fact that our country has a multiple system of financing community services. Federal, state, and local government, as well as private contributions and fees for services, are all involved. Patterns are often confused and frequently inequitable. In his discussion of the financing of the social services, Hipple says, "The pattern of distribution of responsibilities for the administration and financing of the public social services is at best a patchwork. It is, moreover, a patchwork which has been a long time evolving; and which now represents interests dispersed among various local government jurisdictions, the state, and the federal governments; and, therefore, one which offers no easy or simple solutions to the complexities it encompasses." [61] Hipple, like others, makes cogent suggestions for correcting the problems caused by the "patchwork" approach; [62] but it can be assumed that it will take a long time to make a real garment out of the patchwork and boards will have to give thought to the sources of funds, the restrictions attached to their use, the accountability involved, and the potential in their use for basically sound development of program.

On the federal-state relationship level the distinguished Advisory Commission on Intergovernmental Relations makes a number of recommendations worthy of genuine consideration. In calling for a "broadened fiscal mix and great fiscal flexibility in federal aid to states and localities" they say, "The Commission concludes that to meet the needs of twentieth century America with its critical urban problems, the existing intergovernmental fiscal system needs to be significantly improved. Specifically, the Commission recommends that the Federal Government, recognizing the need for flexibility in the type of support it provides, authorize a combination of Federal categorical grants-in-aid, general functional block grants, and per capita general support payments. Each of these mechanisms is designed to, and should be used to, meet specific needs: The categorical grant-in-aid to stimulate and support programs in specific areas of national interest and promote experimentation and demonstration in such areas; block grants, through the consolidation of existing specific grants-in-aid, to give States and localities greater flexibility in meeting needs in broad functional areas; and general support payments on a per capita basis, adjusted for variations in tax effort, to allow States and localities to devise their own programs and set their own priorities to help solve their unique and most crucial problems. Such general support payments could be made to either State or major local units of government if provision is made for insuring that the purposes for which they are spent are not in conflict with any existing comprehensive State plan." [63]

The above is just one example of a policy recommendation in one area. It is likely that agencies and communities will be forced into some kind of coherent policy of financing because the present system, or lack of system, is both inefficient and eventually self-defeating. Finance committees of individual agencies must meet with their counterparts in their fields of service and boards which heretofore thought about only their agency will have to think more about fields of service and the entire community. The lack of financial cooperation between agencies has been a kind of luxury which can no longer be afforded.

6) *The issue of central planning.* Agency financing will be a major element in the realm of centralized planning, which is a reality today.[64] No longer is there any argument about the need for planning. The issue is the planning unit and the planning area. The trend is definitely in the direction of centralized planning with regional, state, and federal groups [65] taking much leadership. The board as a consequence of this movement will have to figure out how it fits into the new pattern and will have to take a much more active role. It is hardly reasonable to assume that any agency can go it alone. Dean points up the issue: "Since America values both economic welfare and political democracy, we are faced as a nation with the necessity for central planning, on the one hand, and maintenance of democratic procedures, on the other. To cope with this dilemma, the United States has thus far opted for a form of national-local collaboration represented by the matching-funds formula, and the requirement that plans (for area redevelopment, urban renewal, vocational training, etc.) be initiated at the local level. It becomes important, therefore, to discover the relevant value orientations which currently prevail among decision making leaders in local communities, with particular reference to their ideas about proper relationships between individual and society. Such knowledge would seem an essential precondition to planning, and instituting, and guiding profound social changes, while simultaneously maximizing the advice, participation, and consent of the governed." [66]

It can be predicted that most boards will spend more time on matters of cooperative planning and most boards will have to have representation on the new planning bodies that are emerging. As Wilson sees it, "U.S. cities confront what is probably the preeminent fact of twentieth-century life: rapid and unceasing change. Complexity is accelerated in the industrial technology, in styles of living, in information available to people, in government and other activities designed to cope with urban society. Sheer size is accelerated—population growth implies that communities not only face complicated social problems but that the number of people whose needs must be met is constantly growing. Stated bluntly and too simply, the community needs industry to employ its citizens and the tax base necessary to urban services; it needs a vast range of services in a bewildering complexity of types, from health to housing to recreation to traffic; and it needs a coordination of governmental and private ideas and facilities to sustain a pattern of fulfilled living for the population. Underlying all these requirements is the imperative planning, for fresh, coherent, and connected thought about how large numbers of men and women can live together in a small space with reasonable civility. . . . U.S. communities appear to be moving, much too rapidly for some and much too slowly for others, toward a form of social organization distinguished by planning, a mixed pattern of public and voluntary institutions, and concern for protecting and cultivating human resources. Perhaps these have always been characteristic of our society, but are becoming more emphatically present in the contemporary situation of urban size and complexity." [67]

The six issues mentioned above are but some of the items with which boards will be concerned in the period ahead. They may result in significant changes on the part of boards as they accept new responsibilities and develop an agenda for action.

Board Responsibilities for the Period Ahead— An Agenda for Action

In closing, it may be helpful to summarize the major tasks which will face boards in the light of the challenges, problems, and issues that are apparent today. The list which follows is a kind of action agenda of board responsibilities. In many cases boards are already assuming these responsibilities. Where they are not, they may wish to review what they are doing and think about the need for change.

While the board may rightly wonder if it can do much about the stern and pressing problems of the hour, Mumford points out that "we shall never succeed in dealing effectively with the complex problems of large units and differentiated groups, unless at the same time we revitalize the *small unit*. We must begin at the beginning; it is here that all life, even the life of big communities and organizations, starts." [68] The board is a small unit, but it is a basic unit in terms of community policy making and it can have a tremendous impact if it will only take leadership. If we can assume that it is the responsibility of our boards to serve as the sensitive conscience of the community and articulate spokesmen for the community's goals and aspirations, if we can assume that boards must take leadership in guaranteeing that the best of knowledge and skill is brought to bear in the provision of human services, then we must start with ourselves and ask, "What must we do to be certain that our board is really meeting its responsibilities?"

1) *The board will look at itself.* Boards will sharpen their selection procedures and will demand the highest of qualifications for all board members. Boards will broaden their base of representation and will endeavor to involve a much wider range of community interest and background in the affairs of the agency. Boards will strive for an orderly flow of new leadership so that new ideas and new vigor will be available at all times. Boards will work together to do a much better job of orientation and training for their members, making sure that everyone is clear about the purpose of the agency and has conviction about the important needs it exists to fill. Boards will clarify their roles and the roles of professional workers and strive for genuine cooperation at all levels.

2) *The board will broaden its frame of reference.* To understand community needs in the areas of health, welfare, education, recreation, and other community services, board members must consider more than their agency. Public and private agencies alike must shift their thinking and their emphasis from the agency alone to the community and community needs. Cooperative interagency and intergovernmental services must take top priority.

3) *Every board will have a long-range planning and development committee.* Too often boards get so busy with the details of current operations that they fail to devote time to thinking about and planning for the future. In the press of day-to-day problems, it is difficult to get a sense of the unfolding future. Yet the board has a responsibility for long-range planning. Every board should have a long-range planning and development committee charged with the responsibility for looking ahead and forecasting long-range needs. As Turner puts it, "I believe leaders in private and public life can no longer permit us, as a people, to 'back into the future.' Long-range forecasting and evaluation of social needs of two or three decades ago might have effectively forestalled many such acute problems of today as core-city deterioration, transportation overload, air and water

pollution, and inadequate training for today's unskilled minorities . . . it should be then of central interest to support one or more major centers of long-range systems research to get on to the social-problem beam of the years ahead." [69]

4) *Boards must work for a combination of physical and social planning.* The various bodies separately concerned with physical, economic, social, and human planning must be combined. Their base must be expanded from the local community to the regional area and to the state as a whole. Boards will seek out proper relationships with these planning groups and will endeavor to exercise leadership in integrating their efforts and in broadening the scope of their concerns.

5) *Boards will work to develop better understanding by the community.* Throughout their long years of service, community agencies have done much to restore people to productive employment, keep families together, care for the disabled and the ill, and help children and youth to grow into responsible citizens. Money invested in these human services has come back to the nation through the contributions made to the common good by productive citizens. In spite of this tangible record, boards must do more in the way of developing a comprehensive and continuous program of interpretation of needs and services so that public understanding will be ever greater and public response ever stronger.

6) *Boards will review and restate purposes.* Because changes in today's world are so rapid, every board and staff is in the position of need to review, clarify, and restate their purposes. Since this exercise cannot be done in a vacuum, boards will have to work within the family of agencies they represent and will have to determine purposes in the light of many new programs that have emerged and will emerge.

7) *Boards will develop a more orderly process of creating new programs and services.* Boards must take responsibility to create a more orderly process of developing new services. The continued authorization of new agencies and new services within established agencies has caused confusion and has raised doubts in the mind of the community. If the community welfare system is ever to become a coordinated system it cannot go on year after year adding new agencies and new services. The boards must give great care to this matter. Thorough research should precede the setting up of new services to make sure that before anything more is added, existing agencies will be evaluated to see if they cannot take on the new program.

8) *Boards will continue their pattern of voluntary-governmental co-*

operation. There are few if any problems today that are strictly local, state, or even regional. Needs that are nationwide in character require national consideration, planning, and financing. However, the actual process of meeting needs and providing services to people must be carried out in the states and communities where people live. The productive partnership between levels of government is a well-established principle. Now there must be a strengthened partnership between voluntary effort and governmental effort because each group shares a common stake in the welfare of the nation.

9) *Boards will develop a better balance of services for the inner city and growing suburban areas.* Remarkable progress has been made in providing enriched services for the inner city. New services and extension services have been made available to the growing suburban areas. Boards will find it necessary to achieve a better balance of services between these two population groups and will be actively engaged in establishing priorities and in setting up better overall program plans.

10) *Boards will concentrate on manpower needs.* The best way for the board to guarantee an economic, efficient and sound program is to see to it that there is an adequate number of well-qualified staff members trained in their fields of specialization. A number of communities [70] have proved that by providing skilled professional service in sufficient numbers, a large proportion of families can be helped back to self-support. These families are on assistance for a shorter period of time and their probability of return to assistance is lessened. Also, unsatisfactory behavior is decreased. Boards must therefore give high priority to all possible measures for strengthening professional personnel in the community and for seeing to it that agencies are adequately staffed. This will call for the sharing of staff in some instances and the joint employment of staff specialists. It will require the development of better staff development programs for those now on the job and an expansion of professional education for new entrants to the various fields of service. Efforts should be made to make possible full professional education for those persons who are expected to provide professional services. Without question, the quality of professional services is determined largely by the quality of professional personnel available to render services.

11) *Boards will strengthen volunteer services.* Inasmuch as volunteers are a most important part of the community service enterprise, strong efforts should be made by the board to strengthen volunteer services. To this end, it is suggested that there be developed more joint programs of

recruitment, training and placement of volunteers and that there be a vastly expanded program of board member training.

12) *Boards will support programs that strengthen family life.* Boards must take leadership in seeing to it that the community welfare enterprise attacks with new vigor the problems of family disorganization, breakdown, and persistent dependency. The attack must be mounted on the level of treatment to rehabilitate people already affected, and on the level of prevention so that the problems will not pyramid and be even more socially devastating in the future. Many, if not most, of the social and personal problems of people develop because the family unit is unable to fulfill its functions adequately. A new and dynamic approach to the strengthening of family life must be the cornerstone of community social welfare endeavors. The very essence of this dynamic approach is the provision of a sufficient number of qualified workers equipped with knowledge and skill through professional education. The concept of rehabilitation is essential to all services designed to improve the welfare of people. Boards must give real support to all programs designed to improve and strengthen family life.

13) *Boards will accent prevention.* It costs the community far less to prevent a problem or deal with it in its early stages than to correct it after it has become serious. Because of this, boards should give high priority to those services which are essentially preventive in character. Such services include: housing, education, mental health, constructive use of leisure, and adequate income maintenance.

14) *Boards will support more research.* Research has become a basic necessity in the community welfare enterprise. It is extremely important that boards take leadership in this area and find ways to strengthen research and evaluation programs.

The objective of citizen boards in community service is not only to make good agencies and provide good services. The fundamental goal of every board is to work for a good society. In speaking about her own commitment to mankind, perhaps the words of Lillian Smith apply to board members and why they serve. She says, "You do what you must do, what seems right, what would make you despise yourself if you did not do it. Or you do it because you love somebody, or a lot of people, so much that you just have to do it." [71]

NOTES

1. Reprinted with permission of The Macmillan Company from *The Year 2000—A Framework For Speculation on the Next Thirty-Three Years,* by Herman Kahn and Anthony J. Weiner, p. 1. Copyright © 1967 by the Hudson Institute, Inc.
2. *Ibid.,* p. 3.
3. Alvin C. Eurich (editor), *Campus 1980—The Shape of the Future in American Higher Education* (New York: Delacorte Press, 1968), p. vii.
4. Lewis Mumford, *The Urban Prospect* (New York: Harcourt, Brace and World, Inc., 1968), p. 3.
5. George Russell Harrison, *What Man May Be.* (New York: William Morrow Co., 1956), pp. 21 and 266. Copyright by George Russell Harrison.
6. Pendleton Herring, "Expand the School," *Saturday Review,* February 1, 1958, © 1958, Saturday Review, Inc.
7. President John F. Kennedy, Speech at Charter Day Exercises, University of California, Berkeley, March 1962.
8. Arnold Toynbee, "The Revolution We Are Living Through," *New York Times Magazine,* July 25, 1954.
9. Dr. Frank R. Leavis, Cambridge University Speech.
10. Rockefeller Brothers Fund, *Annual Report,* 1962.
11. Mumford, *op. cit.,* p. 3.
12. Harold Koontz, *The Board of Directors and Effective Management* (New York: McGraw-Hill, 1967), pp. 11-17. Used with permission of McGraw-Hill Book Company.
13. "Excerpts from Gardner's Statement to Republican Panel on Urban Needs," *New York Times,* July 30, 1968. © 1968 by the New York Times Company. Reprinted by permission.
14. Thomas D. Sherrard (editor), *Social Welfare and Urban Problems* (New York: Columbia University Press, 1968; published for the National Conference on Social Welfare), p. 2.
15. Joseph W. Barr, "The Battle for Resources—Diplomacy versus Domesticity," talk before the Town Hall of California, Los Angeles, June 25, 1968.
16. Edmund K. Faltermayer, *Redoing America—A Nationwide Report on How to Make Our Cities and Surburbs Livable* (New York: Harper & Row, 1968), p. xiii.
17. *The Jewish Community Newsletter* (New York: Council of Jewish Federations and Welfare Funds), June-July, 1968, p. 1.
18. For example see: Robert Dentler, Bernard Mackler, Mary Ellen Warshauer, *The Urban R's—Race Relations as the Problem in Urban Education* (New York: Frederick A. Praeger, Published for the Center for Urban Education, 1967); Lester A. Sobel (editor), *Civil Rights, 1960–66* (New York: Facts on File, 1967); Paul Jacobs, *Prelude to Riot—A View of Urban Education from the Bottom* (New York: Random House, 1967); Irwin Isenberg, *The City in Crisis* (New York: The U. W. Wilson

Co., 1968); *A Time to Listen—A Time to Act—Voices from the Ghettos of the Nation's Cities* (Washington, D.C.: U.S. Commission on Civil Rights, 1967); *Report of the National Advisory Commission on Civil Disorders* (New York: Bantam Books, March 1968); *Supplemental Studies for the National Advisory Commission on Civil Disorders* (Washington, D.C.: Superintendent of Documents, U.S. Government Printing Office, June 1968); Saul Bernstein, *Alternatives to Violence—Alienated Youth and Riots, Race, and Poverty* (New York: Association Press, 1967).

19. Charles Frankel, "The Welfare State: Postscript and Prelude," *Proceedings Fourth Annual Social Work Day,* School of Social Work, University of Buffalo, May 3, 1961.

20. *Poverty and Deprivation in the United States—The Plight of Two-Fifths of a Nation.* Conference on Economic Progress, Washington, D.C., April 1962.

21. *New York Times,* September 22, 1962.

22. Vannevar Bush, "Automation's Awkward Age," *Saturday Review,* August 11, 1962, p. 11. © 1962, Saturday Review, Inc.

23. James B. Conant, *Slums and Suburbs—A Commentary on Schools in Metropolitan Areas* (New York: McGraw-Hill, 1961).

24. Charles Frankel, "The Family in Context," in Fred Delliquardi (editor), *Helping the Family in Urban Society* (New York: Columbia University Press, 1963), p. 20.

25. Leon H. Keyserling, *Progress or Poverty* (Washington, D.C.: Conference on Economic Programs, December 1964).

26. Ronald Sullivan, "Negative Taxes Tested in Jersey—80 Families Are Being Paid Guaranteed Income," *New York Times,* October 27, 1968; Irwin Garfinkel, "Negative Income Tax and Children's Allowance Programs: A Comparison," *Social Work,* October 1968.

27. Marion O. Robinson, *Humanizing the City* (New York: Public Affairs Pamphlet Number 417, April 1968).

28. Alvin L. Schorr, *Slums and Social Insecurity* (Washington, D.C.: U.S. Department of Health, Education and Welfare, Social Security Administration, Division of Research and Statistics, Research Report No. 1, July 1963).

29. Robert Theobald (editor), *Social Policies for America in the Seventies—Nine Divergent Views* (New York: Doubleday and Co., 1968).

30. Barr, *op. cit.*

31. John W. Gardner, "Topics—America in the Twenty-Third Century," *New York Times,* July 27, 1968. © 1968 by the New York Times Company. Reprinted by permission.

32. John D. Rockefeller III, "Responding to the Youth Revolt," *New York Times,* October 27, 1968.

33. "Economic Opportunity Act of 1964," Public Law 88-452, 88th Congress, S. 2642, August 20, 1964, p. 9.

34. Sar A. Levitan, *The Design of Federal Antipoverty Strategy.* Policy Papers in Human Resources and Industrial Relations. The Institute of

Labor and Industrial Relations, The University of Michigan, Wayne State University, March, 1967.

35. See "Maximum Feasible Participation of the Poor—A Hope or a Hustle," New York: Mobilization for Youth, Inc., *News Bulletin*, Vol. 5, No. 2, Summer 1966; Thomas Gladwin, *Poverty U.S.A.* (Boston: Little, Brown & Co., 1967), pp. 176-177; Fred Powledge, "A Role for the Poor—City Ponders How to Give Slum Dwellers a Voice in Its Antipoverty Programs," *New York Times*, May 27, 1965; Ben A. Franklin, "Indigent to Elect Members to Philadelphia's Anti-Poverty Planning Group," *New York Times*, May 9, 1965; James Ridgeway, "Philadelphia Polls the Poor," *New Republic*, June 5, 1965; "Poverty Scramble," *New York Times* editorial, November 9, 1965; Joseph A. Loftus, "Philadelphia's Plan to Give Poor a Voice in Poverty Drive Called a Failure," *New York Times*, July 17, 1966; Rudy Johnson, "Newark Vote Regarded by Some as Defeat for Militant Negroes," *New York Times*, August 16, 1968.

36. Fred M. Hechinger, "Students All Over Challenge the System," *New York Times*, September 1, 1968; Fred M. Hechinger, "How Much Control for the People?" *New York Times*, September 1, 1968; Deirdre Carmody, "Barnard Sets Up New Policy Units," *New York Times*, July 23, 1968.

37. *Annual Report*, Ford Foundation, 1961, p. 6.

38. *New York Times*, November 1, 1968, p. 1.

39. Joseph A. Loftus, "Civic Heads United to Fight Poverty," *New York Times*, November 7, 1965.

40. *Action Report, A Digest of Corporate Approaches to Public Problems*, published by The Chase Manhattan Bank, New York, Volume 1, Number 1, Autumn 1967; Number 2, Winter 1968; Number 3, Spring 1968; "Businessmen Are Urged to Lobby for Social Laws," *New York Times*, October 27, 1968.

41. Kahn and Weiner, *op. cit.*, p. 3.

42. See Leonard Buder, "City Begins Study of School System—Decentralization Is Goal," *New York Times*, March 15, 1960; Fred M. Hechinger, "Sweeping Reform in School Boards Is Urged on State," *New York Times*, October 26, 1965; Leonard Buder, "Regents Propose to Revamp Board of City University," *New York Times*, February 27, 1966; Fred M. Hechinger, "Break-up Is Urged of School Boards," *New York Times*, July 15, 1966; Leonard Buder, "Regents Plan for City Asks Smaller Board, 15 Districts," *New York Times*, March 30, 1968; Fred M. Hechinger, "Decentralization: Progress and Dispute," *New York Times*, August 25, 1968.

43. See Fred M. Hechinger, "Bundy Fears Sea of School Hatred," *New York Times*, October 27, 1968; Harold Laski, *A Grammar of Politics* (London: George Allen and Unwin, Ltd. Fifth Edition, 1967), pp. 412-413; Fred M. Hechinger, "Crisis in Education—A Power Struggle Overwhelms New York's Schools," *New York Times*, September 15, 1968.

44. Janice Falkin, "Teachers Are Backbone," *West Hartford News,* October 31, 1968.

45. National Welfare Rights Organization Conference, Lake Forest, Illinois, August 22-25, 1968, "An Action Proposal—New Organizing Techniques in Flat Grant States"; George Brager, "Two Cheers for Welfare Rights," *Social Work,* October 1968, p. 102; Richard A. Cloward and Frances Fox Piven, "Finessing the Poor," *The Nation,* October 7, 1968, pp. 332-334; Paul Bullock, "On Organizing the Poor—Problems of Morality and Tactics," *Dissent,* January-February 1968; Richard A. Cloward and Frances Fox Piven, "The Weight of the Poor—A Strategy to End Poverty," *The Nation,* May 2, 1966, pp. 510-517; Richard A. Cloward and Frances Fox Piven, "We've Got Rights! The No Longer Silent Welfare Poor," *The New Republic,* August 5, 1967, pp. 23-27.

46. "Legislation to be Sponsored by the State Welfare Department," State of Connecticut, State Welfare Department, October 1968.

47. See Chapter 4 and Chapter 9, *infra.*

48. Gladwin Hill, "Poverty Program Falters on Coast," *New York Times,* March 4, 1966.

49. "Antipoverty Unit Scored on Staffs," *New York Times,* May 15, 1967.

50. Wallace Turner, "Poor Lack Power in Philadelphia—Delegates on Poverty Board Have Little Say on Policy," *New York Times,* November 6, 1965.

51. Sherrard, *op. cit.,* pp. 27-30.

52. Hobart A. Burch and Edward Newman, "A Federal Program for Neighborhood Services," presented at the National Conference on Social Welfare, San Francisco, California, May 27, 1968.

53. Michael S. March, "The Neighborhood Center Concept," *Public Welfare,* January 1968.

54. L. L. Geismar and Michael A. La Sorte, *Understanding the Multi-Problem Family* (New York: Association Press, 1964).

55. *Neighborhood Centers Serve the Troubled Family* (New York: National Federation of Settlements and Neighborhood Centers, 1964).

56. Charles Grosser in *Counseling the Disadvantaged Youth,* William E. Ames and Jean Dresden Grambs, eds., © 1968, Prentice-Hall, Inc., Englewood Cliffs, N.J.

57. Grosser, *ibid.*

58. See *Closing the Gap in Social Work Manpower.* Report of the Departmental Task Force on Social Work Education and Manpower (Washington, D.C.: U.S. Department of Health, Education, and Welfare, Office of the Under Secretary, November 1965); Edward E. Schwartz (editor), *Manpower in Social Welfare—Research Perspectives* (New York: National Association of Social Workers, 1966).

59. See Hilary G. Fry, *Education and Manpower for Community Health* (Pittsburgh: University of Pittsburgh Press, 1967); *Manpower—A Community Responsibility,* 1968 Annual Review, National Commission for Social Work Careers of the National Association of Social Workers in Cooperation with the Council on Social Work Education, New York.

60. See George W. Magner and Thomas L. Briggs (editors), *Staff Development in Mental Health Services* (New York: National Association of Social Workers, 1966); Joseph Soffen, *Faculty Development in Professional Education* (New York: Council on Social Work Education, 1967).

61. Byron T. Hipple, *Fiscal Policy and the Public Social Services* (Graduate School of Public Affairs, State University of New York, Public Affairs Monograph Series, Monograph Number 2, December 1965), p. 1.

62. *Ibid.,* pp. 109-120.

63. *Fiscal Balance in the American Federal System* (Washington, D.C.: Advisory Commission on Intergovernmental Relations, October 1967), Volume I, pp. xxi-xxii.

64. See Robert Morris, *Centrally Planned Change—Prospects and Concepts* (New York: National Association of Social Workers, 1964); Warren G. Bennis, Kenneth D. Benne, Robert Chin, *The Planning of Change—Readings in the Applied Behavorial Sciences* (New York: Holt, Rinehart and Winston, 1966).

65. See *A Proposed Program for National Action to Combat Mental Retardation* (Washington, D.C.: The President's Panel on Mental Retardation, October 1962); *A National Program to Conquer Heart Disease, Cancer and Stroke* (Washington, D.C.: The President's Commission on Heart Disease, Cancer and Stroke, December 1964).

66. Lois Dean, "Minersville: A Study in Socio-economic Stagnation," *Human Organization,* Vol. 24, No. 3, Fall 1965, p. 261.

67. Robert N. Wilson, *Community Structure and Health Action* (Washington, D.C.: Public Affairs Press, 1968), p. 84.

68. Mumford, *op. cit.,* p. 18.

69. W. Homer Turner, "Stewardship Responsibility for Creative Innovation" (New York: United States Steel Foundation, 1968).

70. Elizabeth Wickenden and Winifred Bell, *Public Welfare—Time for a Change* (New York: Columbia University School of Social Work, 1961).

71. George P. Brockway, "You Do It Because You Love Somebody," *Saturday Review,* October 22, 1966, p. 53, © 1966, Saturday Review, Inc.

Bibliography of Selected Readings

Ashby, Lloyd W., *The Effective School Board Member.* Danville, Illinois: The Interstate Printers and Publishers, Inc., 1968.

Brown, C. A., and Smith, E. E., *The Director Looks at His Job.* New York: Columbia University Press, 1957.

Building Board Leadership for the Years Ahead. Proceedings, Advanced Leadership Training Institute, University of Tennessee, School of Social Work, Nashville, Tennessee, September 7-8, 1963. New York: National Jewish Welfare Board.

Burns, Gerald P., *Trustees in Higher Education.* Independent Funds of America, 1966.

Cohen, Nathan, *The Citizen Volunteer.* New York: Harper, 1960.

Dapper, Gloria, and Carter, Barbara, *A Guide for School Board Members.* Chicago: Follett Publishing Company, 1966.

Demorest, Charlotte K., *The Board Members' Manual—How to Produce and Use it in Board Education.* New York: National Publicity Council for Health and Welfare Services, Inc., 1951.

Gardner, John W., *Self-Renewal—The Individual and the Innovative Society.* New York: Harper and Row, 1964.

Glover, Elizabeth E., *Crises in Board-Executive Relationships in Social Agencies.* Doctoral dissertation, University of Pennsylvania, The School of Social Work, 1964.

———, *Guide for Board Organization and Administrative Structure.* New York: Child Welfare League of America, 1963.

Goldhammer, Keith, *The School Board.* New York: The Center for Applied Research in Education, Inc., 1964.

Houle, Cyril O., *The Effective Board.* New York: Association Press, 1960.

James, H. Thomas, *Boardsmanship—A Guide for the School Board Member.* Stanford: Stanford University Press, 1961.

Johns, Ray, *Confronting Organizational Change.* New York: Association Press, 1963.

———, *Executive Responsibility.* New York: Association Press, 1953.

Koontz, Harold, *The Board of Directors and Effective Management.* New York: McGraw-Hill, 1967.

Making Yours a Better Board. New York: Family Service Association of America, 1954.

Martona, S. V., *College Boards of Trustees.* New York: The Center for Applied Research in Education, Inc., 1965.

Naylor, Harriet H., *Volunteers Today—Finding, Training and Working with Them.* New York: Association Press, 1967.

Nominating for Elective Office in a Girl Scout Council. Council Administrative Series No. 3. New York: Girl Scouts of the U.S.A., 1965.

Reeves, Charles E., *School Boards—Their Status, Functions and Activities.* New York: Prentice-Hall, 1954.

Routzahn, Mary Swain, *Better Board Meetings.* New York: National Publicity Council for Health and Welfare Services, 1952.

Rozan, Dorothy, *Board Composition in the Lansing Family Service in Relation to Community Changes, 1920–1957.* Master's thesis. Michigan State University, School of Social Work, 1958.

School Boards and School Board Membership. Recommendations and Report of a Survey. New York Regents Advisory Committee on Educational Leadership, December 1955.

Schmidt, William D., *The Executive and the Board in Social Welfare.* Cleveland: Howard Allen, Inc., 1959.

Sorenson, Roy, *The Art of Board Membership.* New York: Association Press, 1950.

The Board and the Executive Director. New York: National Board, YWCA, 1953.

The Board of Directors of a Neighborhood Center. New York: National Federation of Settlements and Neighborhood Centers, 1960.

The Board Member of a Social Agency. New York: Child Welfare League of America, Inc., 1957.

The Council Manual. New York: Girl Scouts of the U.S.A., 1969.

The Role of the Board of Directors in a Community YWCA. New York: National Board, YWCA, 1957.

Tompkins, Leslie J., *Boards and Committees in the Y.M.C.A.* New York: Association Press, 1958.

Trecker, Harleigh B., *Building the Board.* New York: National Publicity Council for Health and Welfare Services, 1954.

————, *Executive Role with Boards—An Exploratory Study.* University of Connecticut, School of Social Work, 1960.

————, *New Understandings of Administration.* New York: Association Press, 1961.

————, *Social Agency Boards—An Exploratory Study.* University of Connecticut, School of Social Work, 1958.

————, *Social Agency Boards as Viewed by Board Members.* University of Connecticut, School of Social Work, 1959.

————, *Social Agency Board Member Institutes—An Analysis of the Experience of Eighteen Cities.* New York: Community Chests and Councils of America and the National Social Welfare Assembly, Bulletin No. 161, May 1952.

————, and Trecker, Audrey R., *Committee Common Sense.* New York: Whiteside, William Morrow and Co., 1954.

————, *How to Work with Groups.* New York: Association Press, 1952.

Tuttle, Edward M., *School Board Leadership in America.* Danville, Ill.: The Interstate Printers, Revised edition, 1963.

Vance, Stanley C., *Boards of Directors: Structure and Performance.* Eugene: University of Oregon Press, 1964.

Winser, Marian M., *A Handbook for Library Trustees.* New York: R. R. Bowker, 1955.

Young, Virginia G., *The Library Trustee—A Practical Guidebook.* New York: R. R. Bowker, 1964.

Youngdahl, Benjamin E., *Social Action and Social Work.* New York: Association Press, 1966.

Index